FALLEN ANGEL

FALLEN ANGEL

Hell's Angel
to Heaven's Saint

by BARRY MAYSON
with TONY MARCO

Doubleday & Company, Inc.
Garden City, New York

NOTE: The events depicted in this book are true. Only the names and descriptions of certain individuals have been changed, to protect the innocent.

Library of Congress Cataloging in Publication Data

Mayson, Barry.
   Fallen angel.

   1. Mayson, Barry.   2. Converts—United States—
Biography.   3. Hell's Angels.   I. Marco, Tony.   II. Title.
      BV4935.M37A33   248.2'46'0924   [B]   AACR2
   Library of Congress Catalog Card Number: 81-43539
                  ISBN: 0-385-17934-0

I would like to dedicate this book to my mother, Mary Carder, who loved me and prayed for me and Fran through all the years. I love you, Mother!

Also to the leadership and family of Liberty Bible College in Pensacola, Florida, and the churches which God used to mold my first two and a half years with a good foundation in Jesus Christ my Lord. Many thanks to Dan McFarland for his love; to Dub and Marilyn Phillips for their help and love; to all of the true believers in the body of Christ who have kept my family and myself lifted up in prayer, especially to the leadership and family of Forest Drive Baptist Church in Columbia, South Carolina, for their support in hard times.

To Tony Marco, for all his help in telling my story.

And particularly to my wife, Fran, who lived every day of those days and stuck with me through it all. I love you!!

Of course, all credit goes to my first love . . .

To God Be the Glory in Him (John 14:6)

Barry Mayson
January 29, 1982

ACKNOWLEDGMENTS

Thanks: To Dave Hazard of Chosen Books, for initial encouragement and gracious advice; to Peggy Hoyle, who typed the bulk of the manuscript; and to my wife, Joyce, who bore the brunt of it all.

T.M.

CONTENTS

FALLEN ANGEL

BOOK I

1

Ignition!

From out of a shadow under the neon bar-and-grill sign, a thin blade of fire crackled and whizzed past my head. I slammed my foot down and felt 1,200 cc's of Harley-Davidson explode into a roar underneath me. In an instant the hot night air broke into searing headlights and flashing red darts like a pinball machine gone wild. *Cops!*

Sirens wailed to life—no time to think—just *move!*

Four other bikers and I wheeled around, looking for some opening in the street to squeeze through. I only saw one: what looked like a dark alley off to my right. *Might be a dead end in a brick wall? No time to worry about it*—no place else to go.

Bullets spitting all around, I cranked into the darkness so hard I almost snapped my wrists. Behind me Hoss screamed, and I heard his cycle rattle along the sides of the alley. Up ahead a full moon shone through what looked like a rickety fence.

I was rushing at it fast. No stopping now—I just hoped it would give way! It seemed like my front wheel broke the fence in slow motion—flimsy boards scattered around me like a flock of scared birds, and I sailed out into the open air, thinking *Wind, drop me easy!* I hunched into my cycle and braced for the impact.

I landed hard, my head jammed into my chest. I veered left

and right in the open field until I got my balance. My three brother bikers roared to my side. Hoss must be lying back there dead in his own blood—but we were still free! Snake's teeth grinned moonlight at me: "Them cops is gonna pay, brother!"

Ahead a highway wound into the mountains, and we headed for it. My heart thumped hot in my throat as I breathed in the blur of the rushing night and leaned onto the highway with all my weight . . .

"Barry!" I felt a sharp dig to my ribs, and then another, and the vision on the movie screen and in my mind's eye started flaking to pieces, leaving me with aching knuckles, grasping the wheel of my '68 Ford wagon like a dead man.

"Barry, I'm talkin' to you!" Maureen's voice brought me all the way back down—and to the edge of rage. I lashed out from the steering wheel and just missed her lurching, bleached-blond head. "Hey, watchit!" she screamed. "You almost killed the baby!" She smoothed the fuzz on little Jim's head.

"Well, keep the freakin' kid away while I watch this flick!"

"Well, forgive *me*, big man, you don't even care about your own kid. You leanin' and jumpin' made me spill Coke all over him!"

I reached over and grabbed the back of her neck. "Hey! You better get out of this car before I put you through the windshield!"

"You let me go"—she tore herself away—"you stupid animal!" She had the door half open behind her and almost fell out, pulling the now squalling baby with her. She opened the back door on her side and grabbed the diaper bag. "I'm gonna clean this kid up," she said. She leaned her head down to the open window and snarled, "You're no better than them retards on the screen!"—and whirled off.

I thought to light after her and smash her right there. But screw her—she wasn't worth another beating! I flipped up my shirt collar to wipe the sweat off my neck. *Damn bitch and her "nights out"! Her and her little family scenes!* There was nothing left, and she knew it as well as I did. At least she should let me get into a flick and enjoy it now and then. She tried to see to it I didn't get much else in the way of kicks anymore. Little she knew!

In spite of her, it felt good to have gotten really lost in this picture. I couldn't remember ever having clean forgotten where I was at a movie before. But I hadn't ever seen one of those biker epics. We had just sat through *Born to Lose;* this one was *Hell's Angels on Wheels.* Bikers were something new to me. I had glanced once at some pictures of Hell's Angels in a doctor's-office magazine, and I thought they were just California hippies who rode motorcycles. Back here in '68 Georgia, long hair and earrings didn't go too well.

But seeing them now, I realized these guys were anything but hippies. They were more like pirates, with their scraggly beards and cutoff vests and death's-head patches like Jolly Rogers. Yeah, that was it! Pirates, with highways for their high seas, taking what they wanted and going where they pleased, just like the old-time buccaneers. They looked wild and dangerous, like they'd kill in a second, and wherever they went, you could see the fear and respect on people's faces. These guys owned city streets and country blacktops just by being there, flashing color and noise and power.

I had never ridden a motorcycle, but those long choppers dazzled and supercharged my eyes and ears with their chrome flash and thundering speed. It had to take a powerful man to maneuver one of those machines into a forty-foot "wheelie" or jump sand dunes in the desert. Just watching made me feel like that kind of man. I could do that. I *knew* I could do it.

And damn, the way they lived was what I called *living!* There was a party scene on now, with bikers sitting in a circle in a room with a rainbow of lights and loud rock music pounding. They were passing around a hand-rolled smoke, must be marijuana, and guzzling beer in huge gulps. Bikers were yelling and laughing, one so hard he fell over and rolled across the room. Then some women came in and started stripping to the music and running their hands over their own bodies and the bikers' . . .

I heard the car door open to my right. Maureen hesitated, but I kept my eyes glued to the screen. She slid in and stayed as far away from me as possible. When she saw I was ignoring her, she sneered low, "Yeah, you just eat your big ape's heart out! Don't you wish you was in there right now?"

Yeah, I did wish I was there, I wished I could have every bit of it. Anything but this dull mess I was in. What was my life, anyway? At twenty-two, stuck working a night shift in a Ford plant, al-

ways coming home to this same face next to me and crashing out
half the day? Paying installment bills and punching a clock with
nothing else ever to look forward to but a crumbling union card
and a half pension when I got old? I might as well be buried already.

It all never should have happened. Maureen and I had gotten
married on impulse one weekend during one of my long AWOL es-
capes from the Army. I was nineteen, she was only sixteen at the
time. My case of the hots and the nice butt she swayed around
were all we had going for us. I was out of my head and reckless. I
had few interests but to get stinking drunk and party. I cheated her
a lot. It must have been a relief for her when they shipped me off
to Korea.

I was a teletype lineman there, and off-duty it was life in the
raw for me. I got a good taste of rotgut booze and laughing, slanty-
eyed mama-sans with scuzzy teeth, who slithered through the bars
and red-light joints doing anything for a few cents. As time went
on, I raised more and more hell, went AWOL whenever I felt like
it, and ended up doing six extra months in stockade.

When I got back Stateside, it was supposed to be settle-down
time. But there was no way it could work. One night Maureen and
I lay in bed and I made my little confessions. She cried as I told
her, "Hey, I was only nineteen—did you expect me to sit in the bar-
racks starin' at four walls every night?" Same old story. I was getting ready to tell her quits when she told me Ron was on the way.
"I guess you're stuck with me, Barry," she smiled through her tears.

I gritted my teeth and went to work at the Hapeville, Georgia,
Ford plant, and soon we were buying a house outside of Atlanta. I
was inspecting cars and bringing in a good living that paid for the
new station wagon and everything else a family is supposed to have
on credit. Less than a year after Ron was born, Maureen was fat
with Jim. She still had that fine rear end.

But more and more, the responsibilities were gnawing at me.
And there were lots of other nice butts around. I was hitting the
bars after work pretty regularly now, and turning back-seat tricks
when I could get into somebody's pants. Maureen was furious because she was stuck with the kids and I claimed free run of the
town. I let her beg nights out like this to keep her from tearing the

house apart. I had to have someplace to come home to—and her rear end on occasion.

But I knew I couldn't go on this way forever. It was driving me crazy and her, too. Half the time, I wanted to kill her; the other half she "wasn't worth killing." On the job, I despised the routine so much that every time I pulled into the parking lot for my shift, my stomach churned so fiercely I nearly turned around and drove away. As for the kids: I was proud I had them, but they were another kind of trap. In a couple of years they would need a lot of my time, and I had other things I wanted to do with it. And what kind of example would they have in an old man whose whole life was bogged down in a dead end? No, there had to be something better —something more like the kind of life I was seeing in these movies. Whatever it was, I had to find it before it was too late. I had to be free—whether Maureen went along with it or not.

At the end of both movies, there were big battles with the cops, and a lot of bikers got killed or hauled off to jail. The cops and "good citizens" said smug words about justice triumphing. *What justice?* I thought, *All these dudes were doin' was tryin' t' have a good time an' stay free!* So good guys always have to win in the movies. It wouldn't be that way in real life. You couldn't hold down bad guys as bad as the Hell's Angels.

Spotlights beamed out all over the drive-in, and a grainy film on the screen showed a trash barrel filling up. A polite, canned voice said, "Please help keep this theater clean. Make sure the area around your car is litter-free!" I reached for the keys in the ignition, but Maureen asked, "Help pick up this stuff, Barry; the car's a mess."

"Don't tell me what to do," I shot back. "I'll bust your head."

Her eyes narrowed in anger, but she said slowly, "Don't make threats at me, Barry. One o' these days I'm gonna call the cops! Now, will you *please* help pick up this trash?"

I said, "Nope!" and started up the car. I could hear her muttering something under her breath as she reached down for the big popcorn tub. In the rear-view mirror, I saw Ron rubbing his eyes. Somehow he had slept through everything, sprawled across the back seat.

Maureen poked around in front for soda cups and candy wrappers. "Those movies were gross-outs," she said with contempt.

"I don't know," I said, putting the drive-in speaker back on the hook, "I thought them Hell's Angels was pretty neat."

"You *would* think so," she said with a curl of her lip. "Let's go."

I felt my blood start to heat up again, but just as quickly, I packed my rage back down. No use to make a scene and get the kids screaming. I backed up the car and eased into the exiting traffic. I drove slowly past a bent-over old man who swung a red-rimmed flashlight like it weighed fifty pounds and smiled stupidly at nobody. The kid in the car ahead of me looked like he was trying to cop a last feel from his chick before he hit the street. I remembered when drive-ins used to be that kind of fun. Now it was a duty—as much fun as army latrine duty.

We went past the sign reading "Deluxe Drive-In—1st show at dusk" and out onto the "strip," such as it was, of Riverdale, Georgia. It was only a couple of miles to home on Eunice Avenue, gliding by hamburger and barbecue joints, teenagers yelling and bombing around on the pickup scent, a teeming summer Saturday night. I didn't try to hide my eying the little chickies going by. I wondered if Maureen was getting any on the side while I was busting my hump at night. I ought to leave early some night and try to catch her at it. I'd beat her up just on the principle that she still belonged to me—after a fashion.

I did slow zigzags through the neighborhood—mostly ticky-tackies put up in the last five years for working slobs like me. As we turned into the driveway, I nosed a familiar odor floating in from my right: "Shee! That kid reeks!"

"So do you," said Maureen quietly, "only his kind of stink I can clean up."

I wasn't going to answer that one. I got out and helped sleepy Ron step from the back. He lifted his arms and whimpered, "Wan' come up!"

"Oh, all right," I said, and picked him up. His head flopped to rest on my shoulder. He was two now and getting heavy. I held the screen door open with my foot and let it slap shut behind me as I pushed the front door open and stepped into the living room.

"Hey, Barry," Maureen growled as she struggled with the door, the baby, and the diaper bag, "you *could* hold the door open for your wife!"

"Yeah, I could," I said. But I didn't.

By the time she finally got the door, I had dropped Ron into his bed. I left him dressed, just taking off his shoes and socks. Maureen came in the room and turned on the light by the crib. Her face scowling like stone, she started to change Jim's diaper.

I went into the bathroom and dashed cold water on my face and neck. I heard the kids' door shut—and our bedroom door slam and lock. *Screw her!* I thought. I finished up and stepped across the hall.

"Where're the aspirins?" I called through the bedroom door.

"Go to hell!" she shot back coldly.

I gave the door a solid kick.

"Stick it you know where!" she yelled.

Two years before I might have broken it down. Now, *To hell with it,* I thought. I made my way to the kitchen. "God bless this mess!" a plaque said. *Amen!* There was no beer in the refrigerator, only some milk and a little iced tea in a plastic bottle. I fished a dirty glass from the sink and rinsed it out. Two cubes were left in the ice tray. I poured the tea and went for the back door. The kitchen clock was buzzing past twelve-thirty.

I eased the screen door behind me and sat down on the back steps. A whisper of breeze brushed my face in the humid air—just enough to give the swing a slight sway down by Maureen's beetle-eaten rosebush. A sip of tea was good going down, hint of lemon in it. *No stars—rain tonight, maybe? Did I shut the car windows? Check later.*

My anger had almost played itself out now. As it left, I found myself settling into an empty spell that seemed to be climbing from my stomach to my throat. Only my head stayed full—of thoughts that trudged around like soldiers on a forced march. I could do nothing but let my mind go until it quit from exhaustion . . . I set my glass down and lit a cigarette.

I thought it wasn't a bad night to have to sleep on the couch—if I ever got to sleep. I wondered how many more scenes like tonight I could take. Slowly all the life was sapping out of me. Why did I keep letting it happen?

Suddenly that question leaped out and towered over me, like a massive wall that stood in my way and wouldn't budge: *Why do I keep lettin' it happen?* It had never dawned on me before, but I had put myself in a position where everything in my life was running it but me! The Army, Maureen, the job, the kids, the bills—they had all had me by the short hairs, but it was me who put them in their hands! They weren't killing me—I was killing myself!

I heard our bedroom door click open inside, and the bathroom door shut and lock.

A tiny bug of some kind fluttered past my eye, and I turned my head to follow it. I soon lost it in the swarms of moths and insects that pattered against the screen door, drawn by the kitchen light.

Tha's how I've been up t' now, I thought. *Like them bugs. They don't know what they're really after. They jus' keep pushin' t' get out of the night, but everywhere they bounce, there's no way through. But why don't they wise up? It's a whole big night out there, and there's a lot of other lights—ones they can get to, if they jus' try somewhere else.*

The toilet flushed; the doors unlocked and opened, shut and locked again.

I took a last drag and flipped my cigarette to the grass.

Man, I dug those bikers in the flicks tonight! They had found that other light, that way to the other side. Over there they had real brotherhood and excitement, they had real *life*. Hell's Angels. What a weird name! But even if hell was where they were headed, they'd go down burning and not just end up rusting away like I'd been doing.

But hell, why did I have to go on this way? Why couldn't my life change? Who owned me? I did, nobody else. Those bikers weren't basically any different from me. They weren't doing anything I couldn't do. I was just as tough and just as quick-moving. And I could be just as mean, if I let it all out of me. All they had done and I hadn't was make a choice and cut loose for themselves. They made up their minds that life wasn't going to trap them. And after that, with guts and smarts, it was no problem staying free.

So why not me? If I could see all this, what reason was there to keep letting other people tell me who I should be? Even if I decided to be a biker or anything else I wanted to be, who was to say I couldn't make it? Who did I need but me to make up my mind about it?

I reached for another cigarette and puffed it to life. The ice had melted in my tea. I took a sip and tossed the watered-down remains to the lawn. *Hey!* I thought, *Why not me as a biker!* What was standing in my way? I had credit. I could get a bike, start hanging out with other guys who liked to ride. In fact, it was a damned good idea. It would save gas money to and from work. Maureen could have the car, and she'd bug me less about never getting out of the house. *An' if she don't like it, screw her,* I thought. It was my money and my life.

My mind started flashing on some of the country roads I'd been down that would be great to ride. I wondered what kinds of new friends I'd meet. I thought of the bikers' partying and orgying in the movies—maybe some of that was up ahead, too! Who knew? I might even be a Hell's Angel some day. At least I could have some of their freedom. Maybe one day I'd have it all!

This was it: I wasn't going to just run my mouth; I was going to start doing something about this—and right away. I had seen some guys riding to work on scooters. I could ask around the plant and the bars about biking. My workmate Jed was a "lifer" at the Ford plant—maybe he knew somebody who could steer me in the right direction.

All of a sudden, I felt like getting up and taking a long stretch toward the sky. As I rose to my feet, I felt a lightness in my head and a brief shiver of excitement. I flicked my cigarette butt at a huge moth and just missed. For the first time in years, I felt a joy that almost hurt well up in me. My mouth opened up, and I let loose with a soft "Whooeee!"

A neighbor's dog gave a few tired woofs and soon shut up. I decided I'd better go in and get what rest I could. No way the kids would sleep past six-thirty, and after last night, Maureen might not be inclined to keep them quiet.

I walked around front and shut the car windows, went in the

front door and made ready for bed on the couch. As I lay on my back, taking a last few puffs on a smoke, I listened to the locusts shrilling to the night. Before long, they turned into the deeper roars of the gleaming "street choppers" that charged through my dreams.

2

First Gear

It was an especially bad night on the job: A lot of junk was coming down. You could almost tell who'd been drunk the night before by the pattern of work left undone: a loose muffler clamp here, untorqued seat belts there, the same goof-ups by the same hungover guys up the line.

Usually, I had about a minute and a half to inspect the underside of each of the endless stream of Fords that passed over my pit just before being driven off the assembly line. My checklist included underside bolts, seat belts, muffler clamps, emergency brake, seat tightness, as well as anything else down there some earlier inspector had missed.

But tonight, I didn't have Jed behind me to fix what I found wrong. He had come in rubbing his eyes and yawning like a grizzly ready for winter: "Long night las' night, ol' buddy!" About an hour and a half along, he yelled over the racket, "Barry, I got to take me a little break, or I ain't gonna make it."

This was no special favor; he did double duty for me sometimes when I needed a breather, and the foreman didn't mind as long as the job got done. But I was in no mood for double work tonight, and Jed's little breaks often stretched an hour or two. Now he was flat out on his metal chair in a dark corner of the pit, his crew cut sagging over his folded arms. How he could sleep through all the noise—and not fall off!—I never knew.

Still, I wasn't too annoyed because I knew that at lunch I was going over to meet one of the bikers in the plant, a guy named Tom who was Jed's "diet pill" supplier. That, Jed's bribe of two bennies, and the knowledge that he was going to bust his hump the rest of the night, made the time pass a little easier.

One thing that amazed me about Jed was that he didn't mind at all when it was his turn to work double. He was an amiable ol' boy from a one-outhouse Georgia farm town, and for him, working for Ford was big stuff: "Saved me from a life o' shovelin' chicken shit!" he'd say. In fact, he loved for me to sit down so he could drive himself into a furious sweat, twisting and torquing and scribbling, all the while wailing his hillbilly songs above the din like a high-speed drill. He felt he had it in him to be an inspector, not just a repairman, and every now and then, he would glance over his shoulder to see if the foreman was watching his smoke.

He would rebuke me mildly when I complained about the routine: "You don't know what a good thing you got, boy!" I told him routine would never agree with me; I wasn't cut out for it. "Kid," he laughed, "you jus' wish you had the firs' idea what you *are* cut out for!"

Well, he was right about that. I hadn't found a heck of a lot in life that mattered much to me. School never did. I cheated and fought my way along, more eager to be the first to learn smoking and drinking than fractions. For me, school held only one draw: sports. I was always a runt, but I starred against the biggest in football, basketball, and baseball. My idea of a good school lesson was wriggling my way through the arms of big old hog linemen for one-yard touchdowns—and looking back from the end zone for the proud face of my stepdad, Ben Mayson. After he died, when I was sixteen, even sports began to lose my interest. After that, I concentrated on staying drunk, laying chicks, and kicking heads. I didn't like to think about that time in my life . . .

My mother tried to "save me from myself" by enrolling me in a Baptist college up in the Georgia hills. In less than a year, I was kicked out for drinking and flaunting curfew. Then some guy in a bar told me about the high times he'd had in the Army, and I decided that sounded better than going to work. I joined up and soon regretted it. I actually liked the gut challenge of basic training. But taking orders wasn't for me. It was not long after basic that I met Maureen and got on the road to Deadsville—which I'd been tramping till now.

But it felt good to be really excited about something again. Even tonight's junk work was starting to straighten out. Somebody back there must be sobering up!

The bennie I had taken was nudging me into the rhythm of the job and lifting my mood. At least I was in the pit now and not inspecting on top of it. Being sent here was supposed to have been a demotion, but for me it was better than having to do contortions inside the car, torquing the topside of seat belts, and spraining my wrist on hidden emergency brake cables. And soon I was going to see about getting some relief from this drudgery.

I had quit watching time pass when I heard the high-pitched yowl that I knew was Jed's yawn. He stretched his arms down and back so far, he almost fell over on his chair. "Hey, man," he yelled, scratching his bristly head furiously with both hands, "what's the time?"

"Jus' twenty minutes to chow, you hick redneck cracker! You owe me about two hours o' down-time!"

"Shee . . . , Barry, why'd you let me sleep on like that?"

"I got plans to break your ass for the res' of the night," I smiled back. "I hope you got plenty o' them 'vitamins' with you!"

He gave his good-ol'-boy grin, reached into his pocket, and palmed a handful of bennies at me. "Always prepared, man!"

When the whistle blew after lunch, I told Jed I was going to stretch it and find this dude, Tom. Jed winked and said he'd cover for me.

Big Tom was on the other side of the plant where they put the chassis together. Jed was right; I couldn't miss him. He was a hulking guy, gone a little to fat, with a bush of black, curly hair, and heavy eyebrows that ran together over a nose as big as a potato. Soon as it was after lunch, he had stripped off his gray Ford shirt and was sweating already. His double chin dripped as he dovetailed two shanks of metal with surprising grace for his size. I walked up as he was wiping his brow with a porky forearm.

"Your name Tom?"

"That's me. Whadda you want?"

He didn't look too interested in finding out, but I said, "I want to get into bikin'. Jed Tennile says you ride."

He sized me up quickly and said, "You got a scooter?"

"No, man, but I'm lookin' to get one. Maybe you can steer me."

He looked me over again. "You think you can handle it?"

I grinned and said, "I can handle two or three your size."

His jowls shook as he snorted to himself and said, "That's pretty safe talk now that you can't prove it."

I said, "I'll prove it later, anyplace you like."

He reached for a dangling spar of steel and held it steady while he said, "You just might be a fightin' banty rooster. Tell you what: How about the Assembly Line Grill after work?"

"I'll be there if you'll be there."

He nodded and swung a riveting gun into play.

I made my way back to the pit. Jed had things under control, and I sat back to relax for the time he owed me. His nap seemed to have revived him, and he whined away on some honky-tonk tune while he worked.

Jed was okay, just too damned content to be a friend of mine. Now this Tom dude, I felt like he and I were on the same wavelength. He had a smooth energy I could relate to. I could tell he had that same anger and drive in him. We'd get along—or we just might end up killing each other.

Since I had lately been on the prowl for women, I hadn't spent much time at the Assembly Line—the Model T Lounge was the place for that. The Assembly Line was a no-frills auto workers' bar: The decor was plain, so were the girls, if you found any, and the drinks were cheaper.

The place was quiet tonight, a pocket of bass-toned conversation here and there, no jukebox music at the moment, two guys seats apart at the bar huddled over drinks, one brief female giggle from somewhere in the back.

At first I didn't spot Big Tom; he was sitting with another dude just out of the light of the idle pool table. I was almost on top of them before I saw Tom's salami-thick finger dig into his lumpy nose. Intent on their conversation, the two didn't look up at my approach.

The other guy was saying: "My rear wheel is goin' every which-a-way, like, man, a tire's flat—but it ain't. Know what I mean?"

"Yeah, man," Tom said, nodding a fat cigar intently. "That sounds like bad shocks."

"Could be. I tell you, my tailbone is tired of it."

I leaned over the table a few inches, and Tom looked up, jerking his head back sharply. Seeing who I was, he let a chin or two loose and said, "Hey, man, it's the banty rooster! Didn't figure you to show up!"

"It ain't past my crowin' time yet," I said. "Who's your frien'?"

"Oh, this?"—jerking a thumb at the other man—"I hate to introduce you to anybody so ugly, but that's old George. And whadda you call yourself?"

"Barry, Barry Mayson. Pleased," I said, and extended my hand both ways. George was light-haired, with cavernous eyes set atop wide cheekbones that seemed to be trying to scrape through his skin. His face was chipped out from a long, sharp nose to a pointed, jutting jaw like an arrowhead. His mouth was the thinnest gash.

I pulled a chair over, scraped it around backward, and straddled it. Tom asked me what I was drinking and hollered for that, along with refills for him and George. Then he looked at me and said, "So you want to be a biker, eh?"

I said, "Yeah, man," and told them briefly how I'd gotten interested. Tom shifted the dead cigar from side to side of his mouth, and I finally said, "So how do you get into it?"

He said, "You get yourself a bike an' start hangin' out. If you measure up, you'll find your way to the right places. You ain't got what it takes, you'll sell your bike and go back home and baby-sit." He shrugged, picked a book of matches out of his cutoff and started puffing dark clouds out of his stogie.

George leaned over and said sarcastically, "You want to ride, man? Come on and ride! We'll see what you're made out of."

My neck got warm, and I said, "I'm made outa more than you want to know about."

He leaned back and chuckled. "We'll see!"

I said, "Listen, le's cut the crap. I ain't here to play games. Can you tell me where's a good place to get me a deal on a bike?"

George grunted in glee and said, "Man, you ain't ready to think about ridin' yet."

"Why ain't I? I can ride one of them things in five minutes!"

With an amused, patient air, Tom said, "Man, look at you! What's this checked-work-shirt crap? And look at them shoes. If you even stepped on a street where bikers hang out, you'd get the crap stomped out of you by ten guys before you could spit." He held out his cutoff vest with both hands. "You got to make yourself one of these. His is leather," he said, pointing at George. Then he lifted his foot into view and said, "Look at this boot, man. Heavy! You got to walk right, talk right, or you get et alive."

He was right; I was pretty clean-cut. "I can fix that," I said, "an' my looks ain't got a damn thing to do with what I can *do!*"

"Maybe not," George said seriously, "but you end up provin' it ten times as often on the street. And that don't leave no time for ridin' and partyin'."

Tom's cigar was shorter and dead again. He unplugged it from his mouth with a thumb and forefinger and chugged his drink. He replaced the butt and said, "George, why don't we just tell ol' Barry what's happenin', all right?"

"Why not?" said George. "He can't handle it, it's his funeral."

Big Tom spat his stogie to the floor and said, "Some of us at the plant are gettin' together a club. It's gonna be ridin' and partyin' and whatever. Just weekends to start. But we're gonna be brothers, and we're gonna have a patch, and we're gonna ride where some rough dudes go. Six of us been talkin' about it, and we all know what we can do. If you think you want to ride with us, we'll consider it. But you'll have to prove yourself." He smiled at George without showing his teeth, then he sat back and folded his hammy arms.

This is it! I thought to myself, *This is some good timin', stumblin' into somethin' real right off!* I said, "If you can tell me where to get a scooter, I want to be in on it. Tha's all I need to know."

"I'll tell you what," George said, "I know a dealer in Athens who'll give you a break on a BSA if I'm with you. What're you doin' this Saturday?"

I smiled as wide as I felt and said, "I guess I'm headed toward Athens t' get me a BSA!"

He fished a stub of a pencil out of his pants pocket, looked to see if it had a point, then scribbled something on a paper napkin and handed it to me. "This here's my phone number. I live over in Covington. Give me a call, and we can work out when you'll pick me up." He gave a hint of a smile and said, "See if you can't get some of your shit together by then."

I said, "I hear you." I started to get up, but Big Tom lifted up a hand and said, "Hold it a second, man!"

He gave George a knowing glance and said, "Barry, I like your style. I want to give you somethin', but I got it under the scooter seat out back. Let's take a little walk."

I said, "Okay, man," and we got up and headed for the back door. I was feeling high and confident. I could hardly believe these guys were treating me so nice, especially George, who'd been so jeering at first.

On foot, he was shorter than Tom, but not much, and he loped along beside me, lean, slightly hunched over. The hall past the rest rooms to the door was narrow, and being smallest, I slipped in front. Tom fell in behind me, with George after. I reached for the knob and pushed out.

Just then, I felt a chill run up my back, and my shoulders set instinctively. I knew in an instant that I had made a mistake coming out here: I'd been suckered, and I'd better do something fast.

I stepped down from the door and suddenly sprang to my left, just in time to miss the hooking sweep of Tom's brawny right arm. I spun in the air to face him and rolled with a left of his that just grazed my chin. I came back with a left to his belly that had my whole body turned behind it and was designed to thump right through to his backbone. It traveled about two inches of fat and hit what felt as hard as frozen steak. He brought up a knee that just missed its mark but crunched into my rib cage and sent me sprawling back onto the hood of a car. I heard George guffawing his approval in the background.

As Tom charged me, only to meet my flying foot with his forehead, I rolled off the hood into a moving crouch. Hardly dazed, Tom stalked me; I crab-walked, bent low, to my left. He suddenly swung his right foot at me. As it sped past my head, I grabbed his ankle with my right hand and heaved up with everything I had, careening him onto his rear.

With startling quickness, he hurled his whole body forward at me like a popping spring and clutched for my legs with both arms. I leaped straight up, but he snagged one foot enough to make me lose my balance and fall to my elbow by his side. Pain shot up my arm, and I felt Tom's fist crash the side of my face. I scrambled to my feet an instant before him, and we both circled, huffing and puffing.

George broke into a laugh and shouted, "God damn, that's good fightin'!"

Tom glanced his way and started to shake with laughter, too. I stayed in my crouch, wary, and they both looked at me and pointed as they held their sides with glee.

George finally gained enough composure to say, "Relax, man! You passed the test. I'm gonna teach you to ride Saturday!"

Big Tom held out his hand, still trembling with exertion and laughter, and said, "Gimme some skin, boy! Damn if you ain't a one hundred percent banty fightin' cock!"

3

Cranking Down

We couldn't have picked a much nicer day for learning to ride.
The only clouds in the sky were high and feathery. A sprinkle of
rain two days ago had dried up, settling a welcome cool front
around the Atlanta area. I was ready, I thought, for anything at all,
as I drove toward Covington to pick up George.

On my back was my cutoff to which I had sewn some small
patches: a confederate flag, a red devil holding two gold lightning
bolts, a round patch showing a bare butt that said, "Up Yours!" and
a skull chewing greedily on two bloody crossed bones. I had found
all those in joke and hot-rod shops. The cutoff was what used to be
a denim jacket: I told Maureen she could have the sleeves for rags,
and she said, "What a waste!" I had strung a gold watch chain that
used to be my stepdad's across the front of one side.

I had on my dirtiest work T-shirt and some Levi's with big oil
splashes on them. My feet were sweating in the heaviest Marine
issue combat boots available. In fact, it took me a little while to get
sure control of the gas pedal because the soles were so thick. My
red crash helmet rolled around in the back seat.

With me was all my credit information—and five hundred dollars for a down payment. That last had sent Maureen through the
roof. For her, it had been enough when I had strutted around the

house for the past week growling, "Hey, bitch! Do this! Do that!"
and showing off my biker's walk: straight back, chest out, arms
swinging loosely from my sides, legs a taint bowed, steps firm and
strong, a walk designed to show that I meant serious business. She
said she thought it was "stupid and childish," but little Ron just
stared and stared, with his mouth wide open. I'd come up to baby
Jim and say, in a rough and raspy voice, "Your daddy's a biker!
Number one! Top dog!" That would scare him to a howl, but I'd set
him up on my knee facing away and hold his little hands out in
front of him like they were steering a cycle and go "Vrooooom!"
And he chortled and ate it up. I was all biker, I thought—and I
didn't even have a bike yet!

Maureen wasn't so amused. When I ran out before breakfast
the first morning after meeting Tom and George and came back
hours later with armloads of gear, she stormed in from the kitchen
and said, "Where have you been? And what's all this here?"

I was too jubilant to get mad at her. I looked up from my trea-
sures spread out on the bed. "Babe, I'm gonna be a biker!" I saw
heat, but no light, searing in from her eyes. She turned back to the
kitchen, cracking, "Oh, Lord! What next?"

It took a couple of days for her to realize that I was serious. I
was in the backyard, shadowboxing in all my gear. She watched
from the steps, drying a pot. That morning, I had gone out and
bought a big bowie knife, which I had in a sheath at my side out of
her sight. Seeing her standing there, I whipped it out suddenly and
swished it at her. I put the evilest look I could conjure on my face
and snarled, "Gonna cut you to pieces!" and started toward the
steps, flipping the knife from one hand to the other. She kind of
shrugged out a snigger but I kept coming—and for an instant it
flashed across my mind: *Maybe I really should cut her, jus' so she
knows I'm for real!*

Just as quickly, the urge left me, but in that moment, her smirk
turned to a look of sheer terror. She dropped the pot. It clattered
down the stairs, and she rushed through the door. I bounded after
her. The screen door whacked behind me, and I saw her leg disappear into the bedroom. I threw myself at the door and got an iron-
toed boot in it. She screamed and leaned against it with all her
strength, but I bashed it open with a shoulder. She ran by the bed,

picked up an end-table lamp, and pressed herself against the wall, shivering in fear.

"Don't you come near me!" She oozed the words low and mean like a cornered alley cat. I saw she was staring at my right hand and realized I still had the knife in it.

I stepped into the room slowly, held up the knife, and said, "Hey! I'm puttin' it away, see?" I slipped it carefully back in its sheath, held my hands empty out at my side and said, "See? It's gone! Now what'ch you so excited about?"

I took another step toward her, but she held the lamp higher and said, "You stay away!"

I held my hands up and shook my head, saying, "Hey, babe, I was jus' kiddin'!" She lowered the lamp a little but still stood stiff, looking at me sideways without blinking. I moved very gently now, smiling and making soothing sounds, until I was close enough to reach out and touch her face. As my fingers found her cheek, she dropped her shoulders and let out a sigh. I took the lamp by the shade and set it on the floor and folded her into my arms. "See? It's jus' me, Barry!" I said, caressing her hair.

She pushed back from me a bit and looked into my eyes. "No, Barry," she whispered, "that wasn't jus' you. It was you—an' somethin' else, I don't know what." She sat down on the bed and held her face in her hands. I sat beside her and put an arm partway around her back, so I could look at her.

"Barry," she said half-sobbing, "somethin's happenin' to you. It's ugly, it's evil, an' it scares me."

"Babe, it ain't nothin' to worry about." I took her hands softly and lowered them to her lap. I put my right forefinger under her chin and tilted her head up so she could look at me. "I've jus' found a way to be that feels like me—like freedom! An' I got to have it in my life. It's drivin' me nuts, the same thing, day in, day out. My brain's like a friggin' time card tha's been punched into mush. I've got to get free! Can't you understan' that?"

She turned her head aside and said, "I guess so, Barry—but is it bein' free to be rough and hurt people and make everybody afraid of you?"

I said, "If you take away everythin' that rides him, tha's the way a man is!"

She shook her head. "I don't know; I don't think so, Barry!" Suddenly she reached out her hands and took my shoulders and said, pleading in her eyes, "Oh, Barry, maybe the trouble is me! Maybe I haven't made you feel like a man, I know I pick at you sometimes! But maybe I can change! Maybe things can be different! Jus' give me a chance to make things better before you get into this any more!"

I took her hands off my shoulders and held them up in front of me. I searched her face for some sign of understanding. I only saw fear and doubt and begging as she looked through her tears. Something in me hardened. I wasn't going to let her tears get the better of me.

"You jus' don't understan'," I said. "It ain't you. It ain't nothin' but inside me. An' ain't nothin' gonna change it. This *is* the way it's gonna go."

I looked her straight in the eye and nodded my head slowly to make sure she got it. I let her drop her hands to her lap. Her head slumped to her chest, and she stared down at the rug.

In a very small voice, she said, "I don't know whether I can go with this, Barry."

I said, "Sure you can, babe! It's gonna be fun, like ol' times—hangin' out and partyin'—only better. You'll get into it."

"But why the knives and loud talk and . . ."

"Bikers is rough dudes, Maureen. You can't be a candy-ass an' be a biker."

She breathed in deep and let it out in a quick rush. She trembled, then sat very still.

Little Ron toddled into the room, carrying a small plastic truck. He tugged at the knee of Maureen's slacks and said, "Come up!" Maureen smiled a slim trace, reached down, and lifted him into her lap. He looked at her and said, "T'uck!" and proceeded to examine his toy with care.

Without looking at me Maureen said, "So what comes next, Barry?"

I said, "I get me a cycle. I got a buddy who can put me on to a good deal."

"We can't afford no more big bills, Barry, you know that."

"Won't be no big bill if I make a big down payment."

She whipped her head to face me and spat, "And where do you expect to get that from, Barry?"

"You know where I'm gonna get it," I said calmly.

She stood up, furious, and almost let Ron fall. His truck tumbled to the floor, and he pointed at it and started to holler.

"No, Barry," she cried, thin and shrill. "That's my money, and you can't have it—for this, or for nothin' else!"

I got up and put my face close enough to hers to smell the morning's toothpaste on her breath. "You're forgettin' somethin', bitch! That loan is on my credit! I earn every dime of the money, an' I'm gonna damn well do with it what I please!"

She let Ron slip between us to the floor and screamed, "I can't believe you! You don't care about us! That money was for the family and—you can't do this!"

I could feel my blood rising fast. "I could kill you!" I heard the words as a deep, dry rattle in my throat.

"Why don't you then? Why don't you?" she shrieked to my face.

"Shut up, bitch!" I yelled, and stepped back and barehanded her with my right onto the bed.

I stood heaving in and out with rage, and Ron's squalling grated in my ears. I suddenly picked him up by his arm and tossed his squirming body at Maureen. "Take your damn kid!" I shouted and tore out of the room, leaving them both screaming behind me and the baby now screeching in his playpen in the living room, which I kicked the side of as I went out the front door.

I squealed the car out of the driveway and laid rubber halfway down the street. I pulled into the nearest bar and started to get blind drunk until it was time to head for work. I just wanted to see Tom and George again, to have some laughs, to talk about riding and fighting, to forget Maureen and this whole straitjacket world that sucked men dry.

That night, Jed saw I was staggering drunk and offered to let me sit it out. I sneered at him and said, "I'll show you I can work!" I attacked the machinery in a frenzy. After I'd busted an emergency cable, he spoke up again. I held a wrench near his face and said, "I'll bus' your skull if you don't get off my case!" He eased away, with a look as much of sadness as of fear, and clammed up. He didn't sing a song the rest of the night.

After work, I met George and Big Tom at the Assembly Line. With them were Weed and Charlie, a couple of other guys who were going to be with the club. I told them what had been going down, and Tom said, "Man, you got to cool it. If you want to be a biker, you got to be cool. Sometimes things is the way it's doin' with you at first. Straight people don't understand us, man. Till you break 'em in, most bitches don't dig it either. You got to give it time."

Weed piped in, his yellow handlebar mustache bobbing at the corners, "You see, it's another worl', bikin'. It's like wakin' up on Mars. You got to learn your way gradual."

"And you *will* learn it," George added. "Jus' let it all happen easy."

I told the guys it made me feel real good that they understood me and were taking the time to show me the way. "Hey," said Tom, "you're gonna be our brother. We all gonna stick together. All for one, one for all, that's the way it's gonna be. Listen," he said, reaching a hand across the table, "if you feel any time like things is gettin' to you, pop one of these." Between his thumb and forefinger, he held a dark capsule. I put my hand out to take it, and he dropped some more into my palm along with it.

The next few days were tense, both at home and at work. Maureen stayed clear of me, which was all right, as I felt like being by myself anyway. I apologized to Jed for jumping on him; what happened at home wasn't his fault. He said it was all right, but he eyed me warily and kept his distance from then on. Through it all, a few of Tom's red caps were a help.

I kept meeting with my new friends during the rest of the week and began to learn. First there was a whole biker language to pick up. *Crank* was amphetamine or speed. *Jammin'* was riding down the road at a steady fast pace. A *head knocker* was an ax handle, which a lot of bikers used as weapons. A *frog gigger* was a knife. *Hardware, heat, iron,* or *rod* all stood for guns. *Scooter trash* were full-time bikers, which we weren't going to be yet. We were *rooty-poots* or *rinky-dinks,* which is what the *hard-core* bikers called guys who just rode on weekends.

We began to form plans about where we were going to go and things we were going to do: trips down to Florida beaches and motorcycle races, rides to downtown Atlanta biker haunts, and a lot of parties at different guys' houses. And out of our talks came the name for the club: The Rising Sons! One of the guys, Fat Pat, drew a design for the patch on a paper napkin with a four-color pen: a red sun halfway risen over a dark green horizon, shooting long yellow rays into a blue sky with two white clouds. We all agreed it was "bitchin'" and chipped in so Fat Pat could mail away for it to a place that specialized in made-to-order club patches.

On Friday afternoon, I went to the bank and drew out the money in five C-notes. For her information, I told Maureen I had done it and what time I was setting out Saturday for Athens. She just looked away sullenly and made no comment. She didn't turn from the sink to say good-bye to me when I left the next morning.

I leaned twice on the horn outside of George's house in Covington. He had a nice place, light green with darker shutters and shingles. The lawn needed a mowing.

He popped his head out the front door and yelled he'd be right out. He had a late-model Chevy in the driveway—and his Honda, which flashed sky blue in the sunlight. The front door opened, and George stepped out, leaning back to give a peck on the cheek to a blond head that poked out after him. He strolled leisurely over to my wagon, a blue helmet under his arm, and off we took.

On the way to Athens, George told me a little about himself. He was a few years older than I was, and had been working at the plant as a body painter since he got out of high school. So he had some seniority and a rank just below foreman. But like me, it just wasn't doing it for him. He had gotten his Honda about a year ago and had done a lot of weekend riding. He and his wife had no kids, and she liked to ride, though he never took her to the rougher spots. He liked to be where the action was, had even been invited to do a little partying with "heavy-duty" bikers. He was looking forward to being a Rising Son and expanding his horizons. This

way of life, he said, was better if you had "brothers" to share it
with.

He said the boys were impressed with the way I carried myself
and he asked about my past. I filled him in until we hit the outskirts of Athens.

George said as I was parking by the cycle shop, "Don't worry
about nothin', man. I'm tight with the owner here. Jus' pick out
what you want, and I'll Jew him down!" I reminded George of the
five C's I had on me, and he said, "Check, man; I'm gonna use it."

We stepped into the showroom, where my eyes feasted on
chrome and rainbows of color while George fetched the owner.
"Jack," he said, waving a balding, fortyish guy with a straight, thin
mustache toward me, "this here's my friend Barry Mayson, and he
wants to look at yer Beezers."

"Pleased to know you, Barry," said Jack, offering a sweaty
hand. "Any friend of George's is a friend of mine."

"My pleasure likewise," I said.

And he said, "So you want to buy a BSA? Well, come right
over here."

He led me to a long rack of bikes of all shapes, hues, and sizes,
and said, with a sweeping gesture, "Take your pick—if you can
make up your mind!"

It didn't take me long to decide which bike looked right: a
fiery red 650 with lots of chrome, long black leather double seat,
chromed tachometer and fuel gauge, and silver Mag wheels. While
I eyed it, front to rear, George took Jack aside and had some words.

My insides felt tense with excitement. I ran my hands along
the fenders and tailpipes and thrilled to their cool smoothness. I
felt the sharp edges of the Mag wheels. I straddled the bike,
gripped the handlebars and saw wide-open road in my mind's eye.
Man, it looked and felt powerful even standing still!

Jack came over in a while. I had a lot of questions, and he had
a lot of answers, but it wasn't long before he was filling out papers
and I was flipping through the slick new 650 handbook. He was
saying things about guarantees and such, but I wasn't even hearing
him. The only thing on my mind was getting this machine on the
road!

Jack helped George and me load the bike over the tailgate of my wagon. With the back seats down, there was plenty of room for it. Jack shook hands again and wished me good luck. We jumped in the car and headed for countryside, topping off the bike's gas tank on the way.

George had picked out a fairly level stretch of blacktop for my "training course." We were out in farm country: A red barn and silo were hazy in the distance by a stand of tall trees that shaded a white farmhouse. Along the road, it was cows on one side, corn and cotton on the other, as far as you could see, till some pines at the bend of the pavement. Nothing was going on to be heard but the scolding of quails and the ripping of a far-off chain saw.

George was up front on the cycle; I sat behind with my knees pressing into his hips. Out of the side of his mouth that was turned toward me, he said, "Now jus' hold on to me like a tick to a dog and feel the balance. Get ahold of the way I lean my weight when I turn!"

Impatient to get going, I said, "Okay, man, I'm with you—le's burn rubber!" I wrapped my arms around his wiry chest as he began to pump down. One, two! and a deep rumble assaulted the air, drowning out every other sound! Over George's shoulder I saw the cows twitch their ears and quit chewing their cud. A few turned their heads slowly and leveled their huge eyes at us as George revved peals of thunder to the sky.

All of a sudden, I came close to shooting backward, like a mule had kicked me in the stomach. My arms strained at their sockets as George gunned full tilt down the road. I felt surges of power grinding all through me. The green and gold of the summer fields rushed by in split bursts of blur: Cotton fields and cows, standing corn, and deep-green pines all danced by in a shimmering breeze under the blue and mackerel sky. The climbing acceleration yanked at my arms and steadily increased until we reached the wide bend in the shade of the pines.

There, I could feel George let up just a mite and begin to lean over, holding the curve tight. As the bend straightened, he gunned down again, and we whiplashed off, like the follow-through twist at the end of a punch. George really let out now, the road was dead straight, and it was the nearest thing I could think of to hitching on a speeding artillery shell.

By this time, I'd already had enough of this piggyback stuff; I was hungry to ride solo. George started braking down, and I yelled, "Tha's all the lesson I need, man—lemme have a shot at this thing!"

"Not yet, man!" he hollered back. "I got a couple more things to show yuh!"

He pulled off the road into a fallow field and showed me some dirt-biking action. On an overlooking hill, I saw some shapes in blue overalls watching us jump over a few hummocks and slide into some dirt-splattering sideways stops. Then George ground it up the shoulder and back onto the road.

"Now," he yelled. "Hold on tight, 'cause we gonna *buck* this bronco!"

I swear I could feel all my nerve ends pricking out like needles when he opened up full throttle. As we were still gaining speed, I suddenly felt us tilt backward, and I was looking at a cloud! I lowered my eyes and under George's arm I saw the front wheel spinning free of the road. For a second, I thought we were ready to lift off, like riders of some flying horse in a picture book, and just wing over the hills!

At last George let the "wheelie" down, and we went back through the turn, past the cows and corn to the car. He turned the bike around and stopped. He said over the idle, "You think you can handle that, man, or you wanna ride shotgun some more?"

I said, "You can shoot it you know where, man! Lemme in that saddle!"

He put down the kickstand and got off, and I waddled to the front. I grabbed the handlebars and immediately started revving. VROOOM! ROOOOM! ROOOOOM!

"Hey, man!" George yelled in my ear. "Where you think yer goin'? You don't even know the shift yet!"

"Well, damn it, all I'm waitin' for is for you to show it to me!" I cracked, letting her purr to an idle.

He moved my hand from the clutch and said, "All right, cowboy, here it is!"

He showed me the shifting action and the brake and watched me take her out to second, turn around, and bring her back. She felt right and steady underneath me. He nodded approval and told me the rest of the transmission's feel, and then said, "Take it out, man, you're on yer own! Jus' watch you don't go over the high side on that turn!"

"Wha's that, man?"

"That's when you go too far to the outside of the turn—if you do, you'll go flyin' off into knotty pine!"

I winked, "I gotcha, man!" and took off.

I can only describe the release I felt as I turned loose that throttle as like being born, but with no tears! Underneath me, the road was flexing like a muscle: I wasn't riding on it, *it* was pushing *me*, faster and faster, till my ears heard a weird, windy music, and I suddenly realized that the throbbing engine was my real heart, I knew now that I was always ready to explode because it was gasoline pulsing in my veins, I knew now that I was one with the speed of my dreams, my voice's roar was one with an engine's exhaust, my brain was made to rule highways, I *was* the bike and the bike was *me!* I didn't need to learn to ride, my spirit had always been riding, but the rest of me had been asleep, waiting till now—to be born!

I stroked the turn like a hand running over a woman's hip, and sped down to the field George had "plowed." I plunged into it, and I wasn't riding a bike—I was a sneakered child stomping through loose dirt, kicking up clods, leaping into ankle-deep loam in some neighbor's forbidden garden, doing a war dance to the earth and sun and sky. I felt the drudging weight of my old life jar loose and fall away, the anguish of routine pushed from my mouth in a drawn-out scream of joy. I charged back to the road and reared back in a wheelie of my own. What a thrill! It was so new—but as old as my first burst of life: I was born to ride!

As I sped back, I wheelied past George, who rubbernecked, bug-eyed, at my approach. I whirled around and putted up to him, with a proud, hard smile on my face. "I tol' you I didn't need all them lessons, man!"

Shaking a finger at me, he said, "Barry, you shoulda told me you been ridin' a long time!"

"George, I been ridin' ten minutes—but it's like forever!"

"Well, man, you got it!" George said, scratching his head.

George got behind me, and we rode around for miles, getting

our fill of the sun and wind. The cool breeze rippled along my arms, and I understood fully why bikers live to ride motorcycles: It's more than fun to a biker; it's life itself, with no chains on enjoyment. I could see nothing but thrills and good times ahead, an endless highway of adventure and power.

As the afternoon drew on, we headed back to the car. George got off the bike and went to pop the wagon's tailgate. Not hearing me dismount, he turned and said, "Ain't you gonna bring that thing over and help me load it up?"

I reached into my pocket and pulled out my car keys. I tossed them to George and said, "You drive it back, man. I'm *ridin'!*"

He stood fidgeting with the keys for a few seconds, then broke into a smile and said, "All right, man! I can dig it!"

We had a ball on the way back to Covington as we leapfrogged back and forth on the highway, ran up on the tails of old farmers in rusty pickups, chugged beers, and hollered up a storm at a roadside hamburger and gas oasis.

We pulled into George's driveway by late twilight and loaded up the Beezer. George invited me in for some coffee, and we sat and talked awhile. George's wife's name was Jo; she was buttonnosed and perky; though she didn't talk much, she laughed a lot and made it clear that she loved George something fierce. I hoped that one day I'd have an old lady like her, whether it was Maureen with a new attitude or somebody new altogether.

I finally hit the road for home feeling it had been an altogether great day: I had gotten tight with a swell new brother—and I knew beyond a doubt that I was a whole new man!

4

Rooty-Poots and Heavy Duties

The Rising Sons were officially launched a few weeks later when our patches came down from Gastonia, North Carolina. They were as beautiful as we'd imagined, all the colors in silky fabrics, and in white the top and bottom "rockers"—RISING SONS M.C., and ATLANTA, GA.! We were now on the scene as a bike club!

We celebrated with a party at Big Tom's. The whole club was there: By now I had met everybody, including Filthy Fred and Horace the Hog (so-named because he was the only one among us who had a Harley-Davidson bike, though in biking circles, it was debated whether his 1,000 cc Sportster should be considered a real "Hog"). We bought a keg of beer for the occasion, and brought along our wives and girlfriends. None of us was into any drugs but diet pills at that time and a "down" now and then, so we just guzzled the hops and hugged the girls and made a lot of noise.

Tom's pad had Hell's Angels movie posters and pictures from motorcycle magazines all over the walls. He wasn't married, but Rae, whom he introduced as his "old lady," had laid out a spread of pretzels and chips and sandwiches and such, and it was a jubilant evening, filled with beer toasts and lots of happy bragging on each other. Tom had plenty of bluegrass and truck-stop-style records to keep the mood high.

One person, though, obviously wasn't having a good time. Maureen sat by herself under a big, dark poster, sipping on a mug of beer now and then. I had talked her into coming this particular night because I was sure that if she was ever going to enjoy a night with me and my new friends, it would be this one. But I could see that she wasn't about to let herself do that. She just kept that glum look and gave one-word answers to anyone who tried to be friendly to her.

This annoyed me no end, because I had risen rapidly in the gang's estimation in these few weeks, and her behavior signified that she lacked respect for me. We were going to choose officers soon. I knew Tom would be president because he got the club started, but I was hoping I'd get picked for vice-president. She wasn't helping my chances. I did my best to make excuses for her, but it was obvious that she just wasn't with it and didn't want to be.

I went over to her carrying a fresh glass of beer and said cheerfully, "Here, babe, this'll wet your whistle better!" She just looked straight ahead and said a flat, "Thanks," and set it down by her side. I knelt down and said, "Babe, wha's the matter? Why don't you loosen up and get into it? You was always ready for a swingin' party—wha's wrong?"

"These people is pigs, Barry. They's slobs. I can't stand your bein' one of 'em." She hissed it out, with no expression in her voice.

I answered back low, through teeth clenched in white-hot anger: "Woman, watch how you run your mouth! These is my brothers you're talkin' about!"

She went on blankly, "That don't change the truth. It all makes me sick."

I reached out and squeezed her shoulder till my fingers mashed her bones like a steel claw. Her face didn't change as she said, "You can't hurt me any more, Barry." But I saw her forehead break into beads of sweat. "You think so?" I almost couldn't control myself. "I ain't *begun* to hurt you! I'd kill you if we wasn't here!"

"Then kill me later, Barry, if you want to so much. Do it any time—whenever's up to you."

"Screw you!" I whispered, and let her go. Her eyes held steady, but I saw tears welling up in them, and something in me said, *No! I ain't gonna lose my cool! If she wants to get hurt, she'll fin' out what I can do. But dyin'? I won't let 'er have the pleasure!*

I got up and said, "I'll see to you later, bitch!" and rejoined the party. There was no use wishing it or trying to make it happen, I thought—she wasn't going to be a part of my new life.

We drove home from the party in silence. My insides churned, and my brain reeled with thoughts of pulling over and crushing her neck in my hands.

After I drove the baby-sitter home, I found myself turning back toward Eunice Avenue and my house, almost to my surprise. As I got out of the car, I saw a patch of light through the living room window that looked like it was coming from somewhere down the hall.

I went in the front door and tossed my cutoff on the couch. I stepped into the hall and saw, to my amazement, that the bedroom door was open. I said, "Maureen!" No answer.

I stood in the doorway by the light of the end table. I saw Maureen, her tousled head propped up by a pillow. She was looking straight at me with the slightest glimmer in her eyes. Her chest rose and fell slowly and evenly. The bruises my hand had made spread already dark on her shoulder. Her lips turned slightly upward at the corners. She said softly, "I love you, Barry. I don't know why, but I love you!"

She mus' be jokin'! I thought. *Does she want t' get hurt? Is she playin' some kin' of weird mind game?*

She stretched her arms out toward me. *God, she still thinks she owns me! Don't she know yet that she's los' the me she wants—because he's dead?*

I looked at her and despised her. But there *was* one thing she had that I wanted and I could still use—and as long as she was still going to lay it out there like that, I was going to take it. She wanted to be a glutton for punishment? I'd give it to her. What she offered was nothing more to me than a candy bar, and I was going to have it, all of it, my way, as cold as if I took it out of the freezer—before I threw the rest aside as trash.

I took off my clothes and walked to the bed. She didn't move a muscle then.

On one of the Rising Sons' first runs, a couple of weeks later, to a dirt-bike race in South Carolina, the seven of us mapped out a route of two-lane blacktop where we could do the most riding with the least traffic. We'd decided not to stick in a tight bunch all the way but regroup at certain stops for gas and beer.

One of these places was called Wham Bam Sam's Fireworks Barn, on U.S. 378 east of Saluda. Charlie and Tom moved on up ahead after a while, saying they would wait for us there.

The day was cloudless and not too hot, it being early fall, but my throat was dry: I was really looking forward to that frosty-cold beer hitting the back of it!

Bright hand-painted signs had been announcing Wham Bam Sam's for several miles, and there it was up the road, a red and white miniature of a barn with black shingles that looked like they could use some tarring. Two sedans baked in the parking lot. Under a clump of trees by the barn was a picnic table at which Tom and Charlie sat nursing what had to be cans of beer. Their two bikes rested in the shade alongside.

Tom hailed us with a hammy fist as we coasted over to the gas pumps. A broad moonface peered out of the barn window and then came through the door, atop a well-stuffed set of overalls. "What kin I do you fellers fer?" croaked a gravelly voice, chewing vigorously through a golf-ball-sized plug of tobacco.

"You can get out of my face and let me fill up," Weed growled, thrusting down his kickstand. Weed wasn't a loud guy, but he brooked no nonsense. In a fluid motion, he unstraddled his bike, reaching for the hose and flicking on the pump with one hand.

The burly proprietor thrust out his belly and folded his arms over it. "Them mus' be your friends over there," he chewed, nodding his head toward the picnic table. "Sure a couple o' nice fellers."

Hog, who'd opened up another pump, fixed the man in his narrowed eyes and said, "Tha's no guarantee about us." He stared unblinking until the man shifted his chaw and shuffled a step backward.

I was irked by this side of beef still holding his ground. A flash of heat rushed up my back, but I stanched it as I secured my cycle. Then I strolled in front of the man and leaned my face over his belly to within a few inches of his nose. "Boy, you may be worried about whether or not we're gonna pay you." He stopped chewing and shifted his plug to the other cheek. "We may, an' we may not," I went on. "If you leave us alone an' go rustle up three six-packs of Stroh's, we may. If you don't we may jus' stay here till dark an' forget that this ain't the Fourth of July—know what I mean?" I stepped back and fingered the sharp-spiked dog collar I'd recently added around my left wrist.

Eying that, he grinned, his lower lip began to tremble, and he said, "No offense meant!"

"Then don't give none." I poked at his paunch. I did an about-face to my bike and heard him waddle away as I pulled on my dip-stick.

"Damn citizen," George muttered, as he drifted up the pump, replacing Hog, who was putting over by Tom and Charlie.

I felt my temperature cool a bit. More and more, there was no gauging how any one of us might react to a thing like that. It all depended on our mood. At times, looking at us the wrong way could be dangerous. And if one of us set on, the rest would follow. Just a week ago, I had made hamburger out of the face of one dude who bugged me in a bar while I was playing pinball.

The cold Stroh's was waiting for us on the picnic table. I popped one and just chug-a-lugged it, crushed the can, and popped another. The cold throbbed in my temple for a minute and faded away.

"Amazed you waited," I smiled to Charlie.

"All for one an' one for all, Barry!" Charlie scratched the grizzles of a beard he'd started lately. One mean dude, Charlie, ex-Marine with a lot of hand-to-hand combat skills. He had a liking for honky-tonks and whorehouses, where he was fast becoming a well-known and dreaded figure. You got the feeling Charlie wasn't going to stay a root-poot long.

Tom doubled over about something Filthy Fred had cracked. "Damn straight!" he roared. "I kicked that dude's teeth out his ears —an' him with a shiv, too!"

I already knew what Tom could manage. His speed for a big man always amazed me. Had he been bent another way, he might have been a football lineman and a fearsome one.

I admired his old lady, Rae, too. She gave Tom no guff, asked no questions, and was always nice and hospitable to the patch brothers. She looked up to Tom and respected all the rest of us.

About Maureen, I couldn't say the same, but it didn't matter anymore. We'd had our club elections by this time: Tom was president, I got to be vice-president after all, and Charlie was secretary-treasurer. The brothers had been understanding about Maureen: "She jus' ain't one of us," Charlie said. "Some is, an' some ain't. Scooter trash ain't made, it's foun'." Tom and I had a talk about her one night, and he warned me that a day might come when I had to make some tough decisions. He didn't say what he meant, and I didn't feel like pursuing it . . .

Just then a honking horn broke into my thoughts. I turned to see a fresh-faced teenage boy striding quickly in our direction. He had on a cartoon T-shirt, with a big-footed goon exclaiming "Keep on Truckin'!" Other than that, he was straight, with short, sandy hair, pressed corduroy slacks, and white sneakers.

The horn kept on blasting, and then a fatherly voice called out "Jimmy!" But Jimmy kept on coming. His father opened the door of the blue sedan and stood up, looking over the roof. He didn't move or call again. A woman's voice peppered the air anxiously.

We glanced at one another with shared amusement as Jimmy stopped at the end of the table and stammered, "H-hi!"

"Hey, ol' buddy! Wha's shakin'?" The kid turned a little white at Filthy Fred's deep bellow. But he worked up his nerve again, swallowed hard and said, "Are you real Hell-Hell's Angels?" His accent was definitely Yankee.

"Can't you friggin' read, kid?" Fred pointed behind my back. "Wha's that patch say?"

"Rising Sons," the kid piped weakly.

"Hell's Angels!" Filthy Fred jammed a thumb against his nostril, leaned back, and blew his nose at the ground. "Boy, we eat Hell's Angels for breakfas'!"

"Tha's no shit," I snarled, looking as fierce as I could without laughing. "I had grits an' Angel brains jus' this mornin'. Go mighty good stirred up with fresh blood!"

Tom picked up the thread: "We'll roast a young boy like you

on a spit Saturday nights. With a apple in 'is mouth." He licked his lips greedily.

"I save the eyes," George added, "for my ol' lady to make earrings."

"See that nice tan seat? Cop hide," Charlie said.

Again the horn repeated, long and desperately.

Hog strode up, waggling something from the middle finger of his right hand. "Anybody got some use for this?" It was a grotesque "French tickler," I guessed from a rubber machine in Wham Bam Sam's men's room.

Weed slapped his thigh and roared. "Later," I hollered, "I hope!" The kid stood befuddled. Fred turned to him, chuckling: "Kid, some day when you get to be the bigges' an' the baddes', when you get too tough to eat, you stop by Atlanta, Georgia, an' look up the Risin' Sons. Now get the hell out of here before one of us gets hungry!"

By this time, the kid had seen enough. He turned tail and ran to the car, while we hooted and hollered. He jumped in the back door, and I saw his father reach around and wallop him by the ear. Above the din we were making, I heard his mother's angry shrieks. They wasted no time hitting the highway. The car had New Jersey plates.

We finished off the beer and had some snacks. Tom pulled out some pills. He and Weed took a couple each, along with Hog and Filthy Fred. Charlie and George headed for the bathroom.

I went into the barn and scanned the rows of fireworks. Sam busied himself behind the counter and made no comment. I picked out some rockets and ashcans and a cold brew for the road. As the others drifted in, I settled up with old Sam, who knew, politely to the penny, what I owed him. We had joked around about ripping Sam off, now that he was alone. But it was a mellow day, and we didn't need any delays or cop trouble.

We eased out of the lot slowly, and in my rear-view I spotted old Sam standing by the barn door, mopping his face with a big red handkerchief.

As we jammed down the road, I chuckled again over that scrawny little kid back there. He had some spunk, thumbing his nose at his folks like that. I guessed I'd have done what he did, if there'd been bikers around when I was his age. And maybe a lot more. If only I'd discovered biking sooner, how many things I wouldn't have done, and how much time I wouldn't have wasted! But I had real brothers now, I had security and acceptance, and the prospect of all the freedom I wanted. Only I'd have cut loose and become a biker a lot sooner if I'd had the choice that kid had now.

I knew one thing: I wasn't planning on staying a rinky-dink biker for long. A taste of people cringing, like old Sam did, had a way of whetting your appetite for more of the same. No, I was going to have to ride this thing as far as it would go.

Some "bikers" might stay contented career men who rode just as a weekend sideline. They might shock folks at the office, but they wouldn't get into the bar life and drugs and street fighting. Motorcycles would be just toys for them, and they'd never have a need to establish themselves as *bikers*.

We were on our way to watch men who raced bikes as a profession, whether on tracks or dirt courses. Not many of these would be *bikers*—to most of them, riding was just a satisfying way to make a living.

But to a *biker*, how could riding ever be just a sport, or a way to have fun, or even a living? It had to be something more, something like a religion. A *biker*, I thought, had to be a man who discovered himself to be a one hundred percent outcast from society— not unwillingly, but totally *willing* in his rebellion against the straight world and scornful of anyone but another biker. His cycle and his patch brothers were the only things he would put any faith in. Not even all the Rising Sons were this type of man. I had my suspicions already about who might eventually drop out. For right now, though, we all said we wanted to be full-time bikers. Once we learned how to go about it, we'd separate the men from the boys. But it wouldn't be runs like this that would tell the real story . . .

It was mostly a lot of noise and fun at first, the biking life. All of us had been influenced by movies or news media accounts of Hell's Angels or other big bike clubs. So they provided the model we tried to act out.

We'd storm into a bar sometimes and start raising loud hell.

We'd start fights anywhere at the drop of an eyebrow, "duke out" bouncers, do wheelies in the middle of town and generally make as much commotion as we could everywhere we went. In restaurants or on the street, we would outrage "citizens," or "normal" people by hugging each other and kissing on the mouth, as we saw movie bikers do. Sometimes, we'd catch a "citizen" staring at us, and we'd go up and stick our faces in theirs and gravel out "Hey! Whatsa matter, lady? You don't like what you're lookin' at? Beat it!" It was just fun to see people squirm.

If we'd see a chick walking along, we'd pull alongside of her and say things like, "Hey, babe! Them pants is walkin' by themself! How 'bout parkin' that fine body on the back o' this ol' daddy's scooter?" It was surprising how many of them took up our offer.

With those who did, we went to Weed's place. Weed had an old lady, but his apartment had two extra rooms. One had a good bed in it, and we put mattresses on the floor of the other and handed keys to the place all around so any of us could go there and do our thing. Tom's was where we partied most, especially after we began to discover some of the consequences of raising hell in public.

If you tore up a bar too much or got into too many street fights with soldiers or grossed out the wrong people, the police got called. After getting tagged with a few drunk and disorderly charges, we agreed that we just couldn't be as out front as those bikers had been in the movies! We did more of our partying at our own places and hung out in bars where we were respected enough not to get challenged too often. Most disagreements among ourselves were settled in scuffles well-refereed by fellow patch members.

In these situations, it wasn't so important who won the fight as it was that you never backed down from a challenge. Of course, if a fellow patch member was attacked in your presence, it was an all-on-one stomp. If a brother got beat up alone, vengeance was exacted by the whole club as soon as the offender (or offenders) could be found.

Most of this mayhem we carried out after midnight, since our jobs didn't let out till then. But the more we got of this high life, the more we craved. The temptation to lay off work and extend our hours in the night world was getting harder to resist. We were gaining in reputation along the strip; some goodies in the form of exotic drug offers and go-go dancers' company now got waved our way.

I usually got back home around dawn now, if at all, and by the time I had crashed out, it was near time to head for work again. Maureen didn't do much to keep the kids quiet, so my sleep was fitful, contributing to my general nastiness around the house. She knew I was way out of hand, and tried to tell me so a few times, but I either ignored her or walloped her or half-raped her into silence. I paid no attention to the kids anymore, except to bellow at their noise. I was home scarcely at all on weekends. More and more I got to depend on "speed" to keep me working and careening through the nights. I began to front speed deals on the job and sense some of the money potential in drugs.

We all in the Rising Sons had just started to feel like about the coolest of the cool when we began running into some heavy-duty bikers around town. Among the first of these contacts was with a club called the Huns.

As Tom, George, and I were riding down the strip one night, I heard some roaring come up behind us deeper and louder than I was accustomed to. I didn't look around, but it was still back there as we halted for a stoplight down the block. A wild-haired, bearded head right out of a *Teenage Werewolf* flick drifted to my side, atop a long-forked Harley-Davidson fatbob-tanked Superglide.

This "werewolf" looked over at my still crew-cut hair and clean-shaven face. His body started to bob up and down, and a raucous voice clubbed the air: "Haw! Haw! Haw! Haw!"

I twisted my head his way and snarled, "Wha'ch' you laughin' at, hog-eye?"

He broke out a couple more "haws" and shouted, shaking all over, "'Risin' Sons!' Another goddam bunch of rooty-poots cloggin' the road! I thought we done sent the exterminator around already this month—just seems like we can't get the cockroaches off the street! Haw! Haw! Haw!"

He rumbled off on the green, with me shouting to his smoke, "Come on, man, and pull that donkey over! I'll show you who's a cockaroach!" I lit after him for a block or two, but he had more horse than I did, and as he drew on away, I saw that his top rocker read "Huns M.C."

I let up and waited for Tom and George to catch me. George flashed me a green grin on the stoplight and yelled, "Hey, banty Barry! Ready t' take on the Huns! Go at him, jughead!"

I looked back at him sideways and hollered, "You better be glad you're a brother an' smilin' or I'd tack your hide over a baboon's ass!"

Mocking the now long-gone hairy Hun, George gave two Haw! Haw!s and then got serious, "Don't you worry, Barry, the place an' time is gonna come when we show them suckers what we're made of!"

That time came soon enough, but not in the way we expected. It happened something like this: Charlie and Tom were in a bar playing pool a week later, when a blue-collar gutbuster began mouthing off about Charlie's shotmaking. Charlie whipped the side of the dude's head with a pool cue, and up jumped four of his "citizen" friends. Between the two of them, Charlie and Tom laid out the "citizens" and resumed their pool game.

Over from a side table walked two Huns who had been drinking there and seen all the action. "Hey!" one of them gruffed at Tom. Tom didn't answer, just went on lining up his shot. "I said 'Hey!'" said the Hun, a little louder.

Tom sank his ball and looked up. "Who's talkin'?" he said, scanning his next ball.

"A Hun, man," the other dude threw in.

"What's your news?" Tom mumbled, pocketing a six-ball.

"We dug the way you duked them 'citizens,'" said the first Hun.

"You got taste," said Charlie, picking up the chalk.

Pausing a minute, the first Hun said, "You guys mus' think you're cool."

"We're standin' here," Charlie said, as he watched Tom sink the seven and leave himself an impossible play.

"We been seein' you around," said Hun number two. "They call me Froggy, this here's Fungo."

Tom, who had given over to Charlie, returned the intro.

Then Froggy said, "So you guys think you're cool? Come on down tomorrow night and party with us."

"Where at?" Tom said. Fungo told him, and when.

Charlie, who had failed to corner the impossible shot, stepped aside for Tom and said, "You be there—we'll fin' it." Fungo shook his fist in a last tribute to the fighting skill they'd witnessed, and the Huns went back to their drinks.

"Take a toke of this, man," said "Hawk," passing me what I recognized as a joint thick as my middle finger. Not having done dope before, I didn't know quite what to expect, but when dudes as heavy as the Huns make a suggestion, you don't decline.

"Sure, man," I said, smiling eagerly. I took the joint and put it to my lips just like I knew exactly what I was doing. I dragged in as deep as my lungs could hold.

The smoke was on the harsh side and, once in there, tempted me to nearly cough my guts up. I knew you should hold the stuff in, so I somehow swallowed back my gagging impulse. I didn't know what was supposed to happen next. Was I going to feel drunk? Do funny things? Only thing to do was let it happen.

I let the smoke out and felt nothing at all. *Well, hell,* I thought, *there ain't nothin' to this! I jus' mus' be naturally high!* A hand was extended to my left, waiting for the joint. But I decided to play it tough all the way. "Great smoke!" I beamed to all around and took another even deeper drag before sending the joint on its way.

"Haw! Haw! Haw!"

The same beady "werewolf" eyes I had looked into on the street not many days ago were dancing with candle flame across from me. With another "Haw!" the hairy one roared out, "Boy, you ain't got no idea how great that zinger-dinger is—yet! Name's Darryl"—reaching out a hand as hairy as the rest of him—"all the Huns welcome yuh!"

As officers, Tom, Charlie, and myself decided to make this date. We were proud to be asked to party with the Huns. At the same time, we knew we would be tested and challenged, though we didn't know how. Up to this point, everyone had been superfriendly. I wondered if and when there'd be any trouble.

The Huns' clubhouse was a lot more menacing than any of our

places. Posters on the walls were darker and more violent. Near me, a skeleton in leathers and a helmet rode a gleaming black cycle; behind him sat a bony "old lady," who for "hair" had writhing snakes. Garish red lipstick was smeared around her grinning teeth. Her skinny arms curled around his waist, one hand rested in his crotch. The long blade of a scythe curved through the exhaust of the cycle. The planet Saturn, painted in purple and yellow, loomed over a landscape pocked with craters.

Pictures of women weren't slick men's magazine centerfolds like ours; the ones here had men in them, too, and animals, sometimes doing all kinds of kinky things. I hadn't seen shots like these since Korea.

Beer was flowing freely, but also high-proof hard liquor. One hundred plus bourbons disappeared like soda pop. The few girls here weren't wives or old ladies; they were whores, doing after-hours services—in most cases, the Huns were their pimps.

The Huns themselves were rough, loud, and barred no holds. Whether it was a train of five guys on a girl or snorting crystal meth or toying with a pistol, in the clubhouse it all went down, in plain sight. I felt thrills of anticipation running all through me. This was better than the movies had been, deeper, more dangerous. It was all right there, nothing stopping me from touching it.

Somebody turned the lights out. The music had turned strange, like the metal guitar strings were crying out in pain. Now the only light was two candles that flickered lazily in tall red glasses. It seemed like a long way from me the orange-red glow of a joint's tip was arching very slowly through the dark, leaving a trail in the air like a tracer bullet. It bounced and hopped up and gleamed brighter as it cast a glow on the nose and cheeks of its smoker. The jigsawed face dimmed out as the light resumed its journey, shooting straight to my right, hesitating, then doing a little leap again, brightening, and this time more slowly revealing the pieces of a face. Above the tip's fire, flashes from two eyes darted at me, almost causing me to tumble over backward. I felt my head jerk forward on my neck and my body right itself.

The light suddenly floated into view before my face. I saw my hand swim up to meet it, like a fish surfacing from a river bottom for a fly. The light jerked, then stopped in front of my face. Tiny sparks clicked in it, like Roman candles crackling in a distant field.

I heard a deep voice, like a 78 record on 45, roll in my ears: "Haaaaw! Haaaaw! Haaaaaaawuuh! Ta-a-a-ke-ah u-uh-nu-uh-thu-uhhh t-o-o-o-ke-uh, ma-a-an! Haaaaaw! Haaaawuh!"

The light loomed larger, near my nose. The joint's narrow end was wet on my dry lips. I felt myself breathe in and my lungs pull in what seemed to my mind's eye like a black cloud. My eyes closed, and in my lungs the cloud seemed to billow then twist. Then I could feel it shrinking. In my eyelids it was growing smaller; at its edges oozed a field of pure blue. The cloud shrank into the blueness slowly until the blue engulfed it and the cloud disappeared. I felt my whole body lift lightly a few inches into the air, like a blue carny balloon, and just hang there. A thought grinned across my face: *I'm high!*

Pent-up breath rushed out of me in slow snorts of laughter. I felt fingers touch mine and pry the joint loose with determination. I began to fall backward again, but this time, nothing in me wanted to stop. I collapsed like a series of still photos, my mind contemplating the change of position in each one. Each muscle reached out for a day, a year, who knew how long? And let go. Every cell in me felt a pull toward the floor. Bits of words jumbled in my ears, with no meaning. Like a building bashed by a wrecker's ball, everything settled atom by atom in a heap. Finally, every particle came to rest, and was still for what seemed like centuries. Complicated patterns of lines, light, and color formed and fell apart in my mind as I lay in still amazement.

I have no way of knowing how long it was before I began to climb out of the ruin. Everything still moved slowly but was getting faster. I could tell after a while that the speeding-up voices were hung in throbs of laughter. I sensed it wasn't all at me. I rolled over on my side and saw I wasn't the only wreck in the room. Charlie was floored, along with Hawk and another Hun, Bingo. Only Darryl the werewolf sat steady, lost in his everlasting Haw! Haw! Haw!s.

I got an elbow under my head and caught Darryl's eye. Holding his shaking sides, he hollered, "Dynamite dope, huh, Barry? DMT-cured! Haw! Haw! Don't last long, but *how it lasts, while* it lasts!"

I got an arm under me and sat up straight, shaking my head. "I'll say, man. That was some wild ride!" As I looked around, there was still a glow in the air, like a saltshaker of light had been sprinkled on everything. Someone had turned on a black light. The poster with the Grim Reaper and his bony broad quivered like the cycle was really vibrating down the road. "Hey," I cried, pointing at it, "tha's the real International Harvester, man!"

Darryl and I roared with laughter until only a last few yoks were left to squeeze out. By that time, the rest of the room had straightened up. Bingo was offering me a poke at a fifth of Wild Turkey, with which I gladly soaked and seared my throat.

When everybody's head was somewhat together again, Froggy and Tom walked in and sat down next to Charlie. It hadn't struck me that it was getting crowded with Huns in here, but things seemed a bit cooler with Tom back.

We had got to talking about the size of the Huns' drug-dealing network when Froggy suddenly cursed loudly, and pulled at his trouser leg. He said, "This goddam scab is itchin' hell outa me!" He rolled up the pants leg, revealing a big dark blotch. "I had enough." He said, "I'm takin' the damn thing off!" With that, he dug his fingernails around it and ripped it free. As the conversation picked up again, I saw him stuff the scab into his mouth. He slurped it loudly as we talked.

After a while, he took it out of his mouth and passed it away from Charlie to another Hun. None of the Huns seemed to be paying much attention to this action, but all us Rising Sons kept an eye on that scab. Hawk was chewing on it and sucking it just as Froggy had. He soon handed it to Jimson, who waggled it in and out of his mouth with his tongue.

Jimson then leaned over and held the scab out to Tom. "Here, man, take a suck on this." Tom held a hand in front of his face, blocking the idea: "No, man, I don't want it!"

Jimson stretched out his hand toward me and grinned. "How about you, man?"

I thought to myself, *Well, it may be disgustin', but if they can do it, I can do it!* I took it from Jimson and shoved it right in. As I sucked the coldish slime away, I almost laughed out loud at what I discovered: What Froggy had pulled off his leg was a piece of bark, which only looked, in the dim light, like a scab! The Huns had dreamed up the whole thing just to spook us out! Now that I'd done it, Tom had to follow suit. He did: then, wincing just slightly, so did Charlie. Not one of us said anything about this action while it was happening, but I heard Darryl chuckling to himself, "Righteous, man, righteous!"

As we began to hang around with the Huns and other clubs, like the Iron Cross, we got a lot of similar tests of our "righteousness," which we managed to pass. The further you got into it, the more head games got added to physical tests. But with surviving them, we felt that the hard-cores didn't have anything over us. Any superiority they had was just a matter of knowing the ropes. I didn't show any weakness during these ordeals. In fact, I *wasn't* weak. I'd try anything put in front of me, with no fear—and I'd do it.

One of the things that got us a good deal of the Huns' respect happened the night of a sort of fortunate accident. In the back of the Huns' clubhouse was a big oak tree. Some of us were doing our drinking under there, and old Fungo got an urge to climb the tree. We weren't paying much attention as he whooped and hollered his way up, but soon, down came a limb with Fungo crashing right after it, just outside our circle. He landed flush on his back, all his breath knocked out of him.

He lay there, writhing and unable to get any wind, while his brother Huns and the rest of us stood there wondering what to do. I had done some lifeguarding as a teenager and suddenly remembered: mouth-to-mouth resuscitation—that was it!

So I kneeled down and put my mouth to Fungo's and my hands on his chest over his heart and went to work. Soon his breathing started up and got regular again. He sat up after a while and said, "Thanks, man. I might be a goner if you wasn't here!" I told him don't mention it, but it ended up getting mentioned around a lot. Fungo being a patch member, a lot of gratitude came our way for this "cool scene." And with all the Huns I especially was "in."

As our club and the Huns became close, we hung around together, and I began to learn refinements in how to walk and dress and talk, who some of their drug connections were, a few things about pimping, guns, and other weapons—and also what was voodoo—or forbidden—for bikers.

Stealing another biker's drugs, for example, was voodoo. What got somebody high was his alone. Now, you might come to a guy who had, say, some crank (speed) and say, "Brother, I got me some coke here that I'd like to share with you. How about settin' me on to a little of that crank? Le's do it up and hit the town!" And he'd let you in on it most of the time.

The more knowledge I picked up, the more certain I was that I could make it as a full-time biker, but I had some things still holding me back. I didn't yet have enough business interests developed to keep me going without my job. And I had a wife who I knew wouldn't go along with the life I'd chosen.

Anyone who wants to be a hard-core biker has to figure out ways to operate beyond the law. Keeping your bike on the road is everything; getting into crime is the means to that end. Whether your thing is stolen guns, autos, or motorcycle parts; drugs; gambling; or prostitution, it has to allow you maximum freedom and minimum contact with straight society. If you have an old lady and other women, they're there to do their part, whatever that means: dealing dope, stripping, B-drinking, or hooking. Some pickups and "mamas" just hang around to party and get laid, but you don't let them get attached to you unless they set themselves to being productive. While she still turned me on sexually, Maureen wasn't about to work toward my future as a biker.

My job was getting to be a major headache, too. As drugs began to color my thinking, I resented the time and concentration the inspecting demanded. I hated still having to make money in a lifestyle I'd otherwise left behind. I knew I was going to have to make some moves, and fast, to get free for all that I wanted.

5
Cutting Loose

One weekday night, I headed for downtown Atlanta to see what was happening. I had traded a couple of black beauties for a faked doctor's excuse to give me free leave to lay away from work, and I was meeting Weed and the Hog at the Giant Dwarf chicken shack, on the way to whatever the night had in store.

As I pulled up, I spied my two "brothers" outside the joint talking with three girls. My eyes fell immediately on one of the chicks. She was wearing black hiphuggers with wide yellow flanges and a tight black top. Her hair was long and dark brown, and everything about her was moving every which way, because she was wobbling drunk.

I shut down near this group, got off, and swaggered up to the brothers. "Hey, Hog, Weed! Wha's shakin'?"

"What is, man, you see it," said Hog, thumbing toward the girls. Hog never said much, but what came out of his mouth was always to the point. "We got three sisters here, Ellen, Chris, an' this lean one's Fran," he said, pointing at the chick whose looks I liked.

I eyed Fran again. She was swaying from side to side to side, like a snake planning to strike. She didn't look at me, but she waved a hand at my Beezer and said in a low slur, "Man, what a ugly bike! Tha's a rooty-poot bike—ain't no Harley-Davidson!"

I liked the way her dark eyes darted around, both proud and a little nervous. I liked the trim curves and the promises they made as part of her rolled one way and caught itself and then rolled another. I liked her sass and her fresh drawl. I felt like busting her upside the head for what she was saying—but at the same time, I was already thinking about getting into her pants.

I stepped beside her and said, low and sexy as I could, "So you don't like my machine."

She looked straight at me for the first time, from under heavy-blacked lashes, and said, "Don't see much machine to like. An' you don't look like no biker, neither."

She was right, insofar as I was still clean-shaven and short-haired. I was getting ready to start a beard, but I hadn't made up my mind what kind yet.

"Looks can fool you," I said, looking as mean as possible.

She tossed her long hair and drawled, "I ain't fooled. I know real bikers. I had me a ol' man out in California who was a Hell's Angel." I heard Hog and Weed laughing at these goings on, but I ignored them and zeroed in on Fran.

She had taken to twirling her finger around the inside of the big, dark, gypsy-style earrings that dangled against her cheeks. She was messed up—and lying—but I dug the neat way the mess was hanging together.

She went on, her eyes half shut, as if looking off into a private dream world. "Un-huh, an' I'm goin' back West real soon. Ain't no good action in this town."

"That so?" I smiled. "Well, tell me this, li'l Angelette, what happened to that ol' man of yours? Whatever got into him to let you fly the coop?"

"Oh, he never let me loose, I jus' split one night on my own. That ol' man wa'n't bein' near good enough for me." She smoothed her hair back and let me get a good look at her full face. She had smooth and firm-looking lips and soft cheeks that covered wide bones. Her nose was small-nostriled and narrow. Above her dark eye shadow, her brows were thick, well-shaped, and penciled in dark. The pupils of her eyes were wide, pulling in everything and nothing at once.

"So your Angel-man done let you down, huh?" I stroked my
upper lip to half hide my smile.

Her eyes blinked lazily. "Hell, if they ain't up to snuff, ditch
'em, I say."

"Well, what you doin' till somethin' better comes along?" I
couldn't help laughing out loud.

"Fightin' off rinky-dinks with grabby hands," she said, playing
with her earring and looking drunk-smirky.

I was about to answer, when her eyes looked past me and lit
up. I turned and saw Holy Harry's yellow Caddy drive up. Holy
Harry dealt coke and speed, and it was obvious from Fran's interest
that she was one of his customers. She started drifting over to his
car. I moved to follow, and Hog grabbed my arm.

"You like that stuff, Barry?"

"Yeah, I think I'll see what I can do with it."

"Weed and me is gonna bar-hop these two over to his place."

"Okay, man. I'm gonna cut this one out o' the herd an' see how
she rides. Maybe I'll catch you later."

"Dig it." He made over to where Weed was jawing with the
two girls. They had some words, then walked to the street.

Weed and Hog parked the chicks on their bikes and fired up.
I turned my attention back to Fran, who leaned over into Holy
Harry's window. Her butt had some contours I surely wanted to
check out!

I tucked my head beside her in the window and laid an arm on
her back. She didn't move it.

"Hey, Harry," I said, "wha's hot?"

"It's this way, Barry—what's *not?*"

We laughed as I reached in my hand. Fran said, surprised,
"Hey, rooty-poot man, you know Harry?"

"Sure, babe, he an' I have a 'speedin'' acquaintance!"

Harry slapped his thigh and said, "Dig it. Lemme see you two
to a spot of java." Fran and I glanced at each other and nodded,
and Harry said, "Lemme tie up this ol' dinosaur, an' I'll be right in."

We walked into the restaurant and found a booth looking out
the front window. Fran sat down in the seat across from me and
said, "So you know ol' Harry? Maybe you ain't as straight as you
look."

"I'm workin' on gettin' bent," I said, and ordered three coffees.

Harry came in and sat next to Fran. He had on a pencil-thin tan suit; he had the lead-skinny, bug-eyed look of a user of his specialties. His bony fingers traced jagged patterns in front of his face as he started rattling on sprint-rate about recent events along the strip. As usual, he was concerned about narcs and stoolies and how hard they were making it to keep his work righteous.

"It's a holy callin'," he said seriously, "openin' up the vistas of people's heads. There's enemies who don't want to see it happen."

He put an arm around Fran and leaned her over to me. I bowed in, and he looked left and right suspiciously, then whispered: "I got some dynamite crystal meth in a bag in my right pocket. You'd be wise to get a taste of it before they catch up with me!"

I said, "It might make the night more interestin'. You stan' by it?"

"On my righteousness, man, an' you know where that's at."

I asked him how much, and we settled on a price and made the exchange under the table. Just then the waitress brought the coffees. Harry looked up at her, startled.

She left and he whispered, "I got to be movin', man, I feel the vibes gettin' heavy in here." He got to his feet, held a hand spread-fingered in front of his bulging eyes, and said, "May your journeys be galactic!" and strode jerkily to the door. Fran and I shared a chuckle. Out the window, I saw him look quickly both ways and disappear.

I turned to Fran and said, "He never drank his coffee!" She said, "Nope. He never hangs aroun' long." She was unwrapping a stick of gum she had taken from a small pocketbook that she'd set on the table. "Well, babe," I said, "we got some high-test speed here—what we gonna do with it?"

She popped the gum into her mouth and took a couple of chews. She looked at me with her lashes low and said, "What'ch you mean, 'we,' rinky-dink?"

"I mean until your next Angel-man comes along, you ought to check out a Rising Son! Hell's Angels got nothin' on us—we keep a few around the clubhouse jus' to fetch sticks for us." I decided to put it to her directly: "Maybe you'll meet your next ol' man over there eatin' our dog food. Come on and take a ride with me."

She dropped her eyes and snickered, running her front teeth over her lower lip.

I said, "Wha's the matter—you chicken?"

Her eyes shot up at me straight and hard. "I ain't scared o' nothin'!"

I looked back at her just as hard and said, "Only one way to prove that: Le's go!"

Her eyes fell back into their dream state for an instant. Then she floated me a faraway look and slurred, "All right!" She oozed herself out of the booth, and I caught her under the arm and helped her up. She was still on the wobbly side, so I steadied her to the door with a hand under her elbow.

We swayed over to my bike, and I helped her onto the back. She was unsteady, so I got on in front quickly, reached around, and pulled her arms across my chest. I revved up and hollered, "Now you hang on as if you was my shirt!"—which I wasn't real sure she could manage! She was shaky up there, but she put a tight hug on me. When we shoved off, I was surprised that it didn't take her long to learn to move in tandem with me.

I rode her around for a while, away from the usual biker haunts. I didn't want to take any kidding—or do any sharing! She seemed to enjoy the ride. I took her down some back streets and ran a wheelie or two. She squealed with delight: "Stop it, Barry! Not so fas'! Ooh, you ride good!"

I braked at the end of a side street and drew to a halt. I turned and threw an arm around her. I pulled her close and said, "Do I ride as good as your Hell's Angel?"

She smiled and said, "With another lesson or two, you'll do!"

I kissed her softly and said, "Come home and teach me."

She touched my nose with her forefinger and said, "Sure you ain't chicken?"

Letting loose of her, I said, "Baby, le's go!"

Nobody was at Weed's place yet. I winked at Fran and said, "Your sisters mus' still be bar-hoppin'."

Fran said, "Your buddies don't move as fast as you!" I led her down the hall, and she asked, "Where's the bathroom?"

I pointed it out and told her where I'd be. There was a pretty solid double bed in the side room—and I had a skeleton key that locked the door: As I entered the room I put it in the keyhole ready to lock. A shaft of light slanted into the corner near the window. I figured that was enough and didn't reach for a switch.

I hung my cutoff on a chair and took out the bag of crystal. I unbanded it, licked the tip of my little finger, and dipped it in the glistening white powder. I dabbed it on my tongue: It was super-bitter, just the tiniest hint of sweetness. *Bitchin'!* We were going to fly right tonight! I set the speed on the bed. I took off my boots and socks and set them out in the hall so they wouldn't stink up the place. I took off my T-shirt and hung it on the chair and sat on the bed, stretching my feet to let them air out.

Fran peered in at the door and then came in. I pointed to the key behind her and said, "Shut it, an' lock it up." She did that, and I hoped my feet didn't still stink. Now, why was I worried about that? Never had before.

There was a small table near the window, with a mirror on it, and a chair beside. Fran went over and sat down, crossed her legs, and slipped off her shoes. She began taking bobby pins out of her hair and parking them between her lips. Part of her hair was a long fall, which she carefully spread out on the table. I wished she'd hurry; at the same time, I enjoyed watching her. She put the bobby pins in her pocketbook and set it by the mirror. She turned her face from one side to the other, ran both hands back through her hair once and got up slowly.

She came over to the bed and sat down. I held the meth out to her and said, "Take a taste o' that!" She did, and her finger lingered at her lips. "Mmm!" she said, her eyebrows lifting. "Tha's holy!"

"Like Holy Harry said!" I added, and we laughed. I spread a dollar bill and shook the crystal right on George Washington's nose. We snorted up, and I laid the bag on the rug by the bed for later.

A six-foot poster of a Harley street chopper stretched alongside the bed. I was glad for the difference of mid-autumn heat—it didn't boil in all your pores. But the speed was firing in my brain, and I

could see it in Fran's eyes. I took her in my arms and reached
under her top for her bra catch. "Le's let it roll," I said.

"Okay," she whispered. And we were on!

Somewhere during the night, I looked down into Fran's eyes
and saw shifting like a kaleidoscope, pain, pity, desire, strength,
terror, and determination. I ran my fingers all around her eyes and
said, "I want to own you."

A shiny black ball spilled from the corner of her left eye and
streaked toward her ear. "I think you already do, Barry," she said. I
knew I had really found her—someone who had what it took to ride
with me into this life, all the way.

Before dawn, Fran told me she was an army kid, rootless,
hated school and work; she'd had a shotgun wedding and at seven-
teen a son named Rusty who now lived with her parents; she
wanted nothing in life but to stay high and have good times; she'd
never been with a biker or even on a bike before.

I told her how my stepdad had been an airline pilot and my
family had moved a lot, too; how my life had gone bad when he
died; about the Army; about my job; about how I got into biking. I
didn't tell her about Maureen.

At daybreak I smiled to her, "Now don't be surprised if some
angry bitch comes up the fire escape an' smashin' through that window. It's happened before!" That's how I let her know there was
"somebody else" out there—but I also told her that "somebody"
wasn't running my life.

That very night, I laid out of work again and took Fran downtown to Peachtree Street. Everybody seemed to be around, riding
up and down the street, and I introduced Fran here and there.
Some of the Huns and Iron Cross were real rough and scraggly-
looking; I could tell she was a little scared. She commented to me
especially about Scag's crossed eyes and Glugg's coating of dirt and
oil. I told her to just stick close to me and nobody would mess with
her. She could see the respect I enjoyed on the street, and that
impressed her. After a while she began to enjoy herself and all the
loudmouthing and funny goings-on.

"Hey, Barry! Hey, Barry-Barry!" Fungo rolled up and we grabbed forearms. He always called me that—Barry-Barry. "Who's the chick, Barry-Barry?"

I introduced Fran, and Fungo said, "This here's a righteous ol' man—saved my life one night, ain't that so, Barry-Barry?"

"I didn't do nothin'," I said. "If you'd a died, you'd a got up an' been the king of the zombies!"

Fungo doubled over laughing, and when he tailed off, he said, "Man, I got to burn rubber. But hey! I'm onto some fine organic mesc. Come by my place, and we'll get it on! And bring the ol' lady, too!"

"I hear you, man! We'll check it out."

Fungo blasted off, and I thought how good it was to hear him call Fran my old lady. It sure did feel right!

"Barry?"

"Yeah, babe?"

"How come he kep' callin' you Barry-Barry? Ain't that some kinda disease?"

I thought that over for a minute. "You know, I think you're right about that! I remember hearin' somethin' called "Barry-Barry" or "Berry-Berry" in a basic trainin' movie." I turned the idea over in my mind awhile. Then I snapped my fingers and grinned at Fran. "It's right, babe! Tha's who I am! I'm Barry-Barry!" I made my eyes wild and crazy above the grin: "I'm a DISEASE!"

Fran thought that was a gas, and I liked it, I really did. From then on, whenever I met somebody, I'd say, "Hi! I'm Barry-Barry— I'm a DISEEEASE!" It was fun—and no one ever forgot it!

We scuttled around to a few bars that night and managed to run into most of the Rising Sons. I could see Fran was going to be a full part of the scene in no time. What troubled me was what I was going to do about the home situation. I explained it to Fran; she wasn't upset, she just told me to wait on it and it would all work out. I was glad she felt that way. I didn't tell her, but I thought that if I could, I wouldn't mind having both—a wife *and* an old lady. As a biker, I felt like I could have—and mess with—as many women as I could handle. Of course, if they were "property," I didn't want *them* messing with anyone else. But I wasn't quite ready yet to turn loose of Maureen.

About two days later I straggled into the house. Maureen looked up from the couch with a fury in her eyes I'd never seen before. It was about 11 A.M. The TV was on to some soap opera with a sobbing organ; the kids were playing with the toys scrambled on the rug. When he saw me, Ron tripped over and hugged my leg and jumped up and down: "Daddy, Daddy! C'mup!"

"Where've you been?" Maureen shot to her feet and scooped up Jim with one arm. "Lemme get these kids outa here so we can have this out!"

"Hey, no need for that, babe! They want t' see their ol' dad!" I reached my arms down for Ron, and Maureen snapped, "Take your hands off of him!" She grabbed him by the waist and I let her rip him off my leg. He began to scream, and then Jim did, too. Dragging them to the hall, Maureen shouted back, "I don't want them to see you—or what might happen here in a few minutes!"

I sat down heavily in my easy chair. I was tired from the last few hard nights and hoping to crash out for a couple of hours before I went back into work. I was in no mood for this. The shutting door muffled the babies' yowling, and I decided to keep things as low-keyed as possible.

Maureen came in and stayed standing. She got a pack of cigarettes out of her housedress and lit one with an angry puff. She shook the match dead, tossed it at the ash tray, flung her hair back with a jerk of her head, and folded her arms. The cigarette dangled from her mouth. She tapped her foot, waiting for me to say something.

"Don't you make a picture?" I jibed, mouthing a smoke of my own. "Ain't you too young an' pretty to be playin' a angry ol' bag?" I lit up and blew out easy.

She didn't shift position and didn't smile. "Don't even begin tryin' t' sweet-talk me, Barry. Just tell me what you think is goin' on!"

"Well, one thing tha's goin' on is that damn soap suds crap over there," I said, jerking a thumb at the TV. She made a move in its direction and I said, "Maybe you should leave it on—it fits this little scene we're havin'! She paused and then went to it, clicked it off, and sat on the far end of the couch.

"All right," she said, "give!"

I didn't like her tone, but I said, sweet as sugar, "You asked me where I been? Ridin' an' workin'—it's as simple as that."

"It ain't simple, and you're lyin'," she spat out. Before I could answer, she went on, "You ain't been to work in four days. I been checkin' on you. You been out of work a week in the last three. 'How is 'e?' your boss asked me. 'Must be some bout of summer flu that he's havin' such a rough time shakin' it.' I called Jed. He's been tryin' to cover up for you. Says you been comin' in drunk an' hopped up on God knows what. He don't know how much longer he can keep 'em from gettin' on you."

"Woman, you got no call to be messin' in my business!"

"No call! What you think I been doin' here, frettin' myself to death wonderin' when they're gonna come to the door an' say they found you in some alley with a knife in your belly! No call! *You* owe *me* a call at least, so I know you ain't dead . . . ! An' ridin'? Bull! You can't ride no ninety-six hours straight, unless you're ridin' some slut . . ."

"You can't stan' it, can you!" I broke in, jumping to my feet. "You can't stan' that I'm havin' some fun! You can't stan' it that I got freedom! *You* don't want it, but you jus' can't stan' my havin' a *life!*"

"*Life!*" she screamed, rising to her feet, her hands clenched by her waist. "An' what kind of *life* do you think *I've* had, for God's sake! You beat me an' cuss me an' cheat me—an' you ain't even buyin' me off anymore! You left me here to rot in this house while you ride off an' I don't even know anymore whether next week I'll have a roof to rot under!"

"Hey, wait a minute! You got your bills paid!"

"Yeah? An' where you gettin' the money? You ain't been *workin'* for it!"

"Sick pay, babe."

"You ain't got none left—I checked."

"So? Whatta you care, so long as you get yours?"

"Get mine? An' what about that, lover boy? I get you every blue moon like I get a cold Coke bottle, an' you talk to me about livin'!"

"Hey! You got your car. You get a sitter, you got your nights

free. You can go out an' fin' yourself a candy man. Jus' see I don't
catch you!" I winked and she turned away in disgust.

"What's the use talkin' to you?" She shook her head. "There
ain't no way . . ." She faced me and said, "Barry, I've decided
somethin'—an' I got to know right now."

"Right now's awful sudden," I said, acting overshocked, to see
if I couldn't cool things down some.

"It ain't been sudden, Barry. But here it is: You got a choice—
it's either me or that bike club! You either sell that bike, come back
here an' stay put—or you move to the clubhouse or wherever them
barflies light!"

I looked at her calmly. In that moment, for some reason, I
wasn't the slightest bit angry. She had laid it out that clear: Now I
knew what I had to do.

"Choice?" I said. "There ain't no choice. I *know* where *my* real
family is. I'll move out! I got *brothers* who'll put *me* up. I *know*
they care for me. I *know* *they* understan' me. It's good, babe. I
won't have to take this shit no more."

"*You?!*" She blazed up for an instant, then let it die as quick.
"All right," she said, "get your stuff."

She turned and stood, her arms folded, looking out the front
window.

I saw no sense in carrying on further. I hadn't really done any
deciding; it had been done for me. She knew what I would pick. I
went to the bedroom and dug out what I figured I would need.
Without all the straight clothes, it was lot less than I used to need. I
went to the storage room and got my toolbox and my army duffel
bag. I stuffed the clothes and gear in the bag and on the way out
remembered to pick up a pair of work shoes I had left muddy near
the kitchen door. I looked in on the kids. They were asleep, Jim in
his crib, Ron on his blanket on the floor.

I set my gear down in the doorway and picked Ron up. His
sleepy eyes opened, and he said, "Daddy," and yawned and shut
his eyes again.

I said, "So long, li'l buddy!" and put him gently on his bed. He
curled into his blanket and lay on his belly, still.

Maureen wasn't in the living room. I left my stuff there and
found her in the kitchen, laying out the makings for sandwiches. I

said, "I didn't want it this way. It could've been different if you'd understood."

She spread mustard on a piece of bread, didn't look at me. "It never could have been no different," she said quietly.

"Well," I said, "tha's it."

"Good-bye," she said tiredly, and laid on a slice of ham.

"So long," I said, and began to turn. "Say," I said, "I want t' see my kids."

"The law says you can," she said. "I checked."

"Good. I'll be aroun'."

"I don't know what for."

"Because they're *mine*," I said.

I lugged the stuff to my bike, and with belts and the duffel-bag straps secured it to the back. I looked around just once, and saw no face at the window. I fired up and took off. Destination: Weed's.

6

Spark Plug Trouble

I did what I wanted at Weed's, and the freedom was sweet: nobody to answer to, nobody's worry to worry about, and no time-table I didn't make myself. Life was night-to-night, hour-to-hour, "Whatever goes around, comes around," as we used to say. The future we never thought about; it was snort some speed, toke some pot, and take off . . .

Down to Peachtree Street, thunder of exhaust stomping out strip music from honky-tonks . . . Bleary-eyed drunks turning unsteady on the sidewalk to watch us roar by . . . Feeling a wave of power push in front of you as you looked over a bar full of "citizens" . . . The gleam of many-colored capsules shadowed by the crinkle of "long green" passing over the exchange . . . A wise-ass sewer worker spitting out bloody teeth and retching on the bathroom floor, another shot to the belly because he puked on your boot . . . Dance-humping a B-broad with a roll of "jelly" jiggling above her hips and bubble-gum breath . . . Orgying it out at Weed's with Fran, parties of bodies squirming around booze bottles and glassine bags full of white powder . . . Getting ticked at the wrong look in George's eye, panting in rage as brothers held us apart . . . Dim whorehouse lights, stroking a slut's knee, sweet-talking her about coming over to party after work . . . Reputation growing, skinny dude picking a fight just because of who I was . . . Fran, when I wanted her, no questions what I did or where, she knew the terms . . . Bars, by the clear light of meth . . . By the haze of "downs" . . . By the swagger of bourbon . . .

Sleeping late, no Maureen and screaming kids . . . Dropping by once a week, "hi" to kids, few words with Maureen, a few twenties on the kitchen table on the way out . . . Even Ford plant work going better, cracking jokes with Jed again . . . Fun and steady bread, income from dope on the side to gamble on smoke-clouded aces . . . Life in the moment, taking charge . . .

One Friday night at work, a few weeks after I left home, a "gofer" came down from the foreman's office and told me I had a phone call. I wondered who it could be; I had told Fran and the club members not to call me at work unless it was an emergency. I let Jed know what was up, gave him the clipboard, and went upstairs.

From the wide window in the office, I looked out on an overview of just about everything that was happening in our section. The door behind me shut out all but a hum of the plant noise, and I picked up the phone.

"Hello, this is Barry-Barry."

"Hello? Barry?" Damn! It was Maureen.

"What the hell do you want? I tol' you never to call me at work!"

The foreman's fat-faced secretary busied herself at a desk and pretended not to be listening.

There was a pause at the other end, and then: "Barry, you played around long enough. You come home tonight."

I yelled into the phone, "You got to be . . . !!" then hushed. "You got to be jokin'! I ain't comin' home. You laid out the choice, and I made it. Now where you get off tellin' me to come home?"

"I ain't leavin' no choice tonight, Barry. You're comin' home!"

I drew in a breath ready to shout and saw the foreman's secretary take off her glasses and raise her head. I let out in a hoarse whisper: "Bug off, bitch! An' don't you call me here again, y'hear?" I banged the phone down and stormed out of the office.

When I got back to the pit, Jed asked me, "What was that all about?" I said, "Nothin' man!" and clammed up. But inside, I was fuming. *The almighty nerve of her, tellin' me to come home! What is it gonna take to make her give up? Am I gonna have to kill this bitch?*

I didn't get time to think any more about it before the pimple-faced gofer was back again.

"Mr. Mayson, your wife's on the phone."

I turned and roared at him so loud he jumped two feet: "You tell 'er I'm busy and I ain't comin' up there! Now, git!" He showed his heels, and I started trying to work again. The pit of my stomach was like a knot. The feeling sprang up my back, and a smear of blood crossed my eyes. The clipboard went flying, and I sent my torquing wrench clanging to the ground, just missing Jed's quick-skipping foot. He looked at me wide-eyed and then looked at the wrench.

A second later, he picked it up and came over to me cautiously, hefting it in his outstretched hand. "You okay, Barry?"

I shook the tension out of my hands and took the wrench from him. "Yeah," I said, "I guess so."

He said, "You want t' set out for a spell?"

I said, "No, man, I'll feel better workin'."

I picked up the clipboard and tried to find where I had left off. I felt a tap on my shoulder. It was Cochran, the foreman. "Your wife's on the phone, Mayson. She says it's an emergency." I flushed hot, and he said, chewing slowly on his plug of tobacco, "I think you ought to go up there. An'," he added, stabbing me with his piggy eyes, "I don't think you ought to yell at my boy!"

I fairly whooshed by him on the way to the steps. *She had to sic the foreman on me! She's gonna know in no uncertain terms where it's at!* I took the stairs to the office three at a time and charged through the door. I grabbed the phone and didn't give a hang who heard me.

"Listen . . ."

"Barry, are you comin' home?"

"Hey, you ain't talkin' this time, you're listenin'! I ain't comin' home, an' you ain't callin' here again, an' tha's it!"

"I'm comin' down there, Barry!"

"WHAT'D YOU SAY!!"

"I said I'm comin' down there—right now!"

"That better not be what you said! *I'm* tellin' *you* right now, if you come down here an' embarrass me like that, the second I see you, I'll *break your neck!*"

"Don't you threaten me, Barry!"

"I said it—I'll do it. *I'll break your neck!*" I slammed down the phone and glared over at the secretary. "You heard me say it! If she comes down here, don't you tell 'er where I am!"

The door was opening, and I brushed past Cochran and his boy as I raced out.

I had put it to her, and I felt better about it. She knew now where I stood. And that was that.

It was getting near lunch break when I saw Jed's jaw drop and his eyes do a yoyo act. He edged beside me, and still looking up, said from the corner of his mouth, "Barry, we got Law lookin' at us!" I spun around, and Cochran was coming down the steps, followed by two men in khaki, sporting badges.

"Mayson," Cochran said with a grin, "these men got business with you."

He stepped back as they eased forward. The wide, gray-haired one said, "Sheriff's office, Mayson. You're under arrest!"

"What for?"

He pushed a warrant at me and said, "Your wife says you been making threats on her life, Mayson. We got to take you in."

My face stiffened up: "I didn't *do* nothin'—I ain't *sayin'* nothin'!"

He looked me over and said, "Judge'll sort it all out. Frisk 'im, Jim."

The other cop, a younger guy, worked his hands over me while the wide man read my rights in a monotone. Jed stood watching with his hands at his sides; Cochran leaned on the side of the pit with his arms folded.

"You won't find nothin'," I said to the cop at my feet.

"Where's his locker?" said the wide cop, whose name tag read something like "Baxley."

"I'll take you to it," said Cochran, making for the steps.

Jed pivoted like a wooden soldier as he watched us go. About then I started to worry. I had three different kinds of pills in a little slitted patch in my cutoff. If they found them, I was in more trouble than Maureen's complaint.

We went up to the locker room and I pointed out mine. "Open it," Baxley said. I worked the combination and swung the door out. "Let's see your stuff," Baxley nodded. I took my cutoff from the hook and folded it over my arm. I reached for a cycle magazine and a girlie pulp on the shelf. I got my boots, and I felt a tugging at my cutoff. "What've we got here?" Baxley said. He slid it off my arm and turned it around in front of his face. " 'Rising Sons Motor Cycle Club.' How about that? Sure is a lot of fancy patches on this thing! Watch 'im, Jim."

Baxley spread the cutoff from shoulder to shoulder across the locker door. Then he started pressing his fingers all over the patches, including the one with the pills in it. When he was done, he said, "Surprised! Only one hot pocket!" He reached straight for the pill patch and fished around with two fingers. He took the cutoff down and squeezed the pills into his hand. He looked at me beaming and said, "Hey, boy! What're these? M and M's? Some fun for the lab boys! They like all kinds of candy!"

Jim, the other cop, said, "Pick up that stuff and let's go." It was no use saying or doing anything else. On the way out, Baxley said to Cochran, who'd followed along, "We know where we're goin'. Thanks for all the help, Mr. Cochran."

Cochran smiled through his chaw, "Any time, boys, any time."

They didn't arraign anyone on weekends, so I had to spend the next three nights in Jonesboro, at the county jail. I hadn't been behind bars since army days. And by the time they hauled me off to court, I didn't ever want to be in jail again. The company wasn't too much different from what I knew on the streets: drunks, pushers, a petty thief, somebody who had drilled a bouncer with a .38. But what got to me was the frustration of not being able to walk out of that cell when I felt like it. If I wanted a beer or something to eat when it wasn't time, forget it. They weren't giving me any sort of breaks.

Inside I was seething, that the freedom I had fought so hard for had been torn from me. And because of what? Maureen and her trumped up sham of a charge, and I could be locked up like an animal. Straight society was nothing but an ugly trap with iron jaws that cut into anyone who tried to be free. The law? What protection did it give to someone like me?

I made my one phone call to Tom. He told me that the Huns knew a lawyer who'd be there when I saw the judge, and the Rising Sons were ready to post bail. The lawyer said the case was no problem if I played it right. And he said it would go better if no bikers were in the courtroom.

Tom had some other news, too: Word had gone around the Ford plant that I was fired. I told him thanks for not letting me be the last to know—and for everything else—and hung up.

After I finished cursing out Maureen and Cochran, the job thing actually started to feel good. I didn't have to think any more about when and how I was going to make the break from straight life—it had been made for me! I was completely free now—at least I would be once I got out of this jug! And maybe old Jed would even get his shot at my job now. *Good luck, hick!*

"You got it straight, then?" Robins, the lawyer, whispered to me in the holding pen on Monday morning. "You're gonna plead guilty. You're gonna get out because you're really a good family man who had an unfortunate blowup and it's a first offense. This way you'll avoid a trial. Let the judge do all the talking. Just keep saying yes and be a nice guy, okay?"

"Okay, man, I gotcha."

"All right. I'm going out there and see if I can huddle up with the judge and the prosecution. They'll call you in a few minutes. Don't worry, just do what you're told, and we'll have you walking out of here in no time."

He shuffled past the guards toward court. He seemed to know what he was talking about. I sure hoped so—pleading guilty seemed like a funny way to get free.

In a few minutes, a voice called "Charles B. Mayson!" The guards nudged me out, handcuffs and all, into the courtroom. Robins was out there, and I saw Baxley, the cop that arrested me— and two faces in the gallery I surely didn't want to see: Maureen and her mother! *What the hell is she doin' here all the way from*

Fairfield, Alabama? I thought. It couldn't be for any good; that I was certain of. She and I never never had gotten along.

Why did they have to be here? I was getting hotter by the second about it. The guards planted me in front of the judge, but before anybody said anything, I turned around to Maureen and her old lady and shook the cuffs at them. "Take a good look!" I snarled. "You see these? You satisfied, losin' me my job and chainin' me up?"

"Shut up and turn around," one of the guards snapped. "Any more out of you and we'll cuff your legs, too!"

I looked up at the judge, a white-haired, thin-faced guy who tapped something in front of him with a yellow pencil.

A court official asked me was I Charles B. Mayson. I said I was, and he read the charges against me and asked, "How do you plead?"

I said, "Guilty."

The judge looked down at me for a few seconds and said, "It seems as if you've been having some trouble getting along with your wife, Charles. What do you have to say?"

"They call me Barry, sir."

"How's that?"

"Barry. Anyway, sir, things can get tense at home sometimes, you know how it is. I guess I jus' flew off the handle."

"Well—Barry is it? You can't just run off from home when you feel like it if you've got a wife and family, now can you?"

How did he fin' out about that? I wondered. *Did the ol' lady get to 'im somehow?*

"I guess not," I answered.

"It seems to me as if you've got a case of running with the wrong company, too." *Where'd he get that from?*

"I have frien's I hang out with."

"Barry, your friends are your wife's concern, too. You can't just do whatever you want if you're a man with responsibilities." He paused and picked up some papers, scanned them, and put them down. "I see you've never been arrested before."

"No, sir."

He tapped with his pencil again and said, "You understand these are pretty serious charges against you."

"Yes, sir, I guess so."

"You're facing at least six months' imprisonment if you're sentenced; do you realize that?"

I nodded, and he said, "I think you'd better start to straighten up, Barry. That six months is only a minimum." He looked at me seriously, nodding and tapping slowly. Then he said, "If you had a chance, do you think you could go back home and get things fixed up with your wife? Put your affairs in order and stop running around? Do you think you could do that?"

Was he offering me a way out? Facing six months in the hoosegow, I jumped at it quickly: "Yessir, I think I could."

"All right then, here's how it will be. I'm going to suspend your sentence on the condition that you go back home to your family and act like a rational and responsible husband. Are you going to agree to that?"

I said, trying to sound as sincere as I could, "Yes, sir, I'll do it."

He leaned over and said, "If at any time you pull this kind of shenanigans again, you'll be locked up and serve every bit of that sentence, is that clear?"

"Yes, sir, I hear you!"

The judge looked out at the courtroom and said louder, "In view of your plea of guilty, I sentence you, Charles B. Mayson, to six months in Jonesboro county jail on these charges." He looked down at me. "Sentence suspended. Defendant will comply with the ordinance of this court to return home and live with his wife in a peaceable and law-abiding manner. Defendant will not threaten or abuse his wife in any way. If defendant fails to abide by this court's ordinance, sentence will be enforced as heretofore mentioned. Case dismissed."

I was free again—almost! The guards took the handcuffs off. As I rubbed my wrists, the court official came over and called me to a desk, where I signed papers agreeing to what the judge said. Then he told me, "Court costs have been arranged for."

"By who?" I asked. I looked over to the gallery and saw Maureen and her mother smiling and hugging each other. "Never min', man," I said. "I think I know who paid 'em."

Robins, the lawyer, came over and shook my hand. "You had

me sweating there for a minute with your handcuff act. But you did all right."

I said, "So I'm out—on conditions."

He winked and said, "I understand you're a biker. What you do with those conditions is up to you!"

"I hear you, man," I said with a grin.

I didn't know whether anybody'd be keeping an eye on me or not, so I lay around home for about a week. Thank goodness, Maureen's mother was in a hotel and went back to Alabama the day after the arraignment. From the couple of their phone calls I overheard, they seemed to be delighted with the way things had turned out. What they didn't know was, I had no intention of sticking around. When Maureen stepped out to the store, I called Tom and told him I was going to sit home until I felt the heat was off. I told him to tell all the guys not to reveal my whereabouts to anybody once I rejoined them. I was breaking and breaking clean.

I spent the next few days drinking beer, playing a little with the kids, and watching TV. I would miss seeing the kids, but I knew it had to be for now. Maureen was in and out. I said nothing to her and slept on the couch. I didn't want to get into any more set-tos: I was so furious inside over the whole arrest business, I knew the littlest thing might make me want to kill her.

I missed Fran and all the brothers. Being away had already made me feel like some parts of me were missing. When Maureen was out, I called Fran and told her I'd be back on the scene again soon. She said she'd be there waiting for me.

As I clicked the dial of the tube around, all the commercials began to annoy me. I could see why wives got to be like Maureen: TV filled their heads all day with ideas about *things* they had to *get* —and all at whose expense? No wonder she'd been on my back all the time, wanting this and that. The whole system and what it did to people was rotten, locking everyone in with greed to working and buying and debts, like stupid donkeys chasing after a carrot. That wasn't what *life* was, and it would never be that way for me again.

On Friday afternoon Maureen finally got up the nerve to ask me when I was going to go out and look for a job.

"I ain't," I said. "An' I ain't stayin' here neither."

"But the judge said . . ."

"The judge can go to hell. An' you an' your mother, who cooked up this whole thing, can go to hell too!"

"I can get you arrested again . . ."

"Listen!" I turned away from the TV to face her. "Can't you see I don't want to live with you anymore? I don't *want* this kin' of life. I don't want *you!* Hey! You can keep gettin' me arrested! You can have a jailbird husban' if you like! Is that what you want? To put me in a cage where you can come and look at me when you want? 'Cause tha's what it'll be! 'Cause I'm tellin' you right here, an' it'll be the las' time, I don't want to go to jail—but I'll stay there till hell freezes over before I'll come back here an' live with you! An' tha's it!"

Her eyes were down, and she didn't say anything. I went on: "I might's well go now. Now's as good a time as any. So hear me— Stay away from me. Leave me alone. Let me live my life. Don't try to fin' me. If I contac' you, it'll be by mail, with no return address."

She said, "You won't get away with this, Barry!"

"Watch me!" I said.

I got up and put my things together. Neither of us said another word. If she cried, I didn't notice it. I stopped to hug the kids and then split.

I rode to a phone booth and called Fran. I told her I was back and to meet me at Weed's. I called Tom and said, "Spread the word—Barry-Barry's back! An' if anyone comes aroun' lookin' for me, you don't know nothin'!"

I rode into Atlanta and over to Weed's building and went to park in the usual place, the small backyard where we'd opened up the fence. It was so crowded with motorcycles there, I had trouble sandwiching mine in. I heard music blasting from the windows upstairs and said to myself, *Mus' be some wing-ding goin' on up there!* I did the stairs in a flash and opened the door.

"Barry-Barry!" Charlie spotted me first, and then all the brothers and sisters mobbed me, hugging and kissing and backslapping till my ribs ached. "Come on in, man! You're the guest of

honor! We got beer an' coke an' smoke an' eats," Tom said, dragging me with his big arms into the living room, "almost anythin'
your hungry heart desires!"

I yelled, "Where's my ol' lady? Where's Fran?"

I heard her calling and saw her head bobbing up and down in
the mob of bikers, old ladies and mamas: "Here I am, Barry-Barry!
Right over here!" I bulled my way past everybody to where she
was and grabbed her and near hugged the life out of her. With everybody surrounding us, shouting and pounding our backs and
pouring beer over us, I hollered, "I missed you, babe!" I could
barely hear her answer: "I missed you, too, Barry-Barry!"

"Fran!" I yelled, holding her face in my hands, the beer foam
dripping from her chin, "I'm free, gal! One hundred percent free:
It's womb to tomb for us, gal!"

"Womb to tomb, Barry-Barry!" I couldn't tell if it was beer or
tears streaming down her face.

That weekend we all biked down to Panama City, Florida, to
party and ride at the beach. Hog knew of a little cove where we
could sack out in our sleeping bags and ride along the beach and
not be bothered.

After a week of lying around, it felt like I was starting all over
again. The long ride was just as much of a thrill as my first one, and
we really shared the joy of a brotherhood, racing, trick-riding on
the open highway, spooking "citizens," and flaunting the authority
of our patch.

Hog's cove was beautiful, and Fran didn't know it, but I had a
special surprise for her. I'd had Tom's old lady, Rae, make what we
called an "old lady patch." It was long, black-on-white, saying
"Property of Barry-Barry." This made our arrangement official in
bikerdom: Fran was no mama or pig; she belonged to me, and
nobody touched her or messed with her, biker, "citizen," or otherwise, without my say-so. I had the patch rolled up in my sleeping
bag, waiting for sleep-time.

That wasn't a real long time off; when we'd finally arrived, it
was already just about sunset. We gathered some driftwood and
got a fire started, roasted some hot dogs, and broke out the beer. In

a little while, we stripped and skinny-dipped, daylight being gone. By the firelight, we smoked some dope, and Fran and I dropped the mescaline Fungo had laid on me, which I'd kept in the refrigerator for a special occasion.

After a while, I started to feel a little sick to my stomach. First I wondered what I had eaten that didn't agree with me; then I remembered that Fungo had said this was how it would be. The sound of the waves breaking became a deep, tuneless music that was pulling all of me out of my body. I wished I could break into billions of tiny pieces and become extra stars winking in the sky. My head was with me just enough to say to Fran, "I wished we'd a took this stuff when I firs' got it. If we had, we'd be real high right now!" On that last word, I realized I *was . . . real* high! . . . *right now!*

We had a fantastic trip that peaked when I finally said, "Unroll my bag, babe, and le's get it on!" She fetched it and untied it and let it uncurl. I said, "Unzip it, Fran, an' spread it out right there on the san'." As she did, she saw the patch by what was left of the firelight. She picked it up and held it to her chest and breathed a long "Ohhhh!" She came to my arms then. "Oh, Barry-Barry! My Barry-Barry!" she cried over and over again.

We made slow love, and afterward, I thought the whole sea filled her eyes. She whispered to me, "Barry-Barry, las' night I tol' you it was 'womb to tomb' for me with you. I want you to know I mean that with my whole heart an' soul." She began to cry softly. "I can't tell you how happy you've made me, Barry-Barry." She took hold of my arm and clutched it tightly. "I could never live without you, man. The day you die will be the day I die, I don't care how. When they bury you, they're gonna bury me, too, right alongside."

"So be it, babe," I whispered as I stroked her hair. "Womb to tomb!" I loved her hair. And her dark, crazy eyes. There was something in them I couldn't give a name to, a burning, a restless fever. Her big earrings made her look like . . . a gypsy. I suddenly said it aloud: "Gypsy!"

"What was that, Barry-Barry?"

"I don't know; it jus' . . . come out of my mouth: Gypsy." I gazed into her eyes at the red gleam of the fire's embers. "You got the soul of a gypsy."

It seemed right, in the starlight, there on the sand. And Fran *was* Gypsy to me, from then on.

7

Full Throttle

The next few weeks, I blasted off in a doped and boozed-up whirl, trying to cram in everything years of straightness had held scratching and clawing in my mind and body for release. I could have it all now, and I did, full tilt, until . . .

The future is something bikers don't think about. But it arrives anyway, crosshatching into the present with things like winter and suddenly realizing you're broke . . .

. . . "You got somethin' I need—give it to me!" The fish-faced hippie clutched at his thick gold chain. Deep into his trip, his eyes were all pupil and filled now with nothing but fear and me. My knife barely nicked his throat as I reached behind his neck for the clasp. His hands let the chain go limply. "Thanks, freak!" Could those be real gems reflecting the street-light's gleam? "So long, chump!" Never a word from his doofy fish lips . . .

. . . Into the 7-Eleven, Gypsy working behind the counter. She winks, mum. I put up milk, eggs, juice, cereal, potato chips, soda pop, canned stew, beans and more, all on the counter in a pile. "I'm buyin' this Snickers bar!" I wink at Gypsy. She bags the lot, rings up the candy bar. I walk out, a week's food heavier, out a dime . . .

. . . Tom and I rented an old three-story house and came up with a scheme. Gypsy tried to beg out of it—dough and dope and belt licks got her into it. First, get Gypsy a job serving drinks in a bar where she'd meet businessmen and other straights. Then . . .

. . . The whole house was dark now. That's what I'd been waiting for, that last light to go out. I went around front and knocked loud on the door. No answer. I took the key in my hand and opened up. Shut the door, up the stairs to the bedroom, flicked on the light by the door. He was ready, all right, buck naked, going bald, maybe forty. He let go of Gypsy, panic in his eyes and movements. A .357 Magnum did half my talking. I walked over to the bed and grabbed him by the throat. "What the frig d'you think you're doin'? This is my wife!" I started lifting him by the neck: "Get up! I'm gonna kill you!" My gun barrel pressed between his eyes.

"Hey"—he swallowed—"I didn't know she was married or nothin'!"

I sneered, "That don't make no difference, she's still my wife."

He started blubbering then: "Listen, you can have anything you want, just don't kill me!"

Gypsy ran out of the room as I shoved him back onto the bed. "How much money you got, man?"

He pointed, shaking. "My wallet—over there!" Still holding the gun on him, I found the bulge in his pants, pulled it out and threw his pants to him. While he struggled to jam them on, I emptied out his billfold. *Damn good mark, a thick pad of fresh twenties!* Them I pocketed. I tossed his clothes over and demanded his watch. He gave it, no big score, but worth a few. He had enough of his clothes on for me to shout, "Get the hell out of here! An' don't never mess with my wife again, or I'll kill you!" He and his clothes flapped out the door and almost stumbled down the stairs. Gypsy peeked in the door. The front door slammed below. Gypsy came over and put her arms around me. "Did I do right, Barry-Barry?" I patted her on the head. "You did great, babe." She held me tighter. "I don't like it, Barry-Barry." I gave her the hardest look I'd ever given her. "You jus' learnin' what it means to be property, babe . . ."

. . . Southeastern Outlaw Biker's Association forming; we get asked to join, along with the Huns, the Iron Cross, and the Prophets out of Jonesboro. Gypsy sews my "One Percenter's Patch" on my cutoff. I now belong to that one percent of motorcycle riders giving the sport a bad name! Coming down: more dope, more cycle parts to fence, more hookers to pass around . . .

. . . One night, Filthy Fred came over to the big house and blew a couple of joints. After a while, he said, "Barry-Barry, can you drive good?"

"I can handle a car."

"I got my Chevy outside. Help me take care of some business."

"Say when."

"Right now."

"Le's go!"

We drove out to a convenience store in the suburbs. Fred said, "Park over there out of the light." I put the car where he wanted it, and he said, "Wait here an' keep the motor runnin'—I'll be right out."

I idled it, and about a minute later, Fred dashed out of the store with a paper bag in one hand and a pistol in the other. He jumped in, slammed the door, and yelled, "Haul ass, Barry-Barry!"

I laid some fast rubber and floored for the nearest back road. Fred laughed his head off next to me. "Shee . . . was that fun! You shoulda seen that ol' coot's face!" He counted up what was in the bag. It came to over a hundred bucks, and Fred was jolly: "Man, I think I foun' a bitchin' way to get bread!"

He had a good laugh over his job. I didn't say much. I hadn't known what he was up to until I saw the gun in his hand as he exited the store. Somehow it smelled like trouble. I thought maybe I'd be busy if he ever asked me again . . .

Not all the Association members felt the way I did about Fred's kind of fun. He got other members of our club, as well as Iron Crosses and Huns, to drive around knocking off convenience stores. They'd bring back booze and eats, and everybody'd party out. Any money that was left over was divvied up for whatever anyone needed. Fred had an active ring going there for a while. I managed to get some of the goodies but stay out of the driver's seat.

But Fred and his partners showed a pattern that the police picked up on. Fred had a close call with the cops one night, then one of the Huns got hauled in. The Association handled that: some guys put their old ladies on the street and turned a few deals to spring the brother from jail. But it looked like things were starting to get heavy—paranoia setting in!

Filthy Fred got arrested a block from a job. He didn't rat, but he'd been wearing his patch. Soon the cops were keeping a close watch on the Rising Sons. One of Charlie's runners was busted for drugs. Tom's old lady Rae was picked up for hooking. Cops rode along the streets we hung out in. Every time they passed by, they looked straight my way. I was getting a strong "street telegraph" message that the cops were out to bust up the Rising Sons.

As the pressure got heavier, George bugged out. I was angry at my old teacher for turning out a rooty-poot. Fat Pat cut out, too. Weed split town near the end of winter, and I began to think about doing the same until things simmered down.

Filthy Fred was convicted and sent up. Then Charlie's runner ratted on him. Horace the Hog had a serious accident that left him in head-to-toe casts. About this time, the other hard-core outfits in town began to court Tom and me, the Rising Sons' only survivors. Prophets president Marvin argued, "If you don't have but two members, you shouldn't even have a club. You oughta fold your patch up an' be one of us." The Iron Cross and the Huns wanted us as well.

Tom and I agreed we ought to fold up. Tom went Iron Cross. (When he healed up, Hog became a Hun. Charlie did time, and I don't know what happened to him after that. Weed headed west and rode with a club in Arizona.) I really liked the Prophets and had a good thing going with Marvin, but I told him the town was just too hot for me right then. I was going to split for a while, and then come back to prospect for them. We made a deal that the Prophets would help me get a Harley together in return for some services when I got back.

I decided I might as well sell the Beezer. I was going to get a chopper soon, and I planned to travel "incognito" (in straight clothes), so I figured a car would be the best way to get around, least visible, and most comfortable.

One of the Prophets had a junkyard, so car titles came easy for him. He'd take the title and strip the serial number from a junk car and restamp a hot Caddy like it was brand-new. Then he could take that title and get tags for it, not as a wrecked car, but as a new one, put it on a car lot and get thirteen or fourteen thousand bucks for it. He was able to fix me up with a serviceable old Buick for half the price of the Beezer, and give me the rest in cash for traveling money.

With spring stewing into summer, Gypsy and I headed south for New Orleans. I planned to get her a job in a bar and then look around to see what kind of action there was. Gypsy was quiet most of the way down. It was dawning on her that being a biker's old lady was more than just hanging out and good times. She was a part of keeping the old man and his bike going, she was there to make sure money was always coming in. And I could tell she was starting not to like some parts of the arrangement . . .

We didn't stay long in New Orleans, maybe about a month. I just didn't like the scene there that much, I didn't know anyone there, and I didn't make good contacts. But it wasn't a total waste: There, Gypsy began to learn some of the trade secrets of B-drinking. The object was, of course, to get the "marks" soused while the girl stayed sober. One way she did this was with what they called a "spit-cup." It had water in it, and she pretended to use it as a chaser (saying the liquor was too hard). But whatever she drank, she spat into the extra cup. There was a small bucket under each booth, too, where she'd dump booze if the mark went to the john, thus getting him to reorder more quickly.

Some of the B-girls tricked the marks as well. The joint Gypsy worked in had a couple of rooms in the back set up for that purpose. And there were chicks who worked the place primarily as hookers. Some of the go-go girls tricked, too, when they weren't dancing. I saw a lot of money passing hands, which made me think maybe there was something worth looking into in the bar business . . .

I gambled a lot, five-card stud mostly. I was later to find out why I kept losing. At any rate, my bankroll was low, and a place that didn't bring me luck was no place to stay. I spent a night in the hotel room drinking, sifting my way through the problem of what to do next.

Back to Atlanta? Couldn't do it yet, even though by now I'd grown a beard, so I'd be less easily recognized there. If word got

around of my being on the scene before the Rising Sons name had
died out in police headquarters, I'd have no freedom to maneuver.
I needed a place to go where I might hide out if times got tough or
money got short.

About two thirds of the way through the bottle, the answer
floated into place: Charleston! It was a navy town—that meant
sailors, which meant bars, dope, and women. And I had family
there. My mother had remarried, a shipbuilder named Frank
Carder. I could always fall back on her for some support, maybe a
place to stay. She had helped out often in the past, with money for
furniture and kids' clothes. She was easy to sweet-talk. Of course, I
hadn't been in touch with her since I left Maureen, and she might
have some funny ideas about what I was doing. But I was sure I
could talk my way around all that. I got Gypsy from work and told
her to pack up, we were going to Charleston.

"Charleston?" she yawned. "What in hell for?"

I said, "My mother's there, an' she can help us till we get settled in."

She slipped her skirt over her head and said inside it, "You
mean money?"

I picked up the bottle and took a poke of what was left and
said, passing it her way, "Maybe that, maybe other things."

"Some o' what I want?" she sassed back.

"I ain't figured out all o' what you want yet," I said, taking the
bottle back from her. "But if it ain't what I want, forget it!"

8
Sniffing Out Charleston

On the way to Charleston, I ducked for a couple of days into the Prophets' clubhouse in Jonesboro, to talk things over with Marvin. I had wired him money from New Orleans, and some of the parts for my chopper had already come in. I knew it would cost a lot of my own money to build it—but not near as much as the bike would really be worth, because most of the parts would be stolen. The bike I planned would have at least five thousand dollars in it—that kind of expense may explain why bikers are so generally touchy about people messing around with their machines. It's your baby, and woe be to anyone who damages it, or even sits on it without asking permission.

Marvin and I discussed the project. I was aiming for a '49 panhead with a lot of chrome on it: Mag wheels chromed, engine (except the jugs) chromed, even the bottom end chromed. I wanted the hardtail frame painted a light blue, some striping, not loud. I didn't go tor fatbob fuel tanks, didn't like the wide look they gave, or side-fill tanks that looked too "custom." I wanted pull-back handlebars, so I could lean backward for long highway rides. (Some bikers preferred forward-leaning racing bars.) I wanted a Glide front end, twelve inches overextended; tubeless, radial-type tires; a Weber dual-throat carburetor; a swastika-style side-mount taillight; a king-queen seat.

All this was going to be stashed in Marvin's garage. The Prophets would do some of the work. I would come in from Charleston as often as I could to work with them and send money when I couldn't. The bike, we figured, should be ready to assemble around New Year's.

You could tell a lot about a man, Marvin said, just by looking at his bike: his taste, his character, his bankroll, what type of riding he went in for. Flashy or simple, reckless or steady, accessories or no-frills functional, fast and tricky or swift, long jamming, it was all there in steel and leather.

To get the kind of use a biker wants, though, one thing is certain: You can't just ride a "stock" Harley. You have to "chop" it, strip everything that makes for excess weight, and extend the front end. You might modify a number of features to suit your needs. Some bikers want a hardtail frame, no shocks, for example. Hardtail riders generally think they're tougher than shock users. The latter argue that comfort is more important than being tough "and always walking around with a sore ass," as Marvin laughingly said it. A lot of beery debates ensue among bikers over such details.

I reassured Marvin that I wanted to return and prospect for the Prophets as soon as I could. We chewed over a few more loose ends, and I finally left, on good terms, to see what Charleston had to offer.

What I first saw as we drove through the southern end of the town didn't give me much encouragement. The day was steamy, like a hothouse, and everything seemed like nothing but one big antique shop: old ivied and mossy buildings, scenic gardens, expensive restaurants, and historical tourist sights.

But in the north part of town, I perked up considerably. A map of Charleston had showed the location of a navy base, and on the street leading right to that, I found what I was looking for—a thriving stretch of drinking, strip, and gambling joints that spread down Reynolds Avenue right to the base entrance. "Jeez," I said to Gypsy, "all a sailor'd have to do is walk out o' there an' sneeze too hard, an' he'd blow hisself straight into a whorehouse!"

I got a Charleston newspaper from a machine, and we sat in a bar nursing a couple of beers while I looked through the want ads.

"Hey, babe, listen to this: 'Go-go dancers wanted, three hundred dollars a week.' That soun's like what we're lookin' for!"

"I ain't dancin' no topless, Barry-Barry!"

I looked up from the paper. "It don't say 'topless,' Gypsy."

"Maybe not, but tha's what it means!"

"So what? You got nothin' t' be ashamed of. An' you dance as good as any o' them chicks I seen."

She squinched up her brow. "Yeah, but it's different in front of all them horny dudes."

"So? It's no big thing. I can get you some stuff that'll make you forget there's anybody even in the place! Jus' let me call this up . . ."

She tried to say something, but I was already halfway to the phone booth. It turned out she wouldn't even have to start out topless; just wear a little miniskirt and shake her tail a lot. The voice on the other end said he was the bartender; the boss would be in the next night—his name was Jim Rosin. Show Town was the name of the place, on the lower end of Reynolds Avenue.

Gypsy was glad when I told her it wouldn't be topless, but she said, "You're gonna talk me into goin' topless, I know it, Barry-Barry."

"No, I ain't," I lied, "but le's jus' get you started."

The bartender told us there were cheap motels down on Folly Beach, so that's where we headed next. This was a real summer hangout; even though it was late in the season, I could see the ocean front packed with people, mostly young. *What a place to move dope!* I thought. In fact, I saw what looked to me like a couple of deals in progress as we passed by a row of dilapidated beach houses.

We found a cheap place that wasn't too bad and toted our few bags in. Gypsy suggested a swim. We suited up, and carrying a pair of brown-bagged beers we picked up at a little store, we walked to the beach. It was late afternoon, but the sun was still hot, and the salt air clogging my pores made it even more steamy.

The sea smell and the taste of the surf reminded me of that night down in Panama City. The gulls wheeling above the cool

spray reminded me of the freedom I was still after and the pickings
lying around the world to be grabbed. If I had to pick out a place
to hole up, maybe Charleston wasn't a bad one.

We had chili dogs and more beer for dinner. Then it was back
to the motel, where Gypsy and I shared a joint. I felt like going
back downtown and checking out the scene at night, so I left
Gypsy watching an odd-color TV and headed back to Charleston.

Crossing the Ashley River bridge, I didn't see much of a big-
city, light-speckled skyline. Most of Charleston is low-cut, so to
speak. I found my way to Reynolds Avenue and buzzed up and
down the strip for a while, just getting the feel of things. It looked
like the street had some permanent residents, as every strip did,
winos who slumped against the sides of bars and flophouses wherever they'd passed out. Most of the moving traffic was staggering
sailors, working stiffs on the prowl, and streetwalkers, who leaned
into the windows of stopped cars. No smell of roses and polite conversation here. On a street like this, a knife in the guts and a hand
to the wallet were more likely kinds of talk.

I noticed that the farther I got from the navy base, the more
respectable the clubs were. Places like The Dixie Diamond had
neon signs and blow-ups of name strippers lit up with light bulbs.
Business and navy-officer types went in and out of there.

Closer to the base, the joints got rawer; the drinks and tricks
probably moved faster. That was the way to do it, I thought: Bring
'em in, stew 'em, trick 'em, fleece 'em, and bounce 'em to make
room for more. A few good-sized places looked on the shabby side
and like they might be available for owners with more hustle than
the present ones.

Show Town was a place with some class: It had blood-red
black-felted wallpaper, netted candles on the tables, and well-
suited and uniformed customers sitting at them. A mirrored ball on
the ceiling splintered light over the well-dressed B-girls. The bar
was clean, with a veined mirror that let the drinkers get a bleary
view of the go-go dancers and strippers, who tossed and twirled on
strobe-lit platforms. The jukebox blared loudly through a fog of alcohol and nicotine so thick you could almost swim across the room.
I liked it.

We were told by the bartender, who kept glancing warily at my beard, that Jim Rosin was in the back, under the big picture.

Beyond a smaller doorway was a room with a green dice table. Red Arrow slot machines lurked against two walls; men and B-girls sat shadowy at tables.

The big picture was a blow-up of a boxer squaring off, easily recognizable as the man sitting under it. If he was a boxer, he didn't show many marks of it: His nose wasn't flat or his eyes puffy or his ears chewed up. With his dark hair, he looked more like a Plains Indian with a haircut and fancy clothes. He riffled a deck of cards with deft hands.

He looked Gypsy over, and we talked. He said she didn't have to work topless, but the money got better if she did. She could make more money B-drinking when she wasn't dancing. He was happy to hear she had some experience at that. Of course, he added, there was even bigger money to be made in a couple of small trailers parked out back, where some of the girls tricked the customers.

Our talk was interrupted by a dancer's voice on the loud-speakers: "Don't get upset, folks, but we're gonna have a little visit from the po-leece! Just relax and keep it clean, an' they'll be gone soon!"

Rosin said, explaining, "It's Anderson, the vice man. We get a call from him, we stash everything but the mini-bottles. We clean up, he comes, he goes, he gets fifty bucks at the door every night."

Rosin called one of the waitresses over, and she took Gypsy to a back room to try on a micro-miniskirt. Rosin pointed out some of the gambling action: Razzle-dazzle, baccarat at one table, a three-matchbox version of the old shell game at another. "That one causes me some trouble," he said. "The matchbox man pulls a switch on the mark. Sometimes the mark gets mean when he figures that out." Rosin flexed his fingers. "There can be rough stuff."

"You're a boxer," I put in.

"Was," he set me straight. "Hands broke too easy. I had a fighter's punch but a card shark's hands."

He fell silent for a minute. Gypsy was coming from the back just then, and into the room walked two uniformed cops, followed by a chubby guy in plain clothes with a smirk on his face. The smirk's lower half made gum-chewing circles as the small, deep-set eyes above it took in the room. Anderson, as I guessed he was, got over to our table about the same time as Gypsy.

"New babe?" Anderson asked nobody in particular in a high voice.

"Maybe," Rosin said.

"Haven't you got enough here already?" Anderson chewed.

"What's enough?" Rosin looked Anderson in the eye. "You know how it is."

"I'll ignore that remark," said Anderson, chewing a little faster, "but not too many more like it."

The boys in blue lingered at the door, watching the dancers. Anderson made for the bar, and I saw him help himself to a mini-bottle on his way out.

"Pain in the ass," Rosin said. "Wants a payoff *and* respect? Fuck 'im!"

"Some frogs ain't happy with jus' flies," I said.

Rosin looked Gypsy over and thought she had good legs. "Different," he said, squinting, "but she'll do. Be here tomorrow night at seven. The girls will fill you in on everything."

On the way back to Folly Beach, Gypsy asked when I planned on calling my mom.

"Hadn't thought about it," I said. "I'll get aroun' to it."

After a minute or so of silence, Gypsy asked, "Barry-Barry, you got somethin' against your mom?"

I hesitated, then let it out: "She's a liar."

Gypsy pressed: "How'd she lie t' you?"

"She always tol' me my real father was dead. So did my step-dad—but after he died, she tol' me my real dad was alive, doin' life in a pen for murder. I asked 'er why she lied to me. She jus' said she didn't want to hurt my feelin's. I can't stan' a liar."

I was quiet for a while. Then I said, "Don't it scare you to be livin' with a man tha's got a killer's blood?"

"Nah, Barry-Barry," she yawned, "I already knew you was a *disease!*"

I laughed at that and said softly, "But I'll call 'er soon. I may need 'er."

9
Changing Scenes

Gypsy was a little nervous the first night, so I hung around Show Town and kept an eye on her. I watched Rosin carefully, too, and I saw very few guys walk away from his table winners. I spied a lot of big bills going through his hands, most of them on the way to his pockets.

Everywhere I looked in his place, people who worked for him pulled in money. Gypsy's three hundred dollars a week began to look like chicken feed. I wondered how I could get in on it.

As I'd expected, drugs weren't hard to find on Folly Beach. But the season was almost over; soon the beach would be empty. I knew I had to get an apartment in Charleston and a steady drug source. The dealer I copped from mentioned that most of his drugs were fronted through a motorcycle club called the Tribulators. I leaped into a list of questions, but he said he'd never met any of them, just knew by the grapevine where his dope was coming from. This news that there were bikers in town excited me. I knew I'd have to try and find them sooner or later.

That night, Gypsy told me that Rosin had let on he was looking for a bouncer-bodyguard to work Show Town. She had mentioned to him that I could handle myself, and he wanted to talk to me about it the next night. Here was my break; I was ready to jump at it!

But in a couple of hours, I knew it wasn't going to be all that simple. I called Marvin in Jonesboro when we got back to the motel, to see how things were going with my bike. He had some unsettling news: The Outlaws, a powerful club out of Chicago, were moving into Atlanta, and that was probably going to mean trouble.

Right then, Atlanta's turf was a friendly split between the Iron Cross, the Huns, and the Prophets. The Outlaws' coming on the scene meant only one thing: They wanted to absorb the whole area.

Among bikers, the Hell's Angels are generally considered the number one motorcycle club in the country. But there are other large clubs like the Devil's Disciples, the Pagans, and the Outlaws who dispute that claim. And all of these clubs try to increase their power by absorbing smaller bike clubs to get new turf.

It works something like this: A big club comes into an area and meets local club members to size up the situation. If a strong club occupying that turf refuses to give it up, a "war" may take place. As the big club tries to dislodge the locals, bombings, murders, fires—all may come down to settle the issue.

Smaller clubs, partly from being intimidated, partly to gain prestige, will usually elect to join the larger outfit. If so, they hand over their patch to the newcomers and become prospects of the larger outfit. If they refuse to be absorbed, they're usually destroyed.

Marvin said the Hell's Angels had been working east steadily like this. In some places, it was nip and tuck between the Angels and the Outlaws.

Marvin said he thought there'd been talks already between the Outlaws and the Iron Cross. They had been shifty when questioned about it, which led him to believe they were planning to go Outlaw. The Huns were planning to put up a fight, and so, he said, were the Prophets. He didn't know how soon, but he thought my help might be needed if war started.

While he ran the situation by me, I thought about my bike-in-progress down there and started to worry about losing it. I didn't feature being in the law's eye in the Atlanta area, but I realized my scooter (and a lot of money) was at stake. Under pressure, nobody would protect it but me. I had to figure out a way to do that and still stay out of sight.

It might take more trips back and forth from Charleston to Jonesboro, I thought, and more money to get the bike together in a hurry. There was money in sight, with Gypsy working, and probably myself as well. But right now, it was going to be hard to keep eating for the five days till Gypsy got paid. With that in mind, I knew it was time to get in touch with my mother.

On the phone, Mom had sounded just a little more surprised than glad to hear from me. Of course, she asked me what I was doing in Charleston. I told her I'd fill her in when I got there. She said, "Come right on over!" It turned out she was only six miles away on James Island.

The neighborhood I was driving through wasn't ritzy, but it was nice. I found Cornish with no trouble and stopped the car in front of number 28, an average-sized brick house, tree-shaded, with a carport closed over in wood on the side.

When Mother opened the door, she stared at me for a couple of seconds, up and down. Then she took me by the shoulders and examined me at arms' length. "Well, will you look at you! An' what's this?" she asked, taking hold of my beard.

"Some bird come along an' fixed a nest on my chin, Mother!"

She answered the twinkle in my eyes: "I don't know, but I think that's my Barry. Still got a head full o' jokes as always!" She drew me toward her in a hug and twitted, "But where do I kiss you?"

"Try my nose!" I joked, and she did!

She drew me into the living room and shut the door behind us. Part of the room seemed familiar, and part didn't. The old couch I knew, but the easy chair wasn't Ben Mayson's. My sisters Tanya and Tara looked a little older in their gold-framed studio pictures. My high school yearbook shot sure needed updating now!

"Where're the girls?" I asked, pointing to the photos.

"In school, you booby! An' they're young ladies, to you!"

"Oh, sh—yeah! I forgot!"

"That's not all you forgot," she said, wagging a scolding finger. "They were mighty hurt that you didn't remember their last birthdays." And looking sideways at me, she added, "Somebody else was hurt, too."

"I'm sorry, Mother. It's jus' hard to keep track o' them things since—"

"Since you've got nobody t' remind you anymore! I wanta hear some more about the whole mess. Come on in the kitchen and tell me while I finish up some wash!"

Mom offered me something to drink and a sandwich. I knew it was no use asking if she had any beer, so I settled for iced tea and said no to the food. She poured me a tall glass. With her hair colored a dark brown, she looked good, and I told her so. But neither that flattery, nor a few questions about her husband or my sisters or my brother Rick managed to stave off the questions about me for very long.

"Rick's still down there in East Point doin' fine." She looked up from a shirt collar into which she was rubbing liquid soap. "An' where've you been keepin' yourself? Maureen gets nothin' from you but money orders for the kids—an' them none too regular. She says they've all been from Jonesboro or Atlanta, so we didn't figure you'd gone far."

I slid my glass around its pool of water on the Formica table. "I been livin' my own life," I said, "an' that ain't had much to do with her."

"Or your kids, neither. Maureen says they been askin' where their daddy went, an' she's at a loss anymore what t' tell 'em."

"She can tell 'em their ol' man's out bein' free," I said, "'cause tha's the truth of it."

Mom poured soap on a grass-stained shirt elbow and said, "Barry, I wish I could understand what this 'freedom' business is all about. I just don't see why you can't ride your motorcycle an' stay home, too."

I got up and walked over to the sink and leaned on my hands. "Mother, there's no way I can explain it to you. It's more than jus' a cycle—it's a whole way of life. You see, it was no good livin' like I was—I was a rat in a cage. I had to be totally free, an' bikin' full time, you can do that."

"How, Barry? Where do you work at? How do you make a livin'?"

I knew I couldn't begin to tell her that! But I did have Jim Rosin's place waiting. "Well, Mother, I got me a job in a bar, runnin' out customers that get out o' line, keepin' order, kin' o' like a cop."

She gave me a dim view: "That ain't no job, Barry!"

"Well, it's the only one I got. An' it makes good money."

She sighed and started arranging the clothes in the washer. "Barry, you should of thought things over better before you ever got married an' had two kids."

That aggravated me. "Yeah, I should of!" I snapped. "But I was jus' a crazy kid, an' so was she. We didn't know what the—'scuse me!—what we was doin'!"

"So you make it worse by runnin' off an' leavin' her with no support an' your kids with no daddy?"

"She ain't no worse off. You don't know how bad things was, Mother," I pleaded.

"I'm three times married"—she flashed her eyes at me—"I know how bad they can get. But I had two good men, an' we saw it through."

That brought me up short for a moment. All I could come back with was, "Well, things was different. An' I ain't the kin' o' man that can be cut an' stamped. Come to that, don't forget whose hide I was cut out of!"

"That don't excuse you, Barry." She put the top of the washer down and shook her head. "Barry, I don't know how you can have a conscience for this 'freedom' of yours, an' her an' your kids scrapin' to stay alive."

"Better that one of us be free than all of us hog-tied."

"You know better than that, Barry!" She pushed the dial in and started the washer.

I walked back over to the table, sat down, and took a sip of tea. She said, "Don't you want t' know how she's been makin' out?"

I said, "I guess so."

She said, "Well, her mom's been helpin' her, an' we've sent her some. She's been talkin' with her granddaddy about some money to open a beauty parlor."

"Well, I wish her the bes'," I said.

"Barry," Mom said, sitting across the table corner from me,

"you know what'd be best for her. You should go home an' get a good job an' be a father t' your children."

I reached across and put a hand on her arm. "Mother, I know how you feel. An' there's no way I can explain to you where I'm at. But it's jus' somethin' I got to do—an' do all the way." I saw she had a tear in her eye. "There's no turnin' back for me, Mother. Too much has happened for me ever to live that way again. I made my choice, an' this is my life, an' ain't nothin' gonna change it."

She got up, dabbing her eyes with the tip of her apron, and began pulling some undershirts from the dryer into the washbasket. "Some notion of freedom," she said softly. She waved a hand in the dryer, found no stragglers, set the basket by a kitchen chair and sat down to fold the load. "So what brings you to Charleston?" she asked wearily.

"I had to leave Atlanta for a while."

"Why, Barry?"

"Well, it's like this: Some guys I know got into trouble—"

"With the police, Barry?"

"Yeah, but I wasn't in on it. I was afraid I was gonna get dragged into it, though, so I split. Tha's all I can tell you, Mother."

"An' why did you decide to look us up after all this time?"

"'Cause I love y'all," I said with my best smile. "An' because I need some help, Mother."

"What kin' of help, Barry? I thought you said you were workin'."

"I am. But like I tol' you on the phone, I jus' been in town a day or two, an' I don't get paid till nex' week. I don't want no money, Mother, jus' some food to tide me over until payday." I laughed. "I can't toss big ol' drunks out of a bar on a empty stomach!"

She looked at me hesitantly and then pointed and said, "The pantry's over there. There's plenty of canned goods—an' grocery bags folded down below. Help yourself!"

I said, "Thanks, Mom!" and went over to load up.

As I was putting in beans and beef stew and such, Mom said, "Can you stay till your sisters get in from school? I'm sure they'd like to see the sight of you!"

"I jus' can't stay today, Mother. I got things to do before I go to work. But I'll be in town. Maybe I can come by some Saturday."

"That'd be all right," she said. "Jus' let me know ahead of time so I can warn everybody!"

When I had two big bags full on the table, she said, "Barry, your appetite has sure grown!"

"Well, you know I could always eat, Mother."

"Not that much in a week, Barry. You by any chance feedin' a friend, too?"

I could feel my face warm over. "Yeah, I got a frien' along."

"What kin' o' friend, Barry?"

"Le's jus' say a good one, Mother, an' leave it at that."

She shook her head and tisked her tongue. "Barry, what am I goin' to do with you?"

She had the wash all folded and back in the basket, and I was ready to go. She said, "Let me show you somethin' for when you come back an' visit." She took me out a side door and into the made-over carport. It was done up as a rec room, with a stereo and games on shelves; chairs and an old couch; and in the middle, a pool table, with all the balls and accessories.

"You got it fixed up really nice in here, Mother. Tha's nice woodwork an' panelin'."

"Frank's sure handy with wood," she said proudly. "After buildin' boats, he can do work like this in his sleep." She faced me and said, "Barry, I jus' want you t' know: I don't preten' to approve the way you're livin'. But you come an' see us any time. An' bring your friend along, too!"

I said, "Thanks, Mom," and leaned over to give her a kiss.

"Ooh, that tickles, Barry!" she protested, pushing me away.

We went in and I gathered up the two full bags. Mom took the third, light one and walked me out to my car. She bent down to the open window as I started up. "Keep in touch, Barry, y'hear? An' keep out o' trouble!"

"I'll do that, Mother. Tell Frank an' the girls hello. An' thanks for all the chow!"

"You're welcome, son. An' Barry," she said, tugging gently at my chin, "think about goin' back home, will you?"

I said, "Okay, Mother," to get her off of that, and, "you take care now," and took off, relieved that it hadn't been all as bad as

I'd expected. Mom was straight, but she was still as soft a touch as ever.

That night, Gypsy heated up some spaghetti and green beans on a hotplate, and we drove over to Show Town with full stomachs. Gypsy went to work dancing, and Rosin explained the job to me.

Besides bouncing duties, he said, I had to keep an eye out for anyone getting rough with the women, especially the hookers when they went out back. Also, I was to play the "dummy" in some of the gambling routines. In the matchbox game, for example, I would go in halves with the mark when his interest flagged, keep him in it as long as I could, and bounce him if he got rough. Rosin himself liked to "sell a hat," which was what he called a crooked game of five-card stud played in cahoots with a dummy. He said that if I showed more than muscle, he would teach me the tricks he knew and show me how to run things when he took a night off, including how to handle the police.

Within a couple of hours, I had a chance to show him what I could do as a bouncer. A slim businessman got upset with the matchbox game. I doubled him over with an uppercut, fireman-carried him out the door, and shrugged him tail first onto Reynolds Avenue. Rosin liked my work, and we settled on three hundred and fifty dollars a week on full weeks, fifty a night otherwise. I had told him I might have to be out of town some because of my bike.

He said he was happy with Gypsy but asked me to see if I could get her to dance in a bikini. "It's the next step to topless," he said, and I said I understood. He let me know that it would mean more money for her. I said I'd work on her.

Marvin called me about four days later with an update on things in Atlanta: The Iron Cross had gone Outlaw, as he expected, and both were now ganging up on the Huns. He didn't know how long the Huns could hold out, but the Prophets might be the target soon. He said he had "some plans"; what they were, he didn't say. But they might need me down there on weekends to guard the clubhouse. I told him I was ready when he needed me.

Since I might be missing a lot of work, I had no choice but to get Gypsy to make more money. I talked to her about going topless, and she said she didn't feel like showing any more of herself. I got angry and beat her with my fists for the first time. She threatened to leave me, and I said I'd kill her. All that on the negative side and a promise of more speed on the positive side got her working in a bikini the next night.

A few days later, Marvin called again. The Huns had caved in and scattered. The Outlaws' new clubhouse had been blown up, and the Prophets were strongly suspected. I asked if that fit in with his "plans," but he said, "Nobody's talkin', Barry-Barry. I'm expectin' them Outlaws by here any time now, an' you'd be handy to have aroun'. I got a AR-15 automatic an' a Thompson .45 submachine you can use in case you see 'em."

"I'll get down there right away," I said, and hung up. It crossed my mind that I might end up having to shoot old Tom. I wouldn't like that, but if it went that way, I had to be ready.

After explaining to Rosin and making sure Gypsy was into the bikini bit and well supplied with speed, I headed for Jonesboro. I had her holed up in a fleabag near Show Town while I was gone. Now that the beach season was over, cheap places were even cheaper on Folly Beach. But if I was going to hop back and forth from Atlanta, she had to live closer to work. I planned to get us an apartment as soon as I got back.

When I got to the Prophets' clubhouse, things were grim. Marvin and the Outlaws' president, a dude they called Buzzard, were somewhere on "neutral turf" talking things over. Ordinarily, only prospects lived in the clubhouse, but now five other patch members were around as well, just in case. All were armed to the teeth.

While waiting for Marvin to get back, I thought things over and decided I might as well start to prospect for the Prophets at this time. My bike was all right so far. But if I were officially working with the club, it would get more protection, and I'd get more cooperation in putting it together.

A few hours later, Marvin came in. He was glad to see me and quickly told me the news: He had denied knowing anything about the Outlaw clubhouse blowup and told Buzzard that he was willing to negotiate a sort of "peace treaty" whereby the Outlaws and Prophets would divide up the turf and keep out of each other's way. Buzzard had said he'd think it over, and that's where things stood to the minute.

"But that don't mean they won't try to pull somethin'," Marvin said. "We got to be ready."

"I'm with you, man," I said. "I'm even ready to prospec', startin' now."

Marvin grinned and extended a hand. "Hey, man! Tha's all right!"

I added quickly, "But listen, brother, it's jus' one thing."

"What's that?"

"You know what I can do. I'll prospec', but no Mickey Mouse shit!"

I wasn't about to do some of the stuff prospects were usually ordered to perform for patch members, like, say, running down to Florida to buy a pack of cigarettes with a Florida tax stamp to prove they'd done it, in such-and-such time. To me, all that was a bunch of bull. But unless for some reason he was exempt, a prospect had to obey a patch member's orders, no matter how silly.

Marvin agreed to that, though I promised to do the jobs that were important for the club. The whole thing of prospecting involved about six months of constant and strict testing. A prospect had to live at the clubhouse and keep it in some kind of order. And in all kinds of ways, he had to show that he wanted to be a part of the club one hundred percent, or else it was "get on down the road"—the club didn't want him.

Not all the orders were foolish. Sometimes a patch member would tell a prospect, "I need a part for my scooter. Go get me a Harley shovelhead. Give me the jugs, an' you can have the rest." So the prospect would go out and rip off a cycle. It was all part of proving the man was worthy to wear the patch.

In order even to be a prospect, a man had to be voted in by patch members. Then he had to be sponsored by one man who would stick his neck out and bet his reputation on his worthiness. The sponsor's job then was to develop the prospect into full status. This meant he always knew the prospect's whereabouts and kept him under orders.

If the sponsor couldn't control the prospect, or he turned out to be a creator of trouble for the club, the brothers might take action. And the same was just as true of a patch member who couldn't keep cool.

Years later, I was in a bar in Savannah with a brother named Quick, just drinking beer calmly, not bothering anyone. Now, I wasn't toting a gun, but he was, a .22 peashooter.

We were on our second pitcher of beer when Quick started to get loud. He yelled, "Hey, baby, le's get it on!" to a couple of chicks and "What ch'you lookin' at, punk?" to a pretty good-sized dude who had turned around at the bar.

I told him, "Shut up, man! Jus' be cool! Let these people alone; they jus' settin' havin' a good time, an' le's do the same. There's some loose chicks in here; le's pick up a couple of girls an' go. Don't cause no trouble in this place!"

Now he'd been riding with the club a long time, and he said, "Don't tell me what to do! I know what I'm doin'. Nobody's gonna mess with us anyway. An' if they do, I got somethin' that'll handle it!" And he flashed this peashooter.

I said, "Oh, boy! I got a nut here with a .22!" That's like shooting BBs, unless you've got good enough aim to plug somebody in the eye nine times out of ten. But Quick thought he was "bad" because he had that little pistol!

After a while, he got up and started pouring beer on people's heads. He ran around yelling, "Hey! Have some beer!" Thought he was terrorizing the place!

I said, "Boy, tha's it! Le's go! *Come on!*" He knew I meant business. You don't like to have to lay out a brother in public, but I would have done it if he hadn't moved.

But he said, "All right," and we went for the door. This guy walked behind us and said to Quick, "If you ever come back here and mess with my girl again, I'll kill you!"

Quick bellowed, "Oh yeah?" and pulled out his gun. "Who you gonna kill now?" So the dude turned and walked back into the bar.

I said, "Le's go, Quick!" and I put my helmet on and mounted up my bike. We were trying to kick our bikes on when out walked this guy with five more big goons. One of them walked over to me with a .38 snub-nose and stuck it between my eyes. "Get off your bike," he said. "Well," I said, "I don't have much choice, I guess."

So I got off my bike and Quick did, too, as a similar gat was poking at him. Then I made a mistake: I took off my helmet. When

I did, the dude hit me on the side of the face with the .38, and it went off, near blowing my ears away. I couldn't hear a thing at first, the ringing in my ears was so bad, and for a second, I thought he'd shot me.

Then he hit me four or five times on top of the head with the pistol and across the face, chewing up my cheeks and nose. I went to the ground, though I was never knocked out. Quick got the same treatment nearby. I kneeled there just numb with shock, so I didn't feel any pain, and I heard the dude who'd hit me growl, "Don't ever come back here, or you're a dead man!"

Just then, some sirens pulled in close, and a couple of cops rushed over, guns drawn, and asked what was happening. "Hello, Jim," said one of the goons. "It ain't nothin' but a couple of guys causin' trouble."

"Okay, you guys," said Jim the cop, "get out of town and don't let me see you here again!"

We rode on out to a county hospital and got patched up. Now, I was living in Savannah at that time, so I knew I couldn't leave town. But Quick was from Charleston. So I took him back there, and the Tribulators (whom we were both riding with by that time) "held court" on him.

I shared what had happened with the officers there, and he gave his side. I was asked if there was any way the thing could have been prevented. I said, "I believe so—if he hadn't pulled that little peashooter out. We could of left, and there wouldn't of been no hassle."

So the officers got upset with him because he was toting that .22. "If you was gonna carry a gun, carry a *gun*," the president said. "Use somethin' that's gonna do some damage." The outcome was that his patch was pulled, which meant he was through, and we ran him out of town. I ran into him later in another town, and I told him I was sorry about his patch, but that was the way it had to be. And if that was true of a patch member, you know the club wouldn't put up with any nonsense from a prospect. Doing any-thing wrong could mean a sound stomping at least, and often, get-ting kicked out of the club.

There were times when a prospect might challenge a patch member's order. If it was just between the two of them, a one-on-

one battle usually settled it. If it came to that, and a brother was losing, the fight got broken up before the patch member really lost face. The important thing in proving yourself was never backing down. But the challenge was always there. It was hard to get a patch and hard to keep one.

Several qualities tipped you off to a good prospect. First of all, you wanted that cool head. And you wanted somebody who could handle himself well in any kind of fight, be it fists, guns, or knives, and not be afraid to use any of them.

Next, you wanted to know what he could do for the organization. If he could steal motorcycles or cars, you could use him. If he could operate a nightclub or whorehouse, or a drug ring, or a fencing operation, you could use him. And you set him right away to proving he could do what he said he could. If he couldn't, he got laughed out or beaten out pretty quickly.

Going for me now was my friendship with Marvin and my known ability to handle guns. And Marvin knew I'd make good on my promise to protect the Prophets' interest from the Outlaws. He agreed to sponsor me and let it be known around that I wasn't doing any of the donkey stuff.

Only two nights later, I got to show my new loyalty. A bunch of Outlaws dropped by our clubhouse unannounced. We had a campfire going out back, and by its light, I recognized plenty of familiar faces, guys who had been Iron Cross before turning Outlaw. I was sort of glad not to see Tom among them.

But though I knew these dudes, I had a job to do, and I was set to do it. I stood there waving my submachine gun, and some of them looked surprised, after all the partying and riding we'd done together. But I reminded them that since the Outlaws had taken over the scene, all our old friendship was in the past.

This dude named Hornet walked up to me and asked, "What're you doin' with that thing, man?"

I said, "Don't step no closer. One move outa line, an' I'll fill you full of holes!" I meant it, and they knew it. So they kept things cool and went their way soon.

And that was how things stood for a while with the Prophets and the Outlaws: a kind of shaky peace, with nobody making any strong moves. I felt at liberty to go back to Charleston and check things out. My bike needed only a few more parts chromed to be ready for assembly; Marvin figured it would take about three weeks. I agreed to come and stand guard on weekends until then, but no more, because I really needed to make the money to finish the bike.

Marvin was interested in the Tribulators, whom I'd mentioned several times. He said he'd heard of them as one of the stronger clubs in South Carolina, worth getting to know. I said I'd try to make contact with them as soon as I had time.

That's the way it went for the next three weeks: back and forth from Charleston to Jonesboro, bouncing at Jim Rosin's, standing guard for Marvin with my PROSPECT rocker on, getting the parts for the cycle laid out for assembly. I began soaking up everything Rosin had to teach me, not only dummying, but the tricks themselves, as he had the time to show them to me. Gypsy and I moved into a two-room apartment in North Charleston. She taxied back and forth to work when I was gone.

This whole time, I itched to get my hands on my Harley. I had been too long without a bike. I needed to get into the wind like a junkie needs his fix. Anticipation was making me meaner by the minute. I screamed at Gypsy to make more money; from here on, if she made seventy-five dollars one night, it had to be seventy-five dollars every night after that. And constantly handling guns gave me a sense of power; after a while, I was almost eager to shoot somebody, and I let Gypsy know that. Terror became a powerful addition to our life together from then on. The days and nights were tense indeed.

10

Assembly

Three weeks were finally up, and I looked over the gleaming collection of parts in Marvin's garage with hungry excitement. At last I was going to have myself a bona fide chopper. There'd be no place I couldn't go, nothing I couldn't do, nobody I couldn't ride with! This was it! To Marvin, standing beside me, I only said five words: "Le's get on with it!"

Marvin was in and out, so I did most of the work alone. What a pleasure it was to handle all that bright chrome!

I took the frame first and set it up on some concrete blocks. Next, I had to take the engine and set it in the frame and bolt it down. By itself, this took several hours; nearly one hundred and fifty pounds of engine weight is difficult to position.

After that, the back wheel went on. Then I ran the chain and transmission (I had a twenty-two-tooth sprocket, good for long jamming), and topped the back wheel with its fender.

All that took one day. Late the next morning, I attached the "sissy" (or "bitch") bar, where Gypsy was going to ride. The pan cover went on next, over the transmission and chain.

Then I fixed on the front end and began the wiring: All the wires had to be run where they were supposed to go—to coil, clutch, shifter, accessories. End of day two.

On the third day, I finished up the wiring and checked everything out. I didn't have to do any engine work; the boring out and
adjustments had been done at a Harley shop. But as excited as I
was, all the work I did seemed easier to do than telling about it!

It was a proud moment when I first took that bike out on the
road. I'd been happy with the way my BSA moved, but taking off
on the chopper was like switching from a transport plane to a
rocket. I felt a great sense of authority and confidence on that bike,
because it seemed to have the moves of my own body. I'll tell you,
once you've planned and built a bike like this yourself, you really
know what you've got and what it can do.

I made it for the long runs, but it could generate some speed,
too. Gypsy and I were once jamming on a flat stretch of interstate,
and a guy pulled up beside us in a Corvette.

He rolled down his window and hollered, "Hey, man! You
know how fast you're going?"

I said, "No—what're you showin'?"

"One thirty-five!"

We cooked the road like that for some ten miles before he
turned off. Gypsy's moccasins blew off in the swift breeze! And I
believe I could have gone even faster—and probably did, some time
or other.

Marvin had a Polaroid camera, and we took about ten pictures
of the bike and me on it, from different angles. Man, I loved that
bike! No question in my mind, that '49 panhead was the best
chopper I ever owned.

I rode her back to Charleston and brought Gypsy back with
me to pick up the Buick. She thought it was big stuff, tearing down
the road on that big Harley-Davidson. I was glad of that; she'd
been showing signs of getting tired of the life. She needed this little
shot to the brain.

While we were in Jonesboro, Marvin asked me whether I
thought the time was right to come back into Atlanta. Things with
the Outlaws still remained unsettled, and the cops knew the Rising
Sons were a dead patch.

I said it was probably safe, but I wanted some more time to

meet the Tribulators before I left Charleston—and to complete my gambling education under Jim Rosin.

He conceded both of those were good reasons to stay a little longer. Gypsy and I drove the car and chopper back to Charleston that night.

By his cutoff and the way he carried himself, I knew him on sight for a biker. When he walked past me with a mug and pitcher of beer, I knew from his patch he was a Tribulator.

He had long, shaggy red hair and a gray-streaked beard that covered half his chest. Chains jingled on his cutoff. He wasn't much taller than me, but he was wide, his shoulders rolling through the space of two men.

As he paused by the crap table, I got a good look at his colors: An angry-looking buzzard wearing a swastika pendant was crushing a mother, father, and baby in one talon and a city skyline in the other.

He took the mug and pitcher in one hand and with the other hauled over an empty round table and set the beer down on it. He dug in a pocket for a roll of bills and looked over the tumbling of the dice.

Seeing he had a wait before he played, I walked his way slowly and came up to him so he could see me. He glanced at me for an instant, then focused his attention back on the table. He drained half his mug of beer in a couple of gulps.

Jim Rosin was out that night, so I was pretty much running things. It was slow, Thursday night. No harm in sitting down and having a drink with this brother, if he'd do it.

I eased over to his side and said, "Think they'll fall your way tonight, brother?"

He looked surprised to be spoken to as a biker. He didn't answer right off, so I said, "My name is Barry-Barry, an' I'm runnin' the place tonight. You're welcome here, bro'." I extended a hand to him, but he didn't take it.

He said, cagy, "You a biker, man? Where's your patch?"

"I don't wear it on the job, man. But I ride with the Prophets, out of Atlanta. I been lookin' for you Tribulators."

"What for?"

"'Cause I heard you were cool dudes to know."

"What you doin' in Charleston?"

"Bring your beer an' have a drink on me, an' I'll tell you!"

He must have figured I was all right. He stuffed his money in his pocket, gathered up his brew, and followed me to a booth. I signaled a waitress and got us another pitcher of beer, a pair of shot glasses, and a bottle of bourbon from the good stock to chase down.

He nodded at the layout and looked up at me. "They call me Bull Tongue," he grunted. "You can guess how I got that name."

"They call me Barry-Barry," I grinned, "'cause I'm a *disease!*"

He choked, laughing into his sleeve, and this time we put our hands out at the same time and shook. We drank to the Tribulators and the Prophets and settled into a loose conversation.

I had some pictures of my bike in my shirt pocket. Bull looked them over with approval. "Panhead 74," he said knowingly, "solid bike." He had some pictures on him, too, of a fine-looking FX. I pointed out Gypsy bumping on her little stage. He had married his old lady, he said, and showed me a photo of her and their baby.

I told him briefly what had brought me to Charleston and about my hopes of getting something going between the Prophets and the Tribulators.

He thought it might be a good thing, too. The Tribulators were the only biking power in Charleston, and they were seeking other clubs to work and deal with. Bull was acting president of the Tribulators, "until Ice Man gets back," he said.

"Who's he?" I asked.

"One of the dudes who started the club, along with me. He's doin' time now—not enough for my likin'."

"How you mean, man?"

Bull downed another shot and sipped his beer. He said, "He got a short sentence for what he done. An' some other brothers got picked up aroun' that time. I don't know what he had to do with that, but . . . I ain't sayin' nothin' else."

He poured another shot and went on: "Ice's tough, but he can be a punk, mouthin' off an' all. Says I'm gettin' too ol' to ride an' had oughta get out. He don't know nothin'."

It was strange for a biker to talk about a brother like that, and

I didn't press Bull on it. We changed the subject to running bars, and I told him all the stuff I was learning from Rosin.

"Yeah," said Bull, "this place shows he got his shit together, but he ain't one of us."

"I'm hip to that," I said, "but I'm here for shit I can work in my own place."

"I been thinkin' about startin' up a bar," Bull mused, "jus' for us Tribulators to hang out in peace. You know, it's jus' too many hassles in some of these bars. Can't shoot pool or nothin' without somebody lippin' at you."

"Well, you ain't been bothered here," I said.

"No," he snorted, "not with this crowd. But if I brought a few of the brothers in . . ."

"I ain't about to bounce you!"

"One o' these gray-flannel dudes would call the cops right quick."

"You got somethin' there," I agreed.

Bull Tongue sipped his drink and said, "You know, if you was ever to move here, you could get your own place sooner than you think. It's no problem gettin' started, an' the fuzz stays loose—for a price!"

I told him I'd already found that out and said, "So you like the bar business?"

"Yeah," he said, looking at the mirrored ball through his whiskey. "It's a lot o' good marks on these streets." He tipped up his shot and wiped his hand on his forearm. "Man, whatta you say we get into the wind tonight! I got me some crank, an' I know some two-lane that goes to a bar where we can get a little quick action for free!"

I said, "Soun's bitchin', man, but I got duty here, an' the bike's settin' behin' my apartment house."

"Well, I'll tell you," he said, "I gotta split. If you wanta fin' us, try the Crescent Moon Bar down the street toward the base. It's open late."

"I'll be there sometime."

Bull stood up and guzzled his last mugful and held it out toward me. "An' thanks for the drinks, man! I'll get it back to you!"

"Don't worry about it, bro'—a pleasure!"

He weaved out, right steady for a dude who'd put away the booze he had, and I congratulated myself on my good luck. The Tribulators sure hadn't been hard to find!

The next night, we rode to work on the chopper. When Show Town closed, Gypsy was tired, but I told her we were going to drop over and see the Tribulators.

The Crescent Moon Bar had a bulb-lit sign painted in crude yellow letters above a black door. What once had been a window on the street was covered now with a large black-painted square of plywood. Five choppers angled from the curb, including Bull Tongue's, I noticed. I set mine in the lineup, and Gypsy and I walked to the door. Rough voices were laughing inside.

I'd opened the door about a handwidth when I saw that it was pitch dark within. I pushed it a little wider and saw something odd: A single flashlight beam pointed at a small, whitish lump on the floor in a corner. A snicker came from my right. Then the place was still. I nudged Gypsy in and quietly shut the door behind us, wondering, *What the hell is goin' on here?*

We just stood where we were, and the flashlight beam burned steadily into the corner. Nothing stirred. Then I heard a metallic "click," and something glass, maybe a beer mug, touch a table lightly.

Something moved in the lighted corner, several quick pants of breath rustled the room. A rat's head poked out of the shadows, its whiskers twitching eagerly at the lump on the floor.

Suddenly, BOOM! A smoky red-yellow flash belched from my left and momentarily lit up bottles and bearded faces. A strong sulfur smell filled the air, along with raucous cheers. On came the house lights.

"God-dawg, I believe I done got 'im!" Old Bull Tongue ambled out of the laughter toward the corner, an ancient cap-and-ball pistol still smoking in his hand.

"Sure 'nough!" he hollered, swinging some five inches of headless rat by the tail, to more cheers. "Loss his head over that stinky cheese! Haw! Haw! Haw! Gets 'em every time!"

Just then Bull saw me and Gypsy standing by the door. "Hey,

Barry-Barry!" he cried gleefully. "Come on in an' have a drink with my frien' Reddy the rat!"

"I don't know who needs it more, him or me!" I jived.

That got a good laugh all around, and when it died down, Bull said, "This here's the dude I was tellin' you about, rides with the Prophets. This here's Barry-Barry—" and, stealing my line: *"He's a disease!"*

I tried my best to look like one while everybody howled. Then Bull introduced me to the whole contingent, including Slug, Dusty, Whizzer, and Dawg. I showed everybody Gypsy as we all sat around three tables pushed together and talked.

Dusty had heard about what was going down in Atlanta and wondered why I didn't just pack up and settle in Charleston. "Well," I said, "I agreed to probate with them brothers, an' tha's the way it is. If they go, I go."

Bull Tongue took a metal rod and a piece of cloth from his cutoff and set his pistol on the table. He wrapped the cloth around the rod, picked up the pistol again, and jammed the rod and cloth back and forth in the gun, spilling the spent black powder on the floor.

"Neat thin' to have," he said, squinting down the barrel. "These babies is legal in this state. They call 'em antiques, but they can sure put a hole through you jus' the same!"

While we were all still half sober, we agreed that the Prophets and the Tribulators would have to party out together soon. When we got half drunk, we started yelling and getting wild. We shot out a few lights, poured beer over the rat, and in the middle of the hell-raising, I got a notion to try something new.

Gypsy was the only old lady there, and I thought I'd use her to show off to the rest. I picked an empty beer can from a table and handed it to her. She said, "Wha's this for?"

I said, "I want you to go down to the end of the bar an' put this beer can on top of your head an' stay still."

"Whatch'you gonna do, Barry-Barry?"

"You don't need to know—jus' get on down there an' do what I said, an' don't move!"

She was shaky and scared, too, but she got down there, hold-ing onto the chairs and stood with her hip against the bar for balance. I said, "Now put that beer can on your head, an' hol' it steady!" She got it up there, and then I drew my .357 Magnum and cocked it back.

Gypsy's eyes got as big as saucers. "Barry-Barry," she said, all weak and trembly, "what're you doin'?" I took dead aim at the can. She looked like she was ready to faint. "I love you, Barry-Barry!" she said. I said, "I love you, too, Gypsy—now hol' still!"

KAPOW! I blew that thing right off her head. She started to slump down, weak-kneed, but I hollered, "Stan' up there! Hey, Whizzer—give 'er another one!"

Slug said, "The dude's stone crazy!" And heaven knows, I was when I'd done enough drinking. I shot can after can from her head, and this way earned considerable admiration for a stunt that got to be kind of a legend with me and Gypsy. She was as crazy as I was for letting me, but that was part of our being together.

After that, the night broke down in a boozy blur that staggered on until dawn, and I'm not sure to this day how we got home in one piece or who paid for the damages to the bar. But it was a good start of things with the Tribulators that I was sure the Prophets and I could build on.

11

Tribulatin'!

About a week later, after drinking with the Tribulators a few more times, I went back to Jonesboro and told Marvin and the rest of the Prophets all that had gone down of late. The Tribulators had given me a standing invitation to bring the Prophets back with me when I returned, for some partying.

Six of the Prophets piled into a big sedan a day later and followed me down to Charleston: Gut, Lockjaw, Kong, Chinaman, Foul Dan, and a prospect of Kong's named Bald Hill. Kong, Chinaman, and Gut were officers, considered well able to give an account of things to Marvin, who had business keeping him in Atlanta.

The Tribulators' clubhouse at that time was an old frame building in a bad section of Charleston. One advantage to that was, most club activities went on uncomplained of by neighbors. Also, anybody wandering around who looked "wrong" for the neighborhood stood out right away. This made it easier to spot cops and other intruders.

I was familiar enough to the Tribulators not to cause any alarm as I reeled in my chopper in front of the Tribulators' place—with this carload of Prophets piling out after me. The Tribulators were expecting us, and introductions didn't take long. Gut, enforcer (or discipline man) for the Prophets, met his counterpart for the Tribu-

lators, Whizzer. Chinaman, as V.P. of the Prophets, was their rank-
ing officer on this trip, so he got to talking with Bull Tongue. Kong
was the Prophets' secretary-treasurer, same as Dawg for the Tribulators. The rest of the meeting action took care of itself, and soon
we had a solid party going.

I was pleased with the way the two clubs were hitting it off. It
turned out they had the makings of a valuable arrangement, con-
necting the Tribulators' stronghold in Charleston drug traffic with
the Prophets' movement of cars and cycle parts. But a fast series of
events saw to it that nothing got cemented.

The second night, partying moved over to Slug's big apartment
in North Charleston, and things roared along well till about midnight. Then Lockjaw got to talking about some flares he had in the
trunk of his car, which was the one the Prophets had driven from
Jonesboro and I was chauffeuring them around Charleston in.

"Hey!" he shouted. "It would be a gas to set one of them
things off in the middle of the street!"

"Hell, yes!" Bald Hill agreed, jumping up. "Damn thing would
light up the whole block! Le's do it!"

The two of them careened down the stairs and got a flare from
the trunk, while the rest of us shut out the lights and crowded
around the second-story windows looking out on the street.

Lockjaw set off the flare, which splashed bright pink light all
over the block. It was quite a pretty show, and we were all cheer-
ing it on loudly when a car came down the block and stopped, not
being able to get around the spitting flare.

The driver honked his horn repeatedly, and we quieted down
as Baldy and Lockjaw walked over to the car. I heard Lockjaw
taunt the guy: "Wha's the matter, boy? You don't like this fireworks
show?"

A sharp voice came back, "You get that friggin' thing out the
road or I'll run it over!"

"Watch how you talk, boy," I heard Baldy growl. "You better
back that barge offa this street before I back you up the exhaust
pipe!"

The driver swore and shoved open his car door, thumping
Lockjaw in the chest and stomach. Baldy darted around and began
to haul the guy out of the front seat. About this time, the lot of us

upstairs bolted for the door. It looked like a sound stomping was in order!

On the way down, I heard yelling, and two shots rang out. I squeezed out the door just after Whizzer and Kong. The block was alive, with lights flicking on all over, women screaming, and the sound of flesh thumping against metal. Lockjaw was smashing the driver's head against the hood of the car, while Baldy reared back for kicks to the groin. I saw that a car had pulled behind the one whose windows Whizzer and Kong were now smashing with pistol butts. Its front door was open, and a woman ran shrieking down the street.

I shot the tires from under the offending car, while the rest of the brothers worked the driver over. A third car came up the block. I ran over to it, along with Bull Tongue and hollered, "What're you doin' here? Get the hell out o' that car!" I had the juices pumping in me head to toe now, and I wanted to feel some bones crushing!

Bull and I didn't wait for the passengers, two scared citizens, to get out. The guy on the driver's side had his door locked, but Bull broke his window and got his door open. My guy had his door partway open, so I just yanked him to his feet and whipped his face with my pistol barrel. I turned him around and kicked him in the kidney and saw the rest of the brothers charging toward us from what was left of the guy who'd started all the trouble, to help out.

Just then, I heard a siren, and another from a different direction, and still one more! "COPS!" I yelled, and all the brothers looked up, startled.

We dropped the beat-up bodies and started to scatter. I heard Chinaman yell out, "Barry-Barry! Go for the car!" I dodged some flying Tribulators and found myself running alongside Lockjaw. As we neared the car, he tossed the keys at me: "You know the town, man!"

All the Prophets crammed in quick but Baldy. There was no time to wait for him; the sirens were right on top of us. I fired up and laid rubber down the street, away from the scene of the action. At the end of the block, I caught sight of two high beams and a flashing red "bubble-gum machine," racing at me head-on. I veered right onto the sidewalk and shot past the cop car, sending garbage cans crashing all around.

I glanced in my side-view and saw the cops trying to back and turn around. I had a good head start on them. I headed for where I knew there'd be a lot of traffic and I could lose them.

With the sirens wailing behind me, I weaved down the streets, honking cars out of the way and jumping a few citizens to the sidewalks. "What a ride, man!" yelled Kong, and I shouted back, "Jus' keep them eyes glued behin' us an' tell me if they're catchin' up!"

Two blocks later, Chinaman called out, "They's two of 'em now, Barry-Barry—an' they's gainin' on us!"

My side-view told me he was right. We were coming into a congested area, where I'd been hoping to shake them off. "They gettin' closer, Barry-Barry!" It was Foul Dan this time, and I knew he wasn't one to worry. Time had come to do something and do it fast!

Up ahead I spied the fast-moving traffic of Rivers Avenue. I was hitting sixty miles an hour and coming up on a green traffic signal—that suddenly turned yellow, and then flashed red! The lead cop car was but about four car lengths behind me. It was now or never.

I floored her and ripped across Rivers Avenue. A gap opened up as two cars crisscrossed in front of me and a van screeched to a stop. Just behind me, I heard tires squealing and three loud "thuds" and shattering glass.

"You got 'im, Barry-Barry!" screamed Kong, pounding me on the back. "Way to go, man! We home free!"

"Not yet," called Foul Dan. "The other one's still comin'!" I pulled onto Durant and raced alongside some railroad tracks for a second or two. At the corner of Beaufort, I decided to make my move. I hit the brake and spun us into a sweeping U-turn. I floored it again as our tires caught hold, shot across an empty parking lot, and peeled back up Durant.

The cops tried to duplicate this maneuver and couldn't hold it. "Good God!" Kong bellowed. "They done chopped down a telephone pole!" In my side-view, I saw the two cops jump out of the car and live wires sputtering all around them as we made our getaway.

I got a lot of cheers and shakes and backslaps as I doubled back down Rivers Avenue toward Charleston Heights. I was thinking about where we could hide out for a few hours and settling on the trailers in back of Show Town.

When we got there, I cleared things with Jim Rosin, just telling him we'd been speeding. He said we could park in back and use one of the trailers, leaving the other one free for the hookers.

Gypsy brought us back a few pitchers of beer, and I talked Rosin into letting her and a couple of the hookers come in and party with us. Lockjaw backed the car against the wood fence so the license couldn't be seen, then joined us for the rest of a high old night.

Not everybody was as lucky as our carload. One group of Tribulators was busted on a slew of assault and speeding charges, but they kept mum about the rest of us. The Prophets said they'd split the bail costs, and we all agreed it had been a neat caper.

It turned out Baldy got away in a car driven by Whizzer. They had gone over to Whizzer's place and from there to a small bar nearby, where Baldy met an eighteen-year-old chick who was to prove to be the Prophets' undoing.

Under cover of the following night, the Prophets regathered and set off for Jonesboro. I stayed in Charleston. Baldy talked this chick into coming to spend a few days with the Prophets. After they got back to Jonesboro, things went down like this:

Baldy took the chick to the Prophets' clubhouse and got her high and drunk. Some of the other brothers joined in, and they ran a train on her. Baldy being a prospect, after a day or so, he had to lend her out to a patch member named Hook, who transferred her over to his place and just kept her under lock and key for the amusement of anyone who dropped by.

Some brothers came together at Hook's one night and got weird with the chick, sticking pins all over her body and running her through hours of rape. They all got drunk and passed out, and she managed to slip away.

She got hold of the police, and the whole club was raided. Nearly everyone was questioned about it, and only three guys got off scot-free: Marvin, who was out of town at the time, Billy-Bob, who never touched her, and myself.

That was the last straw for me as far as Atlanta was concerned.

I told Marvin as much the last time he called me, and he said he understood. The Prophets were so busted up, he said, that he was probably going to fold up the patch. So few patch members were left to hold off the Outlaws now, they'd never stand a chance.

I was sorry to say so long to Marvin; he'd been a good brother and a lot of help to me. But I knew what future I had lay in Charleston, and I called the Tribulators' clubhouse to let them know I was in town for good.

That night, Gypsy rode off to work in the Buick. I wanted to hole up at home for a few days and stay high. I was halfway through a thick joint when I heard a knock at the door.

I doused the joint with my tongue, laid it aside, and went to the door.

"Who is it?" I said with my hand on the lock.

"Open up, man. It's Quick!"

I didn't know this Tribulator well yet but knew there was no danger in letting him in.

"Wha's happenin'?" I asked as I opened the door and he shouldered by.

He turned and said, "Bull Tongue wants t' see you down at the Crescent Moon." He put on a grim face and added, "He said if you don't come, I'm t' *bring* you!"

I looked down, and he'd pulled out a .45. Panic shot through me for an instant, but I covered it up just as quick. I laughed in Quick's face and said, "You don't need that piece o' junk, man. I ain't afraid to go nowhere!" Whatever went down, I had to let him know I was tougher than he was.

He nudged the gun toward the door, and I said, "Put that thing away. I'm ready; I'll go with you!" He put it up then.

We got on our bikes and rode down to Reynolds Avenue. Outside the Crescent Moon I saw a lot of bikes, looked like the whole club was there. The place was noisy, but everybody shut up the instant I walked through the door.

Bull Tongue was sitting with the rest of the officers at a table, all facing me. I walked toward them smiling and said, "What is it you want, Bull?"

"Jus' stay right where you're at, man," Bull snapped. I stood in my tracks. I thought I heard a snicker from somewhere in the crowded bar, but I kept looking straight at Bull.

He said, "You an' your goddam Prophets cost us a pack o' trouble, man! Ten thousand bucks' worth o' bond."

I said, "No shit! An' a hot little Charleston bitch cos' *them* their patch! I'd say it's fair exchange."

I think even Bull was a little surprised to hear me answer back like that, with the whole room full of Tribulators there. He paused and said, "You know, the cops is still lookin' for the Prophets!"

"They ain't none to fin' no more," I grinned.

"No," he said, and took out his old cap-and-ball pistol, "but I could tell 'em where to fin' one *ex*-Prophet!"

What is goin' on here? I thought, the fear rising up in me again. *But wait a minute! I know this dude. Calm your brains, man!*

I reached over and got an empty chair and straddled it right in front of Bull's table. I cocked my head to the side, smiled, and lit a cigarette. Nobody in the place moved. "Bull," I said, "you jus' wouldn't rat on ol' Barry-Barry!"

"Why not?"

"'Cause you'd have to turn that old cannon aroun' an' blow your own fat head off! I an' you both know what you do to rats!" I pointed my finger like a gun toward the corner, snapping my thumb like a hammer: "Pow!"

Bull tried his best to look serious, but slowly his big head and body began to bob up and down. He bobbed faster and began to snort his laughter through his nose, and the whole bar cracked in a spreading quake of laughter. Soon it felt like the whole place was shaking. With tears streaming down his face, Bull reached across the table. I grabbed his forearm, and we both laughed until it hurt.

When things began to settle, Bull said, "Barry-Barry, how did you know we was puttin' you on?"

I said, "I didn't, man! I jus' had to go with the flow—an' it flowed right!"

"If I hadn't of been foolin' you, you wouldn't be talkin' right now!"

"I know'd that," I said, "but it's better t' go out laughin'. It's more relaxin'! But man, if you gonna keep me alive for a while, how 'bout lettin' me have some beer!"

We partied in there till about sunrise. I brought Gypsy from Show Town after work. Word had gotten around about my driving caper. I spent a lot of time reliving that, to the great amusement of the brothers. They really gave me a royal welcome that night, and I already felt like one of them when Bull Tongue and the rest of the officers got together and asked me, "Hey, why don't you be a Tribulator?"

I said, "I would, but I ain't probatin' for nobody. I don't have to prove nothin' to nobody! I know what I can do."

And Bull said, "That soun's good enough for us!"

So they gave me a patch. I never had to work for it, and this is an honor you don't often see in a bike club. But I was bad, and they all knew it. When I'd get to drinking, I'd do anything, just to prove I wasn't afraid. And once you had a patch, you didn't stop proving yourself, you kept *on* proving it, night after night.

And you proved it with women as well as men. Once a girl poked me in the gut and said, "What happened to your chest—it fell!" She might have been joking, but I was drunk, and it ticked me off. I reached out and backhanded her off her chair. She lay there on the barroom floor, and I said, "Don't talk to me that way, girl. You don't seem to know who you're talkin' to!"

Well, she was somebody else's girl, and this dude came at me, and I said, "Hol' it! Best thing for you to do is get outa here an' take her with you! You got somethin' else to say about it, jus' go ahead an' say it! Do it—or get along!"

He picked her up off the floor and skulked out. But I could be very easygoing, and then the littlest thing set me off. And I didn't get any mellower as time went on.

Three months after I came to Charleston, I left Show Town, though Gypsy stayed on there a while longer. A dude named Jay Younger managed a joint on the strip called the Playpen, and I went to work for him, minding the door to start.

I moved on to bartender in the Playpen, and soon after that became assistant manager. I had learned my gambling well—I no longer did any bouncing; I mainly handled crooked card games and the women. I moved Gypsy over there, too, after a few weeks.

I'd only been there a month and a half when the owner of the place, John Glass, opened up another big club, a whorehouse, and told me, "Okay, this one's yours, Barry—you run it."

The place ran for only two weeks and burned down to the ground. I believe to this day it was torched for insurance. So, with no steady place to work, I went from bar to bar in town, selling a hat and working other card tricks, sometimes with my old boss, Jim Rosin, who liked to spend a couple of his nights a week working other clubs.

I made good money doing this, but after a while, I had an urge to open my own place. And Bull Tongue was right: As far as getting a building and setting up to operate, there was nothing to it. In the upper part of the strip, you could lease a building for only two hundred dollars or so a month. The whole area was just a bunch of bars, one right after the other, with a lot of ownership turnover. (Not too many years later, the Navy bought up several blocks of the strip, probably just to tear it down, which they did right afterward.)

I leased a building, Mims put their Red Arrow machines in on a fifty-fifty split basis, I got a stock of booze, hired some girls, and I was in business. There wasn't much, but I had a little atmosphere in there, with some biking and psychedelic posters lit up with black lights, that kind of thing. I called the place the Mystic Mushroom.

I enjoyed running a bar, being in control of the scene, making a good time for everyone who came in. From here on out, Gypsy and I worked separately. She showed flashes of jealousy that kept me from having the free hand I wanted with the women, and I had to keep her out. I tried to tell her all my messing around was just business. She'd hear from one of the Tribulators' old ladies about someone I was playing with and bring it up to me. I'd tell her I was just after the chick's money (which usually *was* part of my scheme).

If Gypsy could get to her, she would sneak to the chick when I wasn't around and put a knife to her throat and tell her to stay away from me or get her throat slit. She beat up on more than a few of my side chicks. In return, I beat her, viciously sometimes, for every chick she ran off. But it wasn't too much of a hassle; girls seem to gravitate around bikers, and I always had a steady supply.

The Tribulators spent their share of time in my place, but soon Bull and I were talking again about opening up a bar just for the club members. We decided to do it and went in halves on the Tribulator Lounge, just two doors down from the Mystic Mushroom. All the brothers appreciated having this place all their own to relax and do their thing with no interference.

There were a lot of drugs around, but I bought and didn't sell. I lived well off the nightclub life with the booze and gambling, and I was satisfied with that.

Some changes came down not long after. First off, Ice Man came back.

It was clear right away that the dude had a lot of skill and style. He and I were about level in meanness, but we were quite different in other ways. Ice was secretive, liable to punk up and get snappy if you asked him what he was up to. I liked to be open with my brothers; I felt like I had nothing to hide from another patch member, and I bore Ice some resentment for keeping a lot of his activities in the dark.

Ice was the big drug man in the Tribulators. Even after being in prison, he had no trouble setting up his network. Nor did he have any problem taking control of the club as soon as he got back. It was assumed he'd pick up his office, and when he returned, he did.

Ice liked to cultivate a "class" image. He considered himself quite a ladies' man, and you'd often see him running a comb through his retreating red-blond hairline. He wasn't your greasy scooter trash. Ice was lightning quick and smooth with a knife, but felt more at home in dance halls than honky-tonks. He could be as crazy wild as I was when he got drunk—but he was always clean!

I got along all right with Ice. He could see I had a lot of biking knowledge and the respect of all the Tribulators, which was surprising for a fairly new patch member. Though he and I didn't talk a lot, we each knew we were solid bikers and we kept from getting in each other's way.

Gypsy had no use for Ice Man. She thought he was a conceited punk and didn't like the way he treated women. She got especially turned off one night when a girl came up to Ice just to talk. She was being friendly enough, but he hauled off and duked her across the room—not because of anything she said, but just because he didn't like the *way* she spoke! After a while, Gypsy'd just clear out of wherever she was if Ice came around.

Bull Tongue never did settle his beef with Ice. It was clear that the two of them couldn't stand having each other in sight. One night, they almost came to blows in the Tribulator Lounge. A few of the brothers held them back and kept it from happening. But neither of them ever showed signs of making peace, and a month after Ice's return, Bull simply left town without notice, for "parts West." I didn't find out that he'd settled in California till he called me, out of the blue, years later.

I was sorry to hear of Bull's leaving, maybe sorrier for myself than for his troubles with Ice. I was drinking heavily one night when the thought crossed my mind that everybody I got close to seemed to disappear from my life: Big Tom, Marvin, and now Bull. I cursed the fact but shrugged it off to coincidence. I had too many other things going for me to worry about stuff like that.

After Bull left, elections were held for his office, vice-president, and somewhat to my surprise, considering the short time I'd worn the patch, I was elected. To me, this was really sweet! I had struggled and fought—and made my mark as a biker. This was the sign of real recognition, and I was going to take every advantage of it.

To an outsider, a biker's life can seem like a maze of confusion, and at times, mine wasn't any exception. Being named vice-president of the Tribulators wasn't the only unexpected thing that happened to me. Maureen came back into my life for a while.

I made a point of dropping in on my mother about once a month. I didn't see her more than that because I just didn't want to be preached at, and Mom never failed to throw a word or two in suggesting I go back to Maureen. I laughed off that kind of talk, but she and her husband Frank always treated me kindly and with a measure of respect. My sisters were friendly, too—and though Tanya, the older, stayed a little shy and suspicious of me, to Tara I was the cat's meow (much to Mom's annoyance). Tara even tried gleefully to talk Mom into putting a "Support Your Local Tribulator" bumper sticker on the family car (no dice with Mom!).

Mother also stayed in close touch with Maureen and startled me one day by telling me Maureen was moving to Charleston. I asked why in the world she was doing that, and Mom hinted that it had more than a little to do with me!

Strangely enough, at this time, I wasn't at all unhappy to hear this news. I had never gotten tired of Maureen's body, and since I was rolling in the gambling and bar money, I figured I could manage to keep both Gypsy and Maureen as well as the two kids.

So for a while there in Charleston, I was living with both women. I still hadn't brought Gypsy around to meet my mother, so Mom didn't know for sure that I was living with another woman. If Maureen knew, she didn't let on. More than likely, the two of them knew, but didn't say anything about it, hoping against hope to get the marriage back together.

I enjoyed seeing my sons again and taking advantage of Maureen's favors. I lied my way around her questions about my activities. Maureen knew I was in the bar business, and I'd tell her I had to go out of town to swing some deal—and I'd go over and spend a couple of days with Gypsy.

At other times, I'd see Gypsy at night, and since my clubs were running well enough to do without me for short stretches, I'd often spend parts of the nights with Gypsy or other chicks. I'd come back to Maureen at four o'clock or so in the morning and tell her I was just working my "normal" hours.

I was able to keep this song and dance going for quite some time. If it sounds like a busy life, it was! But if you had a lot of money, and were a club officer, the club didn't make many demands on your time. Nobody said, "Hey, man, you ain't been aroun' much lately!" You did what you wanted and answered to nobody.

My "dues" to the club got paid in a lot of ways that kept me appreciated. I was the one who was springing people from jail, posting bonds and all that, throwing the parties—I had the money, and I always had people in the club around me *because* I had it.

So life was good, and it stayed that way until some sudden heat came on the club, and I had to leave town . . . in a hurry!

12

Over the High Side

My good stretch was shattered by some trouble I had nothing to do with. Whizzer, Dusty, Slug, Dawg, and a couple of other patch members were partying with another club, the Dixie Dragons, up in Aiken, South Carolina.

They were all drinking and high on mescaline and acid at the Dragons' clubhouse, and a Dragon said something smart to Whizzer.

Whizzer told him, "Shut up, or we're gonna pull your patches! You got no business wearin' that patch in South Carolina anyway without our say-so. We *own* South Carolina!"

A brawl started, and the Tribulators tied up two guys and two chicks and cut their throats. Whizzer and company came back to Charleston, leaving the Dragons for dead—but the two girls lived!

All the Tribulators were dragged in by the cops. They grilled me over and over about it, claiming I had ordered the killings even though I had airtight proof I'd spent all that night shooting pool in the Black Cat bar in Charleston. They finally let me go, but I knew what my next move had to be: Hit the road!

I told Gypsy to pack some light bags—we were splitting town. The killings generated a mountain of publicity, from newspapers to detective magazines, in short order. I knew that once trial dates

were set, I would get called in as a witness, and I had no intention
of being one, character or otherwise!

I didn't tell Maureen I was leaving, or anyone, even in the
club, where I was going. The most I told anybody was Ice, and that
was: "Man, I'm leavin' town, an' I'll *be* back when I *get* back!"

We had a great cross-country ride, all the way to California. I
was sure glad for the way I'd built my bike—for long-distance jamming. It really felt like flying on some of those desert stretches, the
kind of freedom an eagle must know!

Gypsy was used to dancing topless by this time, and I had no
trouble getting her work in California bars. We hung around for
about two months before I got the itch to go again. And my next
move was to look up Weed in Arizona.

Weed was riding with a club out of Sierra Vista, and we had a
good, high reunion. He helped Gypsy get work dancing in a nightclub thirty miles away in Vincent, where we took a cheap room.
And it was on a stretch of desert road between the two towns that
my story almost ended.

Gypsy had a night off and wanted to spend it with me, but I
told her I had to take care of some business over in Sierra Vista. I
was really going to a party Weed was throwing, where he had some
women who said they wanted to meet me.

The girls were no great shakes, but I managed to get good and
soused, and I headed back toward Vincent around eleven-thirty.

That Arizona highway was straight—and pitch dark except for
dim starlight. There wasn't even a house for miles—at times you
could swear you were riding into a huge black hole, with desert
stretching into nothingness on either side.

I hadn't gotten far from Sierra Vista when I noticed that my
gas gauge was pointing at EMPTY. I started looking for a side road
that might lead to a service station.

I spied an exit up ahead and turned off the main highway and
rode down this stretch for about a mile. I made nothing out but a
low, dark shanty; no sign of a gas station.

I turned around and headed back for the main road. My mind
was spinning with booze and pot, and when I came up on a fork in
the road, I couldn't for the life of me remember its being there or

the right way to go! I decided to turn right, thinking that was at least the general direction I was headed in.

Nothing but black road loomed ahead, so I cranked down, hitting second, then third, moving up around sixty-five or seventy miles an hour.

I suddenly made out a sign to my right that read DEAD END! My headlight shined on what looked like a big dirt pile immediately ahead. I knew it was too late to stop, but I tried to at least gear her down. I had just enough time to drop it into second as I started up the dirt hill.

It didn't look like much; I figured I'd just shoot over it. So I started to give the bike some gas. I flew over that hill, and suddenly found myself in outer space! There was nothing underneath me!

I thought, *God, no! I'm a dead man!* In the darkness I had no idea how far down I was going to plummet, but I could already feel the groundward pull.

That cycle couldn't have dropped more than about ten feet. But when it hit solid earth, it crunched to a dead stop against a rock. The handlebars buckled forward, and I flew over them like I was slingshot. I bounced over rocks and cactus, taking a fierce beating before I slumped still in a heap some distance from my take-off point. I don't think I'd be alive to tell this if I hadn't had a helmet on. As it was, that was torn to shreds by the rocks as I skimmed across them.

I was knocked silly and just lay there in shock for some hours. When I finally moved a little, the first thing I could tell was that my left ankle was badly hurt. I fought the pain and struggled to my feet. I managed to hobble over to my bike to check it out. Because I could do that, I figured the ankle wasn't broken, just badly sprained. That was some relief!

The bike wasn't in as bad shape as my bloody nose. The exhaust had fallen off, the handlebars were bent, and the headlight was smashed. Outside of those, it seemed all right.

I can't say I felt as good as the bike looked. I slumped down and lay in a sort of daze until morning. When it got light, some state troopers spotted me and came down. They helped me into the patrol car and took me back to Sierra Vista. I got hold of Gypsy

and Weed and told them I'd gone over the high side. Weed said
he'd be over soon with a pickup to get me and the bike.

I went into the men's room of the gas station where the cops
had left me to clean up. I looked in the mirror and saw black eyes
and a bruised, cut-up face, but I was plenty happy to be alive!

To me, no more proof was necessary that my luck had run out
in Arizona! I told Gypsy that as soon as I could get the bike on the
road, we would head back to Charleston—if the coast was clear.

Within a few weeks, it was. I called Ice's number, and he told
me what was happening: The state hadn't wasted any time prose-
cuting the brothers involved in the Dixie Dragons killings. Most of
them got sentenced to the electric chair. Ice had been on the
road for a while himself, but now he was back and ready to
start over, he said. Hardly anybody was left, but he was determined, as I told him I was also, to build the patch up again.

By the time I got back to Charleston, it was evident that Ice
had been busy. All the publicity about the murders drew a lot of
hangarounds, including some navy guys who liked to ride and
others who wanted to prove they could run with a tough crowd. I
picked up my officer's rank right where I'd left it, and Ice and I
started making plans.

We decided to prospect weak for a while, let a lot of guys try
for the patch and just weed them out as we went along. With some
forty hangarounds to choose from, we'd surely find a few right
dudes.

That we did! On board came Dick and Black, Moose and Sheb,
who were a few of the best. We found Torrence around that time,
too, and Snag, both of whom I was close with in short order. We
rented a new clubhouse, an out-of-the-way frame dwelling near
I-26, on Ashley-Phosphate Road. In no time, the club was cooking
as well as ever, and we were happy with the new power we
wielded and the new blood we'd recruited. Black became the new
secretary-treasurer, and Moose the enforcer, and we all agreed it
was time to think about expanding our influence even more.

Dick hailed from Savannah, Georgia, where he had graduated
from rooty-poot biking. He told us of a large number of weekend
bike clubs down there that he thought might supply the nucleus of

a new Tribulators' charter. At least, he said, a couple of brothers might be able to steal enough bikes to keep the Tribulators in Charleston well supplied with parts for a while. We had a grave-yard, you see, of old bikes and parts ripped off from all over for club use.

That idea sounded good to me, so I said I'd go down there with Dick and see what I could do to start another charter.

Before I left, I dropped in on my mother again and told her I'd be out of town for a while. She had some news: My latest disap-pearance had been the last straw for Maureen; she was filing for di-vorce. I told Mom I didn't mind, and I'd call her soon and tell her where to send the papers.

She looked at me then kind of sadly and said, "I'm really worried about you, son. You're headed for nothin' but more trouble."

I said, "Mother, don't you get yourself upset on my account. I can take care o' myself."

She put her hand on my cheek and said, "I wish that was true, Barry. But I'm prayin' the angels'll stan' guard over you."

"I don't need no angels guardin' me, Mother," I laughed.

She said, "Maybe you don't think so. But I want you to do somethin' for me."

I said, "Wha's that, Mother?"

She went to her purse and took out a piece of cloth, something like a small square of red silk, and put it in my hand and closed my fist around it. She looked tenderly into my eyes, as she never had before. I was almost startled by the gentleness in her face. I said, "Mother, wha's this?" I opened my hand and looked at the cloth, and she answered, "Son, I want you to carry this with you, every place you go. This cloth has been anointed and prayed over, and God is gonna watch over your life."

I stared at her, flabbergasted, for a few seconds. I shook my head and said, "Mother, I don't believe in all that kin' of stuff. I don't need this thing!" And I tried to hand it back to her.

She raised her eyebrows at me and said, "Just take it!"

"But I don't need it!"

She said then, with that mixture of love and authority a mother never quits using when she thinks something's important, "Give me your billfold!"

And I said to myself, *Why fight her?* and handed it over. She took it and stuck the little piece of cloth into it and handed it back to me. I smiled, "All right, Mother. You happy now?"

She turned away with a look of warm satisfaction and said, "Yes, son, that makes me happy!"

I shrugged my shoulders, tucked my wallet in my pocket, and forgot about it. We said our good-byes, and I went back to my place to pick up Gypsy and head with Dick for Savannah.

Dick and I got a lot done down in Savannah. We established a pipeline for stolen cycle parts that lasted far longer than the year we spent there. And we found about eight reliable bikers, though we never officially set up a charter. Four of these guys we brought back with us to Charleston. Two of them time and trouble weeded out. But the pair who stuck were among the best patch members the Tribulators ever had: Morris (whom we called Shiv) and Hair.

Two incidents stand out in my mind from that year, one sort of comical, and the other, almost fatal—and a little mysterious. Both happened while I was riding my chopper.

One night the eight of us were jamming out of Savannah on Highway 17. We'd been snorting a lot of speed and drinking, and if I remember right, I had taken some mescaline, too.

I was leading the pack as always. We were doing around fifty, still in the city limits. Suddenly, I saw a train up ahead. It looked like a long freighter, crossing the road dead in front of us. I didn't see any railroad signals, no flashing lights or warning bells, just this train.

I hit my brakes hard and tried to wheel around. Everybody behind me tried to do the same, and a couple of guys went down. I came to a stop and looked up again. There was nothing there!

I blinked my eyes, and Hair said, "Wha's the matter with you?" I rubbed my eyes and looked again. Still nothing. I said, "I thought sure I saw a train up there!" Then I thought, *Hey! It must of been that damn mescaline, messin' with my min'!!* And I said aloud, "Man, tha's it! I ain't takin' no more o' that junk!"

The whole thing gave us laughs for some time afterward. But there was something about it that bothered me: For the first time in my experience, I hadn't been able to count on my five senses. With all the drugs I had taken before, including mescaline many times, I had been in control. Now, for just that moment, my judgment had gone haywire. That was a possibility I had never wanted to think about. Now I had to—because it had happened.

Again, I was on Highway 17, this time heading toward Savannah. Gypsy was behind me in the car; I was taking her to the place she worked in, a basement B-drinking spot called The Tender Trap. It was still light, and we planned to stop off at another bar along the way.

I was taking it easy, doing about forty-five, the speed limit. Now, I don't know whether this guy didn't see me because of the pearl blue color of my bike, or what, but with no warning at all, an oncoming car suddenly swerved right in front of me, crossing my lane for a mobile-home sales lot.

For an instant, we looked straight at one another, and we both knew I couldn't stop. My only hope was that he'd get on by before I smashed him sidelong.

But he froze and stopped right in the middle of the street! For me there was no exit, no way to avoid hitting him. I knew the only thing I could do was lay the bike down.

So I leaned it over, and here were six hundred pounds of cycle —WHOOO!—sliding across the asphalt, me kicking away from it— and all I could see was that front bumper heading up on me.

I stuck my hand up, and the bike, as it came sliding in, hit his right front wheel with the forks and slammed—WHAM!—right up underneath the front of his car, with my left leg pinned between the motorcycle and the asphalt, my elbow smashing against the front bumper.

I remember as I was still scraping the pavement, gasoline coming at me from my fuel tank and sparks flying, igniting that gas— and when it hit—WHOOSH!—flames spread up, and here I was, pinned there!

The guy jumped out of his car and started running away. I guess he was sure it was all going to blow any second. "Hey," I

screamed at him, "get this friggin' thing offa me! Come over here
an' get me outa here!" That bike was blazing away, all around my
leg, and I was furiously trying to kick myself free.

I must have called him every foul name in the book, and he
finally came running back over. He lifted up the front end of the
bike, and I managed to pull my leg out. He grabbed me under the
arms and dragged me away, with my pants leg still gasoline-soaked
and burning. I wore high boots, which I'm sure saved my leg, but
as he hauled me, I was slapping away at my leg, trying to put out
the fire.

He barely got me to the sidewalk, and my gas tank went
BOOM! And right after that, his car went FROOOM! We stood
there, and I looked at my Harley-Davidson, and all I could think
was, *Boy, I'd like to wring this guy's neck!* I was seeing my *life*
going up in flames.

I pretty near cussed him into the pavement as the fire department came, TV cameras came, and Gypsy tried to console me. I
told him if I didn't get a new motorcycle out of it, I'd kill him.
The insurance company came to survey the damage, and I heard
an ambulance wailing in the distance. I didn't feel much pain because of shock, and I stumbled around trying to collect the wet
and scattered contents of my billfold.

I found cash cards and receipts here and there, and at last the
limp and torn piece of leather itself. I picked it up, and as I did,
something fluttered out, flimsy and red! The instant it hit the
ground, a thought flashed to me: *Them prayers in that thing saved
my life!* I pushed the idea aside as quickly as it had come, but I
knew I did have little business being alive.

The ambulance arrived and took me to the hospital for patch-
ing up. There wasn't much left of my pants on the left side; my left
leg and rump were badly asphalt-burned. My left arm was skinned
to its length, with a gaping cut by my shoulder. The upper part of
my left boot had burned off, and my leg underneath was cooked a
little—I'm sure that boot is the only reason I still have a leg. But
somehow, nothing was broken!

Of course, I had to put another bike together. It was a good
one, but never did seem as much like *me* as that first Harley 74—I
never felt quite *one* with a bike again.

And brief as it was, I had my first thought that perhaps something beyond me, that I couldn't control, might have an effect on my life.

When we moved back to Charleston, everyone agreed the Savannah trip had been a success. Hair moved up fast in the ranks, soon being named secretary-treasurer of the Tribulators. Shiv and I became fast friends, though, like all my other close friendships, this one didn't last long: Shiv was wiped out in an accident that smashed him and his bike to tiny bits.

Black changed jobs, taking over as enforcer when Moose was out for a while with an injury—and holding on to that office after Moose returned. Dick, who'd worked with me in Savannah, also got killed in an accident (sideswiped by a trailer truck). Dick never had an enemy, in or out of the club, and his funeral drew bikers from all over North and South Carolina. His old lady was all torn up; she was sure the trucker had killed Dick on purpose. She was so drunk at the funeral, she started insulting state troopers and almost caused a riot.

Prospects came, and went mostly. Half the forty we had "prospected weak" dropped out. We picked up Bushy after I got back from Savannah, and he proved himself. Ice and I figured maybe five more would go in a year or so. They did, but we scarcely would have believed the way it finally happened.

I got another couple of bars running, my favorite of them being the Joker Lounge, where I had girls B-drinking and stripping, pool, gambling, and some hooking going on. I tried bringing Gypsy in from time to time to watch things when I was away, and she did a pretty good job of it. When I wasn't there, of course, people stole from me. But Gypsy could always tell me who they were, and I had a way of getting what they owed me when I made the scene again.

The divorce came through at last. I paid child support for the two boys for a while after that. Then there were times when I said, "I ain't gonna pay her nothin'!" But I'd go see the kids, and I'd buy them big things. Once I bought Ron a three-hundred-dollar motorcycle. I spent a lot of money on them. But for months, I'd pay Maureen nothing.

She got mad and told me I couldn't see the kids. Well, I picked up one of the boys at school, and she put out a warrant on me. I went to court, and I paid the bill, and my crooked lawyer got it fixed so she couldn't deny me visitation. The judge told me to pay my child support, so I paid regularly from then on.

Not long after, Maureen married again. But I never would let her husband adopt the two boys—they were mine, and that was all there was to it.

Gypsy, meanwhile, grew into my equal for toughness, only on the female side. She was an excellent liar, a fierce fighter over a good mark, and a super money-maker because of it. She was a pill-head, alcoholic, explosive. But when I told her to do something, she'd do it. The only time she gave me trouble was when she was really high. She might mouth back then, but she usually got beat up for it.

Once in a while, she'd get mad or fed up and take off. Once or twice, I threw her clothes out the door. But always after a few days, I'd feel like a part of me was missing, and I'd get her back. The last time, I picked her up from her mother's in Atlanta—at gunpoint. After that, she was too scared to try it again. She belonged to me, and I was going to be the one who decided what she did with herself.

I worked her like a horse, and now and then she'd just figure "To hell with it!" and let loose. But nothing made me more angry than for her to drink on the job. When she did that, she couldn't bring in the money.

One night, I came to fetch her at a place she was working. She was back in the B-room with a guy. The bartender knew me, so I just walked behind the bar and fixed myself a drink.

She spotted me and got up from her table and came at me staggering. She began smart-mouthing me, the liquor reeking on her breath. I said, "You been drinkin'!" She curled her arms around me and said thickly, "Naw, Barry-Barry, I ain't drunk!"

I just couldn't stand it, her lying barefaced like that, and I just exploded. I reached back and slugged her. I dragged her back to a utility room and threw her inside. She begged, "Don't hit me, don't hit me!" I knocked two of her teeth back into her head. I worked her over, and she let out scream after scream. But nobody in the place interfered with me; they knew what I would do to anyone who stepped in.

I hauled her out and dropped her all bloody on the floor. I said, "Somebody take her to the doctor!" and walked out. A girl drove her to the hospital and they wired her up, and when she came back, our life went on as usual.

I messed around; she didn't mess around. If she did, she got hurt, and she knew it. I did anything I wanted to—if I wanted a couple of women, I had them. I loved Gypsy—in a way. But I loved myself and my way of life a lot more.

We lived one summer again out on Folly Beach, and one night I was driving Gypsy home from work. I was raging high, and she hadn't turned over enough money. She was whining on: "There jus' wasn't enough men, there weren't no business, etc."

I snarled, "You liar!" and started cussing her out. The fury in me rose to a peak, and I pulled out a bowie knife I had at my belt.

I flashed it in her face as I was driving along, and I screamed, "I ought to *kill* you! I'd jus' as soon cut your head off!" And I stabbed that knife again and again into the seat behind her. I was destructive: I thought nothing of going to my own apartment, and if I was mad, taking out my gun and shooting holes in the wall—I just didn't care.

The last time, I jabbed it extra hard, and I heard her breathe out sharply, "Uuhh!" I said, "Wha's eatin' you, bitch?"

She gasped, "You cut me, you cut me!"

I said, "No I didn't! But I ought to! Now shut up!"

She flashed terror in her eyes and shut up. We drove to our apartment building and got out. Gypsy walked in with her arm hanging limp, and once inside, she said, like she was really hurting, "You cut me, Barry-Barry! I'm bleedin'!"

"Let me see!" I said harshly. I took off her navy pile coat, and I could see that she *was* cut, and badly, just under the right shoulderblade.

But I didn't want to bother taking her all the way to the hospital. I was too drunk and too tired to go another step. I said, "Get on the couch." I set her coat under her to soak up the blood and said, "Jus' lay there, an' you'll be okay. I'll take you to the hospital later." And I went over to the bed and passed out.

When I got up, I took her to the hospital, and the doctors and nurses asked her what happened. Actually she had two wounds, one almost two inches deep and another small one. Gypsy told them the knife had been above her on a balcony and fallen off. She didn't rat me out.

The police were there, and I was sitting in the next room sweating! Was she going to do it to me this time? I'd really messed up, I told myself. Of course, I'd been telling her how sorry I was all the way out there—which I was, in my own way.

But she didn't turn me in. They pried her, but she kept on saying it was an accident.

The police came out then, and one cop said to me, "Listen— we *know* this wasn't no accident! You stabbed that girl!" I set my face hard, and he put his so close I could smell his bad breath: "We're gonna get you! If we ever catch you out on Folly Beach again, we're gonna put you *under* the jail!" I didn't blink an eye, and his face turned beet red. "That girl's so scared, she wouldn't say nothin'," he said, low and mean. "But we know you did it!"

I stood up and folded my arms, never saying a word, all sternness. But inside, I was saying, *Whew! She didn't tell on me!* The cops stepped across the room and waited.

Gypsy came out soon, all bandaged up. I told her I loved her, and she said she loved me.

And everything was cool—until we got drunk again. That may be hard to understand, but that's what kept us together—both being the same kind of stone crazy.

So by and large, I had few complaints with life. To my thinking, the Tribulators owned Charleston, and as a brother, I had a piece of it. The piece I wanted. I wasn't looking for a whole lot more, certainly not what soon came my way!

BOOK II

13

Durham Surprise

Thanks to three snorts of good crank, a bluegrass breakdown reeled through my head, just a little louder than the thunder of my brother Tribulators' choppers pulling up alongside.

We were, seven of us, nearly two hours out of Charleston now, on our way to Durham, North Carolina, to party with a club called the Storm Troopers. We had hit it off in the Joker Lounge some eighteen months ago and been partying with them off and on ever since.

It had been six months since we'd seen the Storm Troopers, and the night before, Ice Man got the idea to pay them a visit. We hadn't bothered to call them; we figured we were on friendly enough terms to surprise them without trouble.

Right now, Snag was riding next to me, and Hair, Black, and Bushy tailed us closely. It was a perfect day to ride. We'd picked out a route of mostly two-lane blacktops, with rolling hills and challenging curves, farmland, and not much traffic.

I spied a glint of sun flash from chrome at the bottom of the long hill ahead. There were Moose and Ice Man, speeding out of a lake of hot-air mirage! They had, as usual, left us in the dust a few miles back. Moose and Ice Man were speed demons and loudmouths, couldn't get anywhere fast enough—or resist taunting the rest of us about our "slowness"—as if jamming eighty miles an hour was slow!

I glanced over at Snag and grinned. He showed me his jagged teeth and stuck out a long tongue. We both knew what was coming up and didn't have too much use for Moose's and Ice Man's ego trips.

With his short curly hair and well-burned skin, Snag looked more like a redneck than a biker. But he had earned his patch. He was dirty-mouthed, hard-drinking, and he'd fight you in a second.

He had a sense of humor, though, and that had made for a real closeness between the two of us. We could sit down and talk and laugh and gamble together.

I got a chuckle out of Snag's cutoff: On the front, he had a patch of a mean-looking little red devil holding lightning in one hand and an ax in the other—but below that, just above a rabbit's foot, he had a patch with a little flower on it that said, "Have a nice day!" On the back, of course, was his Tribulators patch.

Moose and Ice Man had slowed down and were waiting up for us. I could see Moose's black hair waving out of his helmet and his droopy eyes darting back to time our approach. Ice Man didn't turn to look.

As we caught up, I heard Moose's high-pitched yell, thin in the wind: "Come on, man! You can't handle it? You can't ride? Them cows up there's gonna beat you-all to Durham!" His big head shook with laughter.

Moose could annoy me no end, but you could take a lot from a brother. He was a punk, and we all knew it. But when a rooty-poot had said that a couple of weeks ago to me in a bar, I had put holes through his cheek with my spiked wristband. Even if Moose and I got on each other's nerves, that tight bond was there . . .

I hauled up on Ice Man, but he kept just ahead of me. He sneered over his shoulder and hollered, "What a bunch o' candies! You call yourselves bikers? We'd be cookin' if it wasn't for you!"

I didn't speed up any; I had nothing to prove. I shot back, "Go ahead an' kill yourself if you want. I'm gonna take my time. I'm gonna do what I wanna do!"

"Yeah, you do that," Moose jeered. "We'll be partied an' back before you get there. Le's jam, Ice!"

"Hey," I shouted. "You think you gonna get there? I *know I'm* gonna get there!" I slowed up just a hair. "Go on—I'll toss a beer can on your dead wreck!"

Ice snickered and moved out, pulling Moose along with him. "Bunch o' rinky-dinks!" he yelled as he and Moose roared steadily away.

"Good riddance!" I said through my teeth. I looked around with only half-mock scorn at Bushy with his big cloud of hair. He had a tattooed arm (marked with a devil and pitchfork and "Born to Raise Hell") lifted in a one-finger salute to Moose and Ice Man. Even in fun, it stung to have your right to wear a patch put down.

I was thirty years old now, and had been riding for over eight years. And after four years with the Tribulators, it was nothing but a joke to question *my* patch.

As the twilight settled over Durham, we weaved our way through the residential streets into shabbier housing. I had figured we were in a colored section before I saw any black faces: I saw frame houses painted a motley of chipping pastels, some with heavy, old-fashioned screens, shaded here and there by a few low trees. Few cars sat on the street or in the driveways that didn't need bodywork.

Old mammies halted their porch swings, and some little woolly heads sprinkled with ribbons, others wearing baseball caps, looked up from the front lawns as we passed by.

I was eager for a good party. Gypsy could worry about the bar for the next couple of nights. Good old Gypsy! Whatever went down tonight would never get back to her. I was "gonna blow it out!" as I told Snag.

The neighborhood was thinning now, as the waning sun splashed gold over the housetops. Up ahead, Ice Man was pointing to a big white house on the left, sitting at the crest of a low hill.

It seemed to be on the edge of a cliff, as some excavation work had scraped away part of the hill to one side. Tufts of grass slumped over the gouged-out hillside, as if any idea of a development had been abandoned years ago. Across from the house, a Piggly Wiggly supermarket sprawled out. I noticed its front windows had been bricked over.

I could see a few bikers talking together on the lawn and some more sitting with cans in their hands on the front porch. There were no bikes out front; they must be parked in back, out of sight.

A red clay driveway curled up the lawn, and we pulled into it, racing our motors to announce our arrival. I didn't see a familiar face. I looked around, trying to spot a Storm Troopers patch, but everybody was facing us—except one thin-faced dude who turned to shout in the direction of the house. On his back, I saw something that took my breath away—a winged skull wearing a crash helmet, and above it, the most feared words in biking: HELL'S ANGELS M.C.!

My heart started pounding, and I felt my neck break out in sweat. *My God!* I thought. *Don't show what you feel inside!*

We had been hearing rumors that the Hell's Angels were moving down the East Coast. Though police had harassed them, these granddaddies of us all had gone underground and moved deep into organized crime. They had a huge charter in Cleveland. They owned a city block in Manhattan. They were soaking up smaller clubs on their way south. And unlike the Tribulators, whose unwritten code forbade killing (or even fighting, unless seriously provoked) a brother, the Angels were contract killers who weeded out even their own kind with murder.

We let down our kickstands, and immediately two men stood by us with drawn pistols. I fingered my .357 Magnum with my left hand while my stomach churned like the first time I'd ever been with a hard-core biker.

"Who're you?" the guy on the right snapped coldly. "Where you from?"

"We're Tribulators," Ice Man answered, "from Charleston, South Carolina."

"What're you doin' here?"

"We come to party with the Storm Troopers."

Our questioner darted his eyes from face to face. I thought to myself, *What the hell is goin' on here? Are the Hell's Angels partyin' with the Storm Troopers? Have the Hell's Angels blowed the Storm Troopers away an' taken over the house? Are they fixin' to pull our patches an' do us in, too?*

I looked over at Snag. His face was set grim, and I could see his forearm bulging rock hard at his side. I knew all of us were ready to go together if we had to. And we might have to! We knew you just didn't rush in on the Angels without notice. I tensed from head to toe, waiting for the next move.

14

Hellbound Train

The two gun-wielding Angels continued to look us over carefully. With my hands in plain sight, I ventured to get off my bike. The Angels didn't stop me, and slowly the rest of the Tribulators followed suit.

Several other Hell's Angels had gathered around us. One was swinging wooden slats twined together. I didn't know what they were, but figured they must be some kind of weapon. From the house, rock music blared loudly, mixed with the shrieks and giggles of women.

For a moment, nobody spoke. Then I said, "Hey, is Bingo here? He can vouch for us." As president of the Storm Troopers, he knew us well enough.

The slim gunman, without taking his eyes from us, said over his shoulder, "Fox, go get Bingo an' tell 'im who's here." The man called Fox walked about halfway to the house and yelled at the top of his voice, "Bingo! Hey Bingo!" I breathed easier to see Bingo's familiar face appear at a first-floor window. "Bingo," Fox hollered, "we've got some Tribulators out here!"

Bingo nodded and a few seconds later strode out the front door, down the porch steps and toward us. He was tall, solidly built, a little younger-looking than some of the men around us, with his long hair and small beard. Both his arms were dark with tat-toos: I made out death's heads, dragons, and on one biceps, a mul-ticolored Grim Reaper. He slouched slightly as he walked slowly over to us.

"These guys are okay," he said with a short wave of a hand. The two Angels with guns put them up; the one with the wood slats kept swinging them while watching us, more out of force of habit than menace. I felt a wave of relief but still not completely at ease. I knew Bingo, but the rest of these faces were unfamiliar and there-fore suspect, even without their being Hell's Angels. Except for Bingo, few guys spoke to us at first. They said a few words to each other and watched us closely, taking our measure (as we did theirs).

We all kind of asked Bingo at once, "Man, wha's happened? Wha's goin' on? Where'd all these Hell's Angels come from?"

He said, "Cool it a minute! Let me tell you. We're not Storm Troopers anymore; we're Hell's Angels now!" He went on to tell how they had partied with the Hell's Angels for the past year and been asked to become part of the Angels' organization. They hadn't broadcast it around.

It was a serious decision to make. The Storm Troopers were a powerful club on their own—they were some thirty strong and well respected. But the Angels had some things going for them that we were only later to discover . . .

We stayed out there on the lawn for some time. Bingo had some beer brought out to us, and we popped a few. Things relaxed as we talked, and gradually, we drifted onto the porch, where we got into some whiskey, coke, smoke, and whatever else was happen-ing. Music kept blasting from a host of speakers hooked up all over the house: "Hellbound Train" by Savoy Brown drummed in my ears as I started to drift into high.

We had been tired and pretty straight when we arrived. Good dope and booze were making the rounds now. I was tempted to let my guard down and just party out. But something inside told me to hold back a little.

Ice Man eased over and sat next to me. He looked straight ahead and talked with a casual air out of the side of his mouth: "Listen, le's stick close together for a while. Don't get off by your-

self. We don't know what's goin' on here. These guys might decide
to try an' pull our patches, an' we'll have to stan' as one."

I told him I had been thinking along those lines. "I can dig it,
man. We'd bes' be cool, don't cause no hassle."

Ice nodded, "Right on. Maybe we can establish a relationship."

I told him I would help spread the word to that effect. "Tha's
cool," he said. Then he moved over and sat down beside Black.

After making sure we all had the same understanding, I decided to check out what was happening in the house. I let Snag
know I was going indoors and stepped in that direction.

Two Hell's Angels met me at the door. "Before you go in
there, man—are you carrying heat?"

"Yeah, I have a pistol." I showed them the Magnum.

"You're gonna have to give that to us. We don't allow no one
to tote a gun on the premises. We'd like for you to put it up."

This is it, I thought to myself. *I'm on the spot. If I don't, some
heavy things are gonna come down. If I do, I'm helpless. This is
bein' between a rock an' a hard place!*

I decided I'd better go along with them. I said, "Okay, whatever's cool!" I handed over the Magnum, and we went inside.

"My name's Stud," said the big guy, "an' this here's Mustang."
He jerked a thumb at our pot-bellied companion.

"Pleased to make your-all acquaintance," I replied as we
turned off into a side room. "I'm Barry-Barry."

Stud said, "This here's my room, man. I'm puttin' your gun
right up here on this mantle with the rest of 'em." He placed it
carefully, letting me see exactly where. He could sense my ner-
vousness and added, "It ain't goin' noplace from here!"

I was leery about having to give up my gun. I knew that it was
us they didn't want carrying weapons. But there were enough of
them to take our guns if they wanted to, whether we liked it or not.
So I put on an act, saying, "Yeah, man; we're brothers. I ain't here
to cause no trouble. But if anythin' comes down from outside, it's
good to know where I can get my gun!"

Mustang and Stud seemed satisfied with my attitude, and they
offered me a "j." As we passed it around, Stud pointed around the
room at his assorted gear: Hell's Angels posters with the devil com-

ing down from Saturn and Jupiter; iron crosses and other medals; whips, chains, and various weapons.

Mustang asked me what was going on with the Tribulators in Charleston. I told them about some of the hassles we were having with the police. The cops were trying to keep us from wearing our patches on the street and otherwise interfering with our operations. I mentioned some hassles with blacks. We hated the blacks: To us, they were less than dirt. We'd sometimes wear "White Power!" T-shirts and Nazi slogans and swastikas. Mustang mentioned that up in Cleveland, the Hell's Angels had some kind of relationship with the American Nazi Party, to help make things tough for blacks there.

The dope and common ground we were sharing loosened us up quickly. Stud and Mustang began to share some about the Storm Troopers and the Hell's Angels. In the house right then were members of several charters from the Midwest and along the East Coast keeping an eye on the young Durham charter.

Prospecting for the Angels, said Stud, involved six months of constant close testing. You had to be up to it and into it all the way. That meant you had to be ready to go anywhere and do anything, on an instant's notice.

I told him that didn't sound any different from the way we prospected, but he said there was more. You had to be willing to accept the presence of one or more Angels representatives at all times, keeping an eye on everything your club did. You might be called upon to kill, steal, go to a run anywhere in the world, handle dangerous shipments of drugs, blow up a building, run guns, anything the club demanded.

I said that outside of killing on orders, which we'd never done, that didn't sound any different, either. He went on: "If once you don't come through, it's proof you ain't one of us. If you ever *stop* comin' through, you *out* that secon'."

As Stud licked another joint together, Mustang said, "It's better never to prospect for Angel than to try it an' fail. You fail, an' it's all over for you as far as your ever bein' a biker. You might as well go straight or kill yourself, 'cause you're dead if they ever see you on the street again."

"It's worst," said Stud, lighting up, "to get the patch an' then blow it. 'Cause it's only one way out of the Hell's Angels, an' tha's six feet under!"

As Mustang and Stud went on about the things the Hell's Angels looked for in a club they decided to bring into the organization, I wondered if the Tribulators might ever be asked to be Angels. I had no doubt that we qualified in every way, but for myself, there was one thing I wasn't sure about—the cold-blooded contract killing.

I wasn't afraid to have to kill someone—for a reason. Threatened, or in a tight spot, I could shoot to kill. I had shot for my life before, though I hadn't happened to kill anyone yet. But to kill someone just because I was ordered to do it—it didn't make sense.

I didn't say a word of this aloud. I didn't want these dudes to think I was a candy in any way. But for the first time, I felt a silent line being drawn inside of me, and I wasn't sure I ever wanted to have to cross it. There was something icy and cruel in these guys when they got to talking hard that I knew wasn't just ego.

Sometimes we Tribulators would joke with one of our prospects or a woman about blowing them away, and we'd carry it off till they got scared. But we never meant it. If a patch member left us, he was disgraced. But he wasn't a dead man. To these Angels, dead seemed to be what a failed brother deserved—it was his right and his destiny.

Talk like this was exciting—and chilling. To be a Hell's Angel— that was the top! That was the dream that had begun my whole life as a biker. But now it looked like it meant a depth of organization, ruthlessness, and secrecy that I hadn't known. Maybe it meant a lot less pleasure and a lot more heaviness than I wanted.

After a while, we got up and walked out into the hall. A chick screamed upstairs. "Jus' a pig!" Stud commented. "Le's fin' some beer!"

The first-floor bathroom had a tubful of icy water floating cans of brew. We grabbed a few and joined Snag and some other Hell's Angels who were smokin' an' cokin' in the living room. We talked, snorted, smoked, and drank until way on in the morning.

In time, everybody began running out of gas and just sat there, listening to the throb of the record player. Over and over again I heard the howl of "Hellbound Train." All through the night, some of the Angels laughed grimly when it came on and said, "Man, we on that train! We on that train now! No gettin' off!"

I was so high, I couldn't help it; I got to laughing along with them. "Listen to that, Barry-Barry! Listen to that!" chuckled Stud again and again.

And I started getting into it—the music more than the words. Somebody turned the lights off, except for a red candle that sat on a low table near the ZigZag papers and a cellophane bag full of grass. I got to grooving as always on the dim light that fell on every face as the joint's tip brightened up before floating to the next man. I felt a spinning in my head that I fought for fear that if I let myself start whirling, I'd never be able to stop.

It was light. I lifted my head from the couch cushion, sized up my headache, and lay back down. I rolled slowly to my side and determined my stomach wasn't in too bad shape. A quick hit of 101 proof would soon straighten me out.

Stud was snoring like a pregnant sow over on the couch whose cushions I had grabbed. Snag was buried in his sleeping bag near the cracked marble fireplace. Others were sprawled across the room.

Mustang was cradling the Wild Turkey I was after. I wondered, could I ease it out of his hand without waking him up? Better leave well enough alone! I remembered I had a piece of gum in my cutoff. I fumbled for it, looking at least to chase the foul taste in my mouth.

I soon had the gum juicing well, and I lay back and let my mind ramble. Through the rough breathing all around me came the ragged hiss of the stereo, digging a deeper groove at the end of a forgotten disc. A spider worked its way down the face of a big poster of Adolf Hitler on one wall.

Things had stayed peaceful all night. Even the Angels we hadn't known as Storm Troopers had treated us in a fairly equal way. A lot of them seemed to be pretty good dudes. But there was something different about them, even the former Troopers. They stayed heavy and just that far distant, even when they got high. They were proud of being Hell's Angels but didn't show a closeness or brotherhood among each other the way we did. Maybe these were just feelings I had; maybe they didn't mean anything. Maybe I was misjudging them. I didn't know, but I planned to keep my eyes wide open.

People stirred around the house before long. When Mustang opened his eyes, I got the whiskey bottle from him and took a good slug of hi-test. He shuffled to the table and rolled a fat joint, "Just to work up a appetite!" The smell of it got Snag moving. He swung an arm and woke up Stud, who joined us in the smoke. Others stretched to life, asked for the booze, and rolled their own smokes.

To my surprise, I found some aspirins in the bathroom. I took two and walked around to see who and what was up.

I hadn't made it to the second floor during the night. Fox was lying naked near the top of the stairs, his head against the wall. He glanced up at me, dazed-eyed. "Hey, Barry-Barry!"

I nodded, "Hey, Fox!" and passed him by. In a room down the hall, a pig sat in her underwear with her back to me, smoke curling around her head. A dude leaned far out the window, retching.

In the next room, a mass of squirming bare limbs was putting a daycap on last night's orgy. Moose's large head lifted out of the pile. His jowls wobbled in rhythm.

I found Ice Man and Black in the room at the end of the hall. Ice was standing fully dressed, passing a comb through his hair. Black sat shirtless on a cot, blowing a joint. I said, "Sweet dreams, Black?"

He looked at me, rolled his heavy-lidded blue eyes, and gazed at the floor. Black claimed he never dreamed when he slept. He was another dude Gypsy thought was weird. In his own place, the room he slept in was painted and decorated in solid black. Even the sheets were black. Black had a big stable of women hooking for him. They'd recently bought him a custom black van.

Ice took a last glance at himself in the mirror. I said, "Get into anythin' good las' night, Ice?"

"A little decent smoke is all," he said, arranging the medals and watchchain on his cutoff. "Couldn't use them stinkin' pigs. But hey!"—and his eyes got brighter—"thin's is super cool with the Angels! They dig us, Barry-Barry!"

"Yeah?" I said. "Tha's cool." I realized by his look that Ice didn't think I was excited enough.

"Are you awake, man? These is *Hell's Angels!*" he said.

"Yeah? An' we're *Tribulators!* They got nothin' on us. We jus' as equal as they are!"

"Hey, man!" he said, putting his hands up. "I ain't downin' our patch. I'm just sayin' give 'em some respect!"

"They show *me* some respec', I'll show *them* some respec', Ice. I don't go by no *name*, man; they got to *prove* who they are!"

"They're who they say, Barry-Barry," Ice said with scorn. "The question is, who are *we?*"

"We don't have to answer that for *nobody!*" I walked off, clenching my hands in anger. I'd never felt so much like smashing a brother's face. But I had to choke it. It wouldn't be in somebody else's clubhouse.

But I couldn't believe he'd said that. *Bein' a Tribulator don't mean nothin' to him,* I thought. *He's already thinkin' Hell's Angel, I can see it in his eyes. We party with these guys jus' one night since they switch their patches from Storm Troopers—how can jus' switchin' patches make 'em so magic to Ice?* Sure, the Hell's Angels were a heavy name. But should we start folding up our patch because they nodded their heads our way? I couldn't see it.

I thought I might feel better if I got a little food in me. I was going to ask Fox where the kitchen was, but he'd evidently peeled himself from the wall, maybe to join the heap of bodies down the hall.

But the kitchen wasn't hard to find. I opened the refrigerator door and was reaching for one of the few cans of beer that were its only contents when I felt a hand on my shoulder.

It was Stud. "How's it goin', man?"

"All right, brother. I was jus' looking for some grub!"

He laughed deep in his throat and said, "Ain't likely t' fin' none aroun' here! Le's go, an' I'll take you to get some good grits an' eggs!"

"Soun's bitchin', man!"

We hopped on our bikes and went to a greasy spoon where we polished off a sizable breakfast. Then Stud led me across town to his house, where he introduced me to a skinny, straw-haired gal he said was his wife. "Jus' hitched!" She jumped on behind him, and we rode over to a department store.

"I want t' get you somethin'," Stud said. He picked out a dark blue bandanna, and I tied it around my head. He looked me over, pleased.

We scooted around town for a while. Stud showed me some of the bars and massage parlors the Angels owned. Then we headed back toward the clubhouse. I felt just a tinge of shame for the way I'd been thinking about the Angels. Stud, at least, was just all right!

Everybody was up and around by the time we got back. Someone had gone and gotten a keg of beer, which sat available on the front porch. A few old ladies were in evidence now; last night's mamas had split. Groups of bikers sat around talking over joints and crank. A lot of the Angels' reserve seemed to have melted. They were bending over backward to be friendly. *Could jus' be I was wrong,* I thought.

I found the dude named Alley playing with his wood slats again and asked him what they were.

"These is called 'noonchuks,'" he said, without missing a flip. "I picked 'em up in Hong Kong. Some ol' Chink taught me how to use 'em. Man, they can tear your face up—but they ain't ruled concealed weapons if they fin' 'em on you!"

He put on a razzle-dazzle demonstration, then said he'd show me how to work them. I did my best but didn't manage much more than to smash up my knuckles pretty badly. We laughed about it, and I told him he'd have to give me some more lessons when my calluses got fatter.

The afternoon passed agreeably, and that night the Angels took us out barhopping in groups. They showed us a good time, and here and there we even ran into bikers from other clubs we knew. I ended up in a bar sitting across from Slim, now vice-president of the Durham charter. I had known him as a Storm Trooper; as officers, we had spent time together before.

We got to taking about the rapid growth of the Hell's Angels, and after a while Slim asked me, "Whadda you think about droppin' your patch an' bein' a Hell's Angel?"

I had a feeling an invitation would be coming and already had an answer made up. I said, "Tha's somethin' we'd have to give a lot of discussion. We won't *give* our patch to nobody. Our patch is too powerful. But I'll say this: As far as I'm concerned, the Hell's Angels is number one! An' if I ever was to let my patch go, it would be for a Hell's Angel patch an' nothin' else!"

He nodded behind his dark glasses and then said, "It's very possible that you guys could *become* Hell's Angels."

I wished I could see what his eyes were saying. As officer to officer, this was serious talk. Slim was the type of guy who meant exactly what he said, and you knew it. And he had a stillness about him that was menacing: He would cut you in a second and walk away without giving it another thought.

We left it at that, and the conversation passed on to other things. But before I slept that night, I spent some time mulling the idea over.

Now that an offer had actually been made, I had to come to grips with what to do about it. There was more to this than just picking up another club name. This was the big one—what would we have to go through to get it?

Would the Hell's Angels start choosing among the Tribulators which ones they were going to let wear the patch? There were twenty of us, almost every one important to the club and to me. We were brothers, together for a long time, some of us. If they planned to break us apart—it would be no way! We should stay Tribulators before doing that. It would have to be all or none of us—if we became Hell's Angels at all. That was going to be my position.

Around noon the next day, we headed back to Charleston. Stud and Mustang came along, saying they wanted to see our clubhouse and check out what was happening with us. It wasn't hard to figure out that their trip wasn't just for pleasure, though we told them we'd party them. They were surely on orders to give our operation a good look-see and bring back a report.

We rode in a tight group the whole way down. We didn't do much joking or horsing around. I hadn't told any of the brothers what Slim had said to me, but I could tell we all sensed it: We were now under the microscope as potential prospects of the Hell's Angels.

15

Business—As Unusual!

While Stud and Mustang were still around, the Tribulators were too busy seeing they were entertained to spend time talking about the possibility of being Hell's Angels. I gave the two free run of my place and a couple of the hookers for a night.

That was cool. But they weren't so friendly on our turf as they'd been in Durham. I had the feeling again that they were looking things over with the idea of it soon being the Angels'. As they looked around, it seemed like they were absorbing *my place* into *their thing*.

As Tribulators, we were brothers; but what was *mine* was *mine*, and we all respected that of one another. What we had, we shared out of comradeship and appreciation, never because we were made to. If we were going to become Hell's Angels, I wanted to make sure things stayed that way.

All in all, I had a good setup, and the more I thought about it, the less I could see how becoming a Hell's Angel could make it any better. Most of what I was doing was local trade. The Angels name might even hurt it by drawing more heat from the cops. Status was all I was being offered.

After Mustang and Stud left, Ice Man, Black, Hair, and I met in a bar as officers to hash the whole thing out.

Ice leaned over his beer and said, "Here it is: Stud an' Mustang like what they seen here. Stud tol' me they're bringin' a good report back to Durham. Tha's gonna probably mean they'll offer to let us prospec' for 'em. As officers, we gotta decide what our nex' move is."

We agreed to work at that, and I started off with an account of my conversation with Slim. When I finished, I said I would wait to hear what the rest had to say.

Nobody had made an offer to Hair or Black, but they had heard about it from Ice. He'd been approached by Bingo with the possibility of the Tribulators becoming Hell's Angels. Ice Man, as I expected, saw nothing but benefits: "First, they got a big organization. As part of a bigger 'family,' we'll get all their weight an' help on call if we ever need it. Second, we can only beef up our own power by addin' theirs *to* it. Right here in Charleston, we automatically get a bigger name an' more clout! The only question is, what we have to do to make it happen."

I said, "But tha's jus' it, Ice: You thinkin' too much about what they can do for us—an' not enough about what we might have to do for them! I think all you said is neat, it's good. We need more power an' things like that, but—will we have to give them our patch?

"We been wearin' these patches a long time. Ain't there some way we can keep our patch, but have theirs, too? Maybe we can wear their patch but not burn ours or turn it over to them— especially turn it over to 'em! To me, that'd be like sayin' they were better, an' I feel like we jus' as good as they are! The only difference is the name 'Hell's Angels.' If we ain't as good as they are, why they want us to come in?"

Everybody thought that was right, and along that line, Hair said, "If we have to prospec' for 'em, will we wear our patch while we're doin' it, or will we have to take our patch off? If we have to wear their prospec' patch, we'd *lose* some respec' here in Charleston!"

We agreed we didn't want to do that. If they were going to ask that, forget it. They hadn't said we *had* to join; it was an *offer* they'd made. And we decided to lay it out to them just that way. If they couldn't go along with it, we'd stay friends with them but keep our patch. If they didn't want to be friends, maybe we'd have to fight it out with them.

We ended the meeting on that note, and I stopped by the club Gypsy was working at to take her home.

In the car, I mentioned the Hell's Angels offer to her for the first time. Tired as she was, her eyes lit up. She gushed, "Barry-Barry! My man a Hell's Angel! I'm so *proud!* You always did wanna be number one—an' now you got it!"

"Ain't got it yet, babe!"

"Oh, you will, Barry-Barry, you will!"

I grinned at her and said, "Shouldn't be no thrill to you! You already been a Hell's Angel's old lady before I met you!"

She pushed my shoulder playfully and purred, "Quit funnin' me, Barry-Barry!"

She bubbled away, and I decided to keep my suspicions about the Angels taking us over to myself for a while. Nobody seemed to fear it but me. Still, I wasn't sure my judgment was wrong. Each of the other three Tribulators officers had some reasons for wanting to be Hell's Angels that I didn't share.

A lot of Black's girls were very young. He had them on the street, not in bars, like I did. The Angels could help him by supplying—and discarding—runaway teens from the Midwest. Hair was into drugs and fencing. The Hell's Angels had a coast-to-coast network for moving stolen cars, guns, and motorcycle parts.

Ice Man, of course, was the biggest drug mover in the club. As president of the charter, he would get a lion's share of new business, which the Angels could give him lots of!

The move to Hell's Angels looked good for them and for others like Moose, who wheeled and dealed in stolen goods. All of them stood to gain. The Tribulators patch seemed to be all there was to lose.

But there's a catch in it somewhere, I thought. *Greed might draw us all in—but before long, we might get dependent on them. They'll become the heart an' brains, an' we'll lose our own!*

When we got home, I palmed a downer and two aspirins. Gypsy crashed out. I was headachy-tired, but my mind was still tying knots. I popped a beer in the kitchen and pushed down the pills.

I sat on the couch and flipped on the TV—Jap horror flick. I got my stash of grass from under the chair and rolled a joint. But even a few tokes and *Godzilla vs. Rodan* didn't ease my brain.

We had one more meeting before presenting the offer to the whole club. This time Moose and Bushy and Snag sat in, because they'd been to Durham and could add their piece about how we'd been treated.

I didn't share my misgivings, but I held that we ought to make the Angels agree to prospect all the Tribulators and not just some. I said, "We shouldn't break up our family to become a part of theirs."

Ice was a little hesitant about that, but we finally okayed this idea and set a time to lay the whole thing on the rest of the brothers.

After the meeting, Snag and I went to another bar to have a few drinks. He was excited about the idea of being a Hell's Angel, but sad, like me, about no longer being a Tribulator. He was about as serious as I'd ever seen him.

"One thing about it," he said. "I hope it don't mean no change in the way we're all together as brothers. We've had good times, Barry-Barry!"

Snag and I had had our share of them together. I did a lot of my drinking with Snag now. Gypsy would always say, "Oh no!" when Snag came by. Not that she didn't like Snag—but she knew whenever he and I went off together, I more often than not came back broke: He was by far my best gambling buddy.

"Yeah," he said, "I hope it don't change nothin'."

He grinned one of his sawtooth grins, but his eyes looked sad. I decided to tell him just a little of what was on my mind. I told him I was afraid, too, that being a Hell's Angel might bring something between the brothers. "It's bitchin' to be tops if it brings you what you really want. But it's got to add, brother, not take away. I jus' ain't sure this is gonna add nothin' but trouble."

"Well, that could be, Barry-Barry, could be." Snag looked at me then with one of his real grins: "But whatever goes aroun', comes aroun', right, man?"

"I guess I'll have t' drink t' that, Snag!"

I tipped my shot up, but not with a full heart. I wished I could see it as simply as Snag and the rest did. Something was eating at me. I didn't like the feeling. But there it was, and I couldn't lose it.

Snag pointed out a poker game starting up at another table and said, "Le's get in on it!"

I said, "No, man, you go on. I jus' ain't into it tonight."

Snag cocked his head and looked at me, puzzled. "Hey, man! Wha's with you?"

"I don't know, man," I said. "I jus' got this *tension* in me. You go on, do your thing."

Snag leaned toward me and said, "It's true we might see some changes, man. But don't be makin' 'em yourself with no call!"

"You right, Snag. I jus' got t' cool my head. I'm goin' home an' crash out."

"You do that, man. Me? I'm stayin' here an' palm some aces!"

I went on home, still heavy, my stomach like lead. I sifted the whole thing through my mind again and again and again and finally realized that the feeling was bigger than all my reasons for having it. What was causing it? I couldn't add it up.

General meetings with required attendance of all patch members weren't called very often, so the clubhouse was in quite a stir the next afternoon. Everybody knew through the grapevine that we had partied with the Hell's Angels, and a lot of the guys had met Stud and Mustang during their stay in Charleston. But we'd kept the prospecting offer among the inner circle to this point, so amid the loud greetings and backslapping, there was a steady hammer of questions as to what it was all about.

We soon let everyone know. Ice announced the offer and laid out the advantages to be gained in accepting it. Great excitement and cheers started up when he took his seat, and when they died down, I stood up.

It was my job to explain the conditions we were going to give the Angels for joining them. A lot of "Right on, man!'s" and "Yeah, brother!'s" piped up as I spoke. I finished up: "Sure it's a great honor for us t' be asked to be Hell's Angels. But it's jus' as great a honor for *them* to get *us!* We ain't jus' any club—an' if they want us, they ain't gettin' us cheap! An' we gonna let 'em know that right from the start!"

I sat down to a lot of applause. Then Bushy and Snag each got up and gave their "amens," telling how cool things had been when we partied with the Angels in Durham. Ice Man finished up: "We're gonna party with 'em, feel 'em out, an' play it all whichever way it lays. But however it comes down, we all in it together—an' you can count on that!"

Laughter and congratulations flew all around then. Somebody rolled out a keg of beer, and the record player started up, blowing banjo through the house's six speakers.

Somehow, the noise was aggravating me. I stepped out the front door for a little air. The music blared from the porch speakers —mournful and slow for bluegrass, a tune about some little black news boy's troubles.

Man, it's loud! I thought. *Well, it ain't gonna bother nobody but them ghos's in the ol' graveyard!*

Hardly anybody ever visited that colored cemetery since we moved in across the road. The grass and weeds around the stones almost hid some of them; a few had leaned over, a few had cracked.

A shadow moved across the little graveyard, and a second later, a jet plane's scream drowned out the music and rattled the clubhouse windows. I looked up and watched the big jet rise off into the blue, and half wished I was on it.

16

So Long, Snag

A man can scarcely afford to lose a friend anytime. If I ever needed one, it was now. I couldn't understand what was going through me. Partying was going on all around me, night after night. Every man was strutting like a rooster. I was, too—on the outside.

But my insides were wrong. I knew what I *should* feel: pride, accomplishment, a new sense of strength. And all those *were* in me, but more like ideas written on my brain rather than in my guts. I longed to try to explain it all to someone. Snag was closest to me now. I wasn't sure he'd understand. Maybe he was right, that I was making myself miserable. But at least I knew he'd listen. And I could count on him finding a funny side to it all.

I never again got the chance. I had just come over to the clubhouse from a night's work in my bar and was sipping a beer when a hangaround we all knew came in the door out of breath and said, "Snag's been shot!"

We all jumped up and hollered at him at once: "Where, man? Who did it? How many of 'em was there?"

He said, "Hol' it! I don't know all that. I jus' heard on the street an' hightailed it out here!"

I said, "Man, what *do* you know?"

He said, "They say it happened down at the Sailors Hornpipe
—tha's all I heard!"

Now, most of us present had been drinking, some doing drugs,
and tempers flared up like straw burning. Guys were going for their
guns and yelling, "Le's go down there an' get 'em!"

I held up my hand and hollered, "Cool it, cool it, cool it!" Everybody looked around, and I said, "Le's fin' out wha's goin' on before we go runnin' off killin' a whole bunch of people!" I always did
my best to keep peace, to keep things together, in situations like
this.

So I sent a dude named Elrod down incognito, with no colors,
to find out just what, if anything, was happening and give us a call
as soon as he had the story.

I kept everybody calm while we waited until the call came.
When the phone rang, I picked it up. The brother laid it out like
this:

"He's blowed away, man! An' here's how it happened. Snag
come into this bar with a couple o' rednecks he done some bouncin'
with. Snag set at the bar for a drink, but these other two dudes
went an' started messin' with some guy's woman.

"The dude got pissed an' said somethin' to 'em. So these two
guys who was with Snag took this dude outside an' beat 'im up an'
lef' 'im an' went an' got in their car an' drove off. All this time, Snag
was settin' at the bar, min'in' his own business.

"Well, the dude that got beat up, it went through his head that
Snag was with them because they come in together. So he goes out
an' gets 'im a gun from the bartender's car.

"An' 'e comes back in an' walks over to Snag an' taps 'im on
the shoulder. Snag sees the gun an' throws up 'is hands an' says,
'Whoah, whoah, man! Be cool!' The dude never says a word to 'im,
jus' pulls the trigger an' wastes 'im, right through the heart."

I said, "Is the dude that done it on the loose?"

He said, "No, man, the cops picked 'im up."

"Damn!" I muttered.

"Wha's that?" he asked.

"Nothin'! Forget it!" I said and hung up.

I just sat there for a few seconds and didn't say anything. I
couldn't believe it. I felt like somebody'd jabbed me suddenly

with a pin: knowing it was coming, but still waiting for the pain to hit. "What happened, Barry-Barry? Is he dead?" I heard the voice like it was a long way away. "Yeah, they killed 'im. In col' blood."

I looked up and I said, "Well, he's gonna pay." And then the anger came. My hands shook and my voice choked with it: "We'll get 'im! The cops done took 'im off. Maybe he'll get out on bond, an' we'll snuff 'im!"

But all our scheming for revenge came to nothing. The killer was held without bail, and all we could do was drink away our frustration. Which we did. I must have downed gallons of vodka.

I went down to the coroner's at the hospital and identified him. No mistake, it was Snag. His mouth was open a little bit, showing that shark set of teeth. But they were set in a sneer, something Snag never did in life. Made me sick to see him that way.

We got his billfold and cutoff, everything that had been on him. We just took charge, told them we were his patch brothers and had a right to the stuff. One thing we wanted to make sure of was that there was nothing on him the newspapers could play up and nothing that would incriminate anyone in the club. We put it all back together and gave it to his mother when she came to get his body.

Snag's funeral took place in his hometown, Chester, South Carolina. About seventy-five bikers got together for it, many of them Tribulators or ex-brothers who knew and loved Snag, as well as members of other clubs we'd partied with over the years. We'd invited the Hell's Angels, but they didn't show.

Some of us rode up on our bikes, some came in cars. When we got there, the town of Chester was ready for us. State police were stationed all over. The sheriff had the routes to the funeral home and the cemetery all sawhorsed off and traffic redirected.

People stood and watched from behind the barricades and leaned out of their windows waving. Little kids cheered us on. It was like a parade. The authorities motioned us on through town, against traffic lights and stop signs. They wanted us in and out as quickly as possible.

We all paid our respects to Snag where he was laid out in the mortuary. Old friends passed by and threw rings and swastikas and medals into the coffin. By the time I got to it, Snag looked like a pi-

rate ready to be buried in a treasure chest. They'd put some color
on his cheeks and taken the sneer off his face. Good as he looked,
he might have been passed out from a hard drunk.

I thought to myself, *These undertakers is gonna make a haul
from all this junk before they shut the lid!* I had my own token I
wanted to drop in. I palmed it, a bright new silver dollar, so nobody could see it and brought it down in my hand over his chest.
He had his cutoff on, and I slipped the dollar into one of the little
pockets. I patted it and said, "So long, Snag! You ain't never gonna
be broke no more!" As I took my hand off the pocket, I caught sight
of the patch sewed on it: "Have a nice day!"

I whispered. "Thanks, Snag—you too, wherever you're goin'!" I
liked to think the morticians missed that dollar, though they probably didn't.

Out at the burial site, we were all drunk and choked up. Gypsy
was with me, and she and a lot of the other old ladies were crying.
I could easily have cried, but I knew it was voodoo to show any of
that kind of weakness. Quite a few town folks, neighbors, relatives,
former teachers, that sort, were there, along with Snag's mom.

A preacher said some words over him, just so much junk to us:
how he was basically a good-hearted guy and all that. Heaven and
hell went in one ear and out the other. We were more worried
about the square-jawed guys in hats and dark suits who walked all
around us taking pictures: FBI men, as there are near every hard-
core biker gathering of any size.

When they lowered the casket, we all passed by and threw a
handful of dirt in there. There was no shooting or anything. The
groundskeepers must have had a job picking up all the empty beer
and whiskey bottles, though.

We went our ways peacefully after that, no fights, no trouble.
With all that was on my mind, I was just sort of numb. Gypsy and I
got into our car and drove off. We didn't say anything to each other
for a long time.

I thought to myself as we rode down highway 321, *What is
happenin' all around me? Firs' Dick, then Morris, now Snag—why
do all my good brothers die on me? When is it gonna be my turn?*

I stopped myself right there. What was I doing, thinking stuff
like that? Sure, my time would come. But I didn't have to go look-

ing for a bullet! If you choose to live like a biker, accept the chance you'll die like a biker. Snag had done that.

What a way to die, though: blown away for something he didn't even do! Well, the bullet may have been aimed wrong—but it still had Snag's name on it. Whatever went around, came around.

Somehow, that's how I was going to have to look at this whole trip with the Hell's Angels. What choice did I have about it? I had no bridges behind me I could recross. I had said a long time ago it was all the way for me. So, all the way it would be.

Stop cryin' inside, I told myself. *Be a man!*

But the more I tried to be a man, the less I felt like one—and less I knew why all of a sudden I was turning soft.

17

On the Run

For the next couple of months, it was back and forth between Durham and Charleston, sometimes three or four Hell's Angels coming down to stay with us, sometimes a number of us going up there, partying, getting to know one another, feeling each other out. When the Angels were around, things got more serious, and I could tell that the few navy guys and merchant seamen we still had around were getting uneasy.

Eventually, the Angels invited us to be guests at a run that was being held at a bluegrass festival in Union Grove, North Carolina.

Ice didn't make it, but I went in charge of ten Tribulators. As we pulled up to the camp, I had never seen so many bikers assembled in one place. Representatives came from Angels charters in Omaha, Nebraska; Oakland and other California chapters; New York City, Binghampton, and Rochester, New York; Bridgeport, Connecticut; Salem, Massachusetts; Cleveland, Ohio; and, of course, Durham; probably upward of one hundred fifty Hell's Angels in all, some with old ladies, some alone.

We didn't know anyone but Durham, so we just walked around, taking in the scene. Authorities had roped off the whole Angels' camping area, trying to keep spectators from getting too close to the action and maybe getting dragged in. And action there was a lot of! It was a typical run, with a tremendous amount of drinking, drugs circulating freely, and plenty of abuse of girls.

The Hell's Angels had prospects patrolling the area, armed with long ax handles. A lot of Angels had brought fighting dogs with them, and the sound of snarling was frequent, as one Angel would let his dog loose on another one.

We all sort of stuck together, with me as leader since Ice wasn't there. Every now and then, a Hell's Angel from somewhere or other would come over and talk to us, mostly asking questions. The patch members were friendly enough, but the prospects seemed determined to give *us* a taste of the old "dog-eat-dog," too.

We were passing by a tent, and a prospect with a shaved head came out and hollered at Jace, one of our guys, "Hey, man! Come over here an' pick up this load!" Jace got ticked and said, "I ain't gonna do it!"

The two of them started shouting at each other and nearly came to blows. But Jace backed down, which was the one thing you don't do in that kind of situation. Of course, their yelling had attracted attention, and a lot of Angels saw Jace back down.

Shouts and hoots came from all around: "You Tribulators are a bunch of sissies!" The bald prospect sneered, "You candies ain't no bikers!" The jeering was pretty heavy, and we had to hustle Jace out of that part of the camp. We kept him out of sight for the rest of the weekend, and when we got back to Charleston, ordered him to either turn in his patch or get it stripped off his back. He handed it in and left town in disgrace.

After that, we were challenged a lot during the whole run. It was always prospects, I guessed on the orders of patch members—to test the prospects as well as us. I was challenged once, by the same prospect that had bugged Jace.

As the run folded up, some prospects were taking down tents. This same bald-headed guy spotted us and yelled, "Hey, you Tribulators! How about givin' us a hand with these tents?"

I just stood there, and nobody else moved either. So he came up to me and said, "Hey! You give me a friggin' hand!"

I said, "Listen! I'm no prospec'. I'm a guest here. If I'm gonna do anything, I'm gonna do it on my own. You ain't gonna tell me what to do." And I stood my ground.

He put his face near me and said, "Oh, yeah?"

And I said, "Tha's right! An' if you want t' get it on, man, we'll get it on! But you don't tell me what t' do!"

He stood there a second and then said, "Yeah, okay!" And he turned away. I stood there for a minute, with everybody watching me, until he went back to his work.

Then I got our guys together, and we walked around for a little. At last I said to the brothers, "Come on, le's give 'em a han'!" So we went over to him and I said, "Hey! We'll give you a han'—but don't tell us what t' do!" And we helped him take the tents down. This showed them something: that we were willing to be helpful, but we weren't going to be pushovers for anybody.

We knew they were checking us out pretty closely then, but we didn't know that at this run, we were officially voted on as prospects by all the charters represented. We passed muster, because we got notice soon after we got back to Charleston that we could prospect under our terms.

After the run, a couple of guys went back to Durham with Bingo and company. The rest went back to Charleston with me. A lot of Tribulators dropped out after this run. The reports of the Angels' constant testing and the scenes at the run were enough to scare them off. Several told me, "This is just too heavy. I want no part of it."

I argued, "It's nothin' to worry about! It's jus' bein' strong, standin' up, an' not lettin' 'em push you. As long as you don't show no weakness, you got it made!" I had more than a little fear in me, too! But whatever fear I had, I couldn't let anyone see it. I was an officer, and I had to stay on top. So I'd tell everyone else, "They's nothin' t' be afraid of. These guys are okay! Just stan' your groun', man! Be a man!"

All the while I was telling them this, I was busy psyching myself: *I'm probably gonna get whupped. But I'm still gonna stan' my groun'! No matter what it takes, I'm goin' through this. I'm gonna prove to 'em all I'm jus' as good as they are!* The fear I had in me was of losing my patch. I was at the place where I was ready to give my life rather than have that patch taken.

Twelve of us stayed with it, the ones who wanted more than

just riding on Harleys and hitting the bars. I still had my doubts, but my pride drove me on. I squelched that heavy feeling and just kept going forward. Being a Hell's Angel might not be just what I wanted it to be. But being on top was more important.

Not long after the Union Grove run and starting to prospect for the Angels, the atmosphere around the club began to change. Not only had a lot of members left, a sense of growing secrecy began to creep in. All of a sudden, even among us officers, a lot of things became "top secret."

It seemed like Ice Man was traveling all the time, to some run or meeting or other. I could have gone with him, but I had my nightclubs to take care of and just wasn't able to get around. Ice would come back from these trips with huge quantities of drugs. The Hell's Angels were pouring them into his lap, and he'd give the rest of us some of them—but he was making a killing, mountains of money suddenly, compared to us.

There started to be a lot of backbiting and jealousy among us. With me, it was more a matter of principle than anything else: It just wasn't fair for Ice Man to be getting everything. Pretty soon *I* was making secret deals with other Hell's Angels, and everybody else did, too! And as one brother began to find out what the other was doing, a lot of squabbling got to taking place—over who was selling what, and for how much. Discord settled in and deepened all the time.

Every once in a while, I would step back from it all and think I could see the Angels' game: They would court this guy, then that guy; throw this brother a good deal and the other one not as solid; play us off against one another; drive us into competition with one another, and break down our brotherhood.

I knew they had to be behind it. As Tribulators, we had all gotten along well for years; now, everybody was at his brother's throat. And it didn't happen gradually or subtly; it moved in right from the start and just got more intense.

Soon, there were no more good times when the Hell's Angels were around. Everything was business. As I got caught up in the scramble for drugs, I neglected my own businesses and found myself short of the kind of money I'd always been making. I felt myself going downhill. I felt myself losing my authority and power. I felt like a puppet being used. I had a title, that was all.

Ice Man seemed to be getting more and more of the power. He even came around and attacked my worthiness to wear my patch. One night I told him, "Well, all you got t' do is take it! If you can take my patch, you got it!" He just laughed and walked away.

He was getting on other guys' nerves, too, the way he strutted around, flashing his success. Hair and Moose said things to me now and then about it. Black didn't mention it, but then, he steered clear of the drugs. He had his women, and he got drugs just for them.

Moose would take his drugs and trade for hot guns and TV sets and do a lot of dealing up in Cleveland, so his complaints didn't hold much water. And Hair was just bitching for bitching's sake, too.

I did have my nightclubs and whorehouses and gambling, and I should have stuck with those as my income. But I wanted a cut of all those drugs, too; there was just too much money in it for me to pass it by. I'd see Ice with a new custom van or furnishing his house and just burn with envy. His wheeling and dealing was hopping; mine wasn't doing so well. My nightclub operations seemed to be fading out, and when I looked at it all, I knew the Angels' web was closing around me, too.

A few of us went on another run some months after our first one, this time up to the Outlaw Mountains up in Maine, only forty miles from the Canadian border. There I got into my first and only fight with a Hell's Angels patch member.

I was totally messed up and managed to trip over an electrical cord plugged into the amplifier of a band they'd hired to play just for the night. Immediately the music cut out, and this dude snapped at me, "Hey you! Plug that back up!"

I mouthed at him, "You plug it up!" and stumbled on my way.

I was wobbly and hardly saw him coming over to me. He leveled a punch and knocked me down. I got up and jumped on him, and we went to it! He tripped me up, I fell on my back, and he came down on me, with his two spiked wristbands pressed against my face. He said, "Man, I like you! I don't want you to walk away from here with no face! I know you're fucked up right now. And we can both get up and forget about it. But, if you want to keep on, well, I'll take your face off with these!"

I was bleary, but I still had some sense. I said, "Okay, le's get up!" And we got to our feet, shook hands, and that was it.

As prospects, we had to attend a lot of runs and do the dirty work: building fires, cutting wood, setting up and breaking down camp. And soon we were drawn into challenging other small visiting clubs, just as we'd been challenged on our first run.

I remember the U.S.A. run up in South Dakota, a big one, with Angels from all over the United States—and from charters in foreign countries, too. It lasted about three weeks, with a lot of high-level meetings and plans made that I knew nothing about.

I remember one night there seeing a bright shooting star cross the sky. "Hey!" somebody shouted. "There goes another one of our brothers!" Years later, I was to realize what he meant: a fallen Angel!

During the whole time we prospected, a Hell's Angel named Rattler stayed with us. We didn't know he was a spy for the Angels at first; we thought he was just on the run. We were told that he had killed a few people and needed a place to hide. So he wore one of our patches (and then a South Carolina Hell's Angels patch later) and acted like one of us—but he was checking us out all the while.

Rattler was a big horse of a guy, light-brown-haired and dirty. He could be wild, but he always had his wits about him. His five-year patch said he'd been with the Angels that long. It was rumored he was one of the Filthy Few, who're the eliminators of the Hell's Angels. These are dudes who've killed somebody on orders, with brother Angels as witnesses.

He had another patch a lot of the Hell's Angels like to wear: the red wings. That one signified certain "achievements" as a lover.

From Rattler, I learned bits and pieces of the Hell's Angels' long-range plans. He'd get drunk sometimes and launch into long rambles about all the things the Angels were going to do "when we take over." The Angels had big dreams, according to Rattler, which they were already working out.

He talked about the Angels getting past organized crime and into "legitimate" businesses and government. "Right now," he said, "there's Hell's Angels incognito everywhere. People think Hell's Angels are just low-life, ignorant dudes who don't know how to wash their asses. It ain't that way anymore. We've got college graduates in business offices wearing three-piece suits. We've got Angels in sports. Some big rock bands are Hell's Angels incognito. You'd be amazed.

"And some day, we're gonna take it all over! You laugh? It's gonna happen! Bit by bit, man, little by little, by terror and skill, we'll do it!

"It'll be great when we get charge! Anybody will do any damn thing they want. You want to spend your whole day smokin' hash, you'll do it. Hell, you can even be straight if you want.

"Only, straights will be just like old ladies; they'll bust their balls while we do our thing. Hey, they want to work? We'll give 'em work! If work is their thing, they'll do their thing—everybody'll do his thing. Citizens, bitches, and machines'll keep it all going. And we'll just stay high and give all the orders."

And he'd go on and on like that. Rattler had it all figured out. I wondered how much there was to it. I knew for a fact that there were a lot of Hell's Angels moving around incognito. But did what they were doing match up at all with the size of Rattler's pipe dreams? I don't know to this day.

18

Angel with Lead Wings

Right after the U.S.A. run, the Tribulators had another officers' meeting. Ice said that he understood from sources on the inside that we had been elected Hell's Angels up in Maine and could claim our patches any time. But I still had my doubts. I knew we had proved ourselves. But I didn't like what it had cost us.

We were down to only a handful now. And we were hardly what I considered brothers anymore. I decided then and there to say my piece. I reminded them of all the fighting that had been going on, all the discord between us. I said I thought all the enjoyment of being a biker was gone. Sure, some of us had more money. But we were losing our respect for each other. We were losing our loyalty. "I think," I said in conclusion, "that in takin' their patch, we might be makin' a mistake."

Ice Man almost went through the roof. "What're you talkin' about, man?" he shouted. "You've already committed yourself! How can you say it's a mistake?"

I said, "I feel like that they gonna infiltrate us an' take over the city, an' then do us away an' bring their own people in."

Hair kind of took my side—for a while. He said, "You know, it's jus' possible they could do that. I noticed some of what you been talkin' about. But Barry-Barry, we already a part o' them. Ain't no way we can back off now!"

Black said nothing. He'd made it clear that he was all for being a Hell's Angel. And once Black made up his mind, you never heard him say anything more about a subject.

Ice got up and stormed around the room. He pointed his finger at me and said, "Man, you can get outa here any time you want to!"

But I knew I couldn't do that. This was my life; all I had, and all I could imagine wanting was wrapped up in biking. I *had* to go ahead. I said, "No, no. I'm with it all the way."

So we agreed to take the patch. And a couple of weeks later we had a visit from Jumbo Jim, president of the Cleveland charter, who confirmed Ice's rumor: "You guys is Hell's Angels now. You got voted up in Maine. All it is now is waiting for your patches to come down!"

In a few days, they did. Only six of us gathered around a small fire to burn our Tribulators patches: Ice Man, Black, Hair, Bushy, Moose, and myself—the same group who'd first gone up to Durham and met the Angels—minus Snag, of course.

I felt as I watched my patch go up that the flames were licking at me. In flames were all the reasons why I'd wanted to be a biker: the fun, the closeness of brothers, the freedom to do my thing. On my back, I was going to put a skull. *A skull done et up a buzzard!* I thought. *Ain't that a bitch!*

I knew the gleam in everyone else's eyes was real as we hugged each other. The only light in mine was a reflection of the flames.

By the time I put on the Hell's Angels patch, I'd dropped the last of my nightclubs. I still had Gypsy working the bars, but the Angels' demands on my time were so great, I couldn't keep a place running right. More and more, I was getting Gypsy to sell drugs for me. And it was becoming clear that she was soon going to have to sell her body, too.

But once my clubs were gone, I had to rely most on hustling drugs. I took the drugs and started dealing outside of Charleston with small bike clubs throughout the state. They saw the Hell's

Angel patch and went on the same kind of ego trip we had, and I channeled them drugs—using them just as I'd been used, passing the ball on down.

As an Angel, you couldn't use your brother. You had to steer clear of his territory. I staked my claim in Beaufort, a club called Heaven's Own; in Fayetteville, North Carolina; another bike club in Columbia, South Carolina.

I realized that I, like the rest of what used to be the Tribulators, had gone down to dog-eat-dog—but I had to do it in order to survive.

I finally told Gypsy to start hooking. She was tired, burned out, and didn't put up any resistance when she heard it. But I saw hatred and contempt in her eyes for me. She took a lot of beatings during that time, because she got back at me by dogging it, no longer caring what price she'd have to pay.

She'd come home night after night without much money. I'd grab her and shake her, trying to get out of her why she wasn't turning the dough. She'd lie about the trade being scarce, the marks being cheap. Now and then when she was broken up, she begged me not to send her out there. She said she couldn't stand to have anyone touch her but me. But we had to have money. She had to go.

I heard at last through the grapevine that she was cheating me by getting a mark on the hook—and then spending hours talking him out of the trick! When I found out about that, the beatings got worse, to the point that I got disgusted with hitting her. But I had to keep on because I needed whatever I could get out of her.

She came home with just a few bucks again one night, and I got ready to lay into her. She sat down on the couch and started to cry. I said, "Get up an' take your medicine! You done earned it!" She buried her face in her hands and moaned. I said, "Get up, while you still can, or it's gonna be worse!" My hand was cocked to let her have it.

She sobbed out, "Go ahead, Barry-Barry! Get it over with! Kill me this time, it don't matter no more."

I came closer. "Don't make me do it! You know if I got to I will!"

"I say go ahead! I ain't doin' no more hookin', Barry-Barry, kill me or no!" She looked up wide-eyed through her tear-dripping fingers. "Barry-Barry, I'm pregnant!"

My hands dropped to my side. I let myself slowly down onto the couch. Her eyes had told me she was speaking truth. "It can't be! You tol' me the doctor said after Rusty . . ."

"He *done* said it, Barry-Barry! An' all these years we done nothin' t' stop it. But it's there, Barry-Barry."

I glared at her. "You *sure?*"

"I been to the doctor. It's in there. An' I'm startin' to show."

"How long?"

"Three months." She squeezed my arm with both hands. "Barry-Barry, I jus' couldn't tell you! I know how hard pressed you been! But with it in there, I ain't gonna hook no more. An' I can't dance no more!"

"Don't give me that shit—you can hook *an'* dance!"

"I ain't gonna do it, Barry-Barry! You'll have t' kill me firs'! I mean it—I ain't losin' this baby!"

I ripped my arm loose from her hands and stalked across the room. I turned and pointed my finger at her. "It ain't mine! You got to get rid of it!"

"It's yours! It's yours, Barry-Barry! I asked the doctor when it started, an' I knowed it was a time when I didn't have nobody but you for two weeks!"

"You're lyin'!"

"No!" she screamed, tears pouring out of her. "I ain't lyin'! Would I lie if I knew it wasn't yours an' you'd kill me if I didn't undo it? You *know* me, Barry-Barry! I wouldn't let it *live* for nobody but you!"

I slumped down in a chair, staring at the floor. There was nothing I could do. I couldn't prove it wasn't mine. And if it was mine, I couldn't kill it. I found myself saying, "What're we gonna do?"

Gypsy rushed over to me, kneeled down and threw her arms around my waist. "Barry-Barry, I can work harder at sellin' the drugs—I don't care if they catch me, I'll go to jail, I'll never rat on you, Barry-Barry! Please don't make me kill it, Barry-Barry, please!"

I turned my face away from her. Tears were trying to burn out

the corners of my eyes. I didn't care what she did, she would never
see me cry. I heard a hoarse whisper slide through my teeth: "All
right! Have it!"

I tore myself away from her. She was sobbing in gasps now. I
flung myself out the door, got on my bike, and rode into the wind
for miles all alone, till the brick in my throat shrank to nothing.

Word got out pretty quickly about Gypsy's pregnancy, and I
soon had a lot of people kidding me. Moose howled with laughter:
"You ain't never home, she's out hookin'—who you tryin' to put on
that tha's your kid?" That made me mad enough to fight—and I
would have, if Bushy and Black hadn't held me back. Sometimes
they'd say, "Aw, we're jus' kiddin' you, Barry-Barry!" And once a
smart-mouth prospect said, "It's *my* kid!" I beat him something
fierce for that.

Sometimes I'd get high and drunk at home and tell Gypsy,
"That probably ain't my kid, it's probably somebody's off the
street." Then she'd get upset, with anger and tears.

Other times, I'd say to myself, "So what? So what if it ain't
mine? I'd *like* to have a kid!" And that surprised me. A lot of things
I was feeling surprised me. That I was letting her have the kid.
That I wasn't beating up on her anymore. That I felt like a well of
tears was springing up in me when I saw a little hand or foot kicking out of Gypsy's belly. That I wanted to spend time with Gypsy.
Some of those things I had never felt before, even about my two
boys when they were born. My insides were breaking up, and I
couldn't do anything about it. I think Gypsy could tell, but I wasn't
about to let anyone else know.

I still sent her around the bars, this time to deal heavy. I gave
her crystal meth and coke and had her sell them at twenty-five dollars a gram. She did some waitress work as well in the nightclubs
and sold drugs to the other girls who were hustling. She actually
started bringing in a lot of money, because the hookers and B-girls
all around town knew her, and they kind of put her under their
wings and took care of her. They made sure she got big tips, till she
was bringing in fifty to sixty dollars a night in tips alone.

But with all she was making, it wasn't nearly enough to keep us going—and not nearly what she made in the old days. So I was still forced to hit the road.

But as Gypsy and I began to spend more time together, I started learning what she thought of the whole Hell's Angels thing. At first she had followed along with the pumping-up job I was doing about it. She took my word that it was great, and the right thing to do. And I kept up that rap for a long time.

But as things got rougher, I started confiding in her: "Oh, I wish I didn't have to go to that place, I wish I didn't have to do that thing!" She told me she had come close to hating me, that almost all her love had gone, especially when I had forced her to hook. She told me that she didn't trust the Hell's Angels. They weren't like other bikers, they were so grim and scheming, and crazy in a dark, morbid way. We both recalled one guy who had visited for a while, from the Midwest. He always wore a black cape, and his eyes stared out glassily, like he wasn't alive. He was a gifted artist, did most of the posters for the Angels. But they were always Grim Reapers or devils, always steeped in death and torture. He was spaced out on acid, speed, coke, PCP, often all at once—all the time. A lot of the Angels sent chills up and down her, Gypsy said. She just didn't want to be around them.

Part of her opinion was an echo of things I was telling her. But enough of it was her own to let me know I wasn't alone in my suspicions of the Angels. And the more I knew them, the less human they seemed to be.

I'd complain to Gypsy about a run I didn't want to go on, and she'd say, "Don't go to it, Barry-Barry! You don't have t' go!" I'd answer, "But I got to! I *got* to!"

But one time, I didn't. The Angels were holding a run in Virginia, where they were going to check out a club called the Rat Patrol—the same kind of ordeal they'd put us through when we were hangarounds with them. Ice told us about it and said, "Everybody goes on this one, nobody stays!"

I felt a clutch inside myself. I just didn't want to go. To me, these runs had just become a hassle. I knew I'd have to go up there and defend myself again. There'd be challenges and fights, and it just wasn't worth it to me. The thought crossed my mind for the first time that evening: *I wish to hell I could get out of this whole damn life! If this is all there is to bein' tops, to hell with it!*

It was like a loud voice speaking inside me. I almost turned to see where it came from. I hoped nobody else had heard it! I hoped it hadn't come out of my mouth!

I knew at that moment that I wasn't going to go on that run. I found myself saying, "Hey! I got some business down in Beaufort I gotta take care of. I ain't makin' this one!"

Ice Man's eyes bulged. "What'd you say?"

"I said I ain't goin' on this run!"

He paused for a minute and sat back. "Listen, man," he said quietly, "I been noticin' you actin' funny lately. You don't care no more. You ain't interested no more." He leaned forward, "I don't think you're really one of us! You're jus' hangin' here, man!"

I saw Black staring at me, his head just barely nodding. I said, "Man, I'm jus' as much a Hell's Angel as you are! But I got other things I got to do besides pleasin' everybody. I got to get some money in. You want t' go on a run, tha's fine—you got plenty o' dough, you can do things. I don't. I gotta get out an' hustle—I ain't got time t' party!"

I knew from the looks on their faces I was writing a bad ticket for myself. But inside I knew it was true: I did want out. There was no more joy in the life I was living. All I could see ahead was hustling to make a living, trying to keep out of my brothers' ways, preying on other bike clubs, fear and frustration, killing—and likely being killed!

Where was I going to end up five years from now? Only one of two places: a jail cell or a grave. It wouldn't matter how I got to either, it'd have to be one of them. The cops would get me, I'd go over the high side, get snuffed by some punk in a bar like Snag had, or the Hell's Angels would wipe me out.

What about Gypsy and the baby on the way? The kid might never see its old man. I could imagine Gypsy down at the morgue trying to recognize what was left of my shot-up body. And what if I lived? Gypsy holding up the baby on the other side of a piece of glass in prison? Gypsy trying to pay for the kid's food go-go dancing and hooking? The kid trying to look up to an old man who wasn't even proud of himself anymore?

What was I doing to myself? I was thinking about the future! A crazy man! Wanting out? There was no way out—except six feet under. I could do only one thing: set my one foot in front of the other in the direction I was already heading and meet whatever shiv or bullet or cell door was waiting for me.

19

Moses

The kitchen window was open as usual, and I could smell coffee brewing inside. I peeked over the sill and saw Mom, her hair up in a kerchief, wiping off the kitchen table. I stood on my tiptoes and cleared my throat loudly.

Mom looked up quickly and saw me. She smiled and threw her hands over her head and cried, "Here comes Moses!"

"Aw, go on, Mother!"

"Well, get your head out of my window an' come on in!"

As I stepped through the kitchen door, she said, "Ah, there's my prophet!"

I said, "Mother, cut out that 'prophet' stuff an' give me a hug!"

I reached out for her, but she held me at arm's length. "Yup. You look more like ol' Moses all the time! Your beard's gettin' grayer every time I see you."

"Well, I sure ain't no prophet," I said, pulling her into my arms. She pushed me to arm's length again and looked up into my eyes. "Oh, yes, you are," she said. "Son, you don't know it, but you *are* just like Moses. You're not a Hell's Angel."

"Get off this preachin', Mother, you know I'm a Hell's Angel. You seen this tattoo!" I rolled up my T-shirt sleeve to show her the helmeted winged skull again. My cutoff I'd folded up and put under my cycle seat—just before combing the bugs out of my beard. For some reason, I never wore the patch in Mom's house anymore.

"No, son," she said. "You're not a Hell's Angel—you're not an angel from hell! You're a child of God, an' I've claimed you for the kingdom of God!"

"Mother, you know I don't wanna hear that stuff. Could I please have a cup o' that coffee—an' could we change the subjec'?"

She smiled and said, "Sure, son!" She went over to the stove for the coffee pot. "But you're not a Hell's Angel!"

I didn't want to argue the point anymore. It was her craziness and not mine. It didn't matter. I kept finding myself over here in spite of it of late. In all the torment I was going through, Mother's was the one place I could relax for an hour or two. At first I brought friends along, and we played pool in the carport, or Mom would make us breakfast. She never turned us away. I got tired of making excuses over her saying a blessing before the meal, and after a while, I didn't bring the brothers anymore. And anyway, I just wanted to be there by myself.

Mom set two cups on the table and poured the coffee. Before she sat down, she said, "You had somethin' to eat?"

"Yeah, I had some cereal for breakfast, Mother. But you know me!" I said.

"All right, all right! I got some leftover roast beef. Will that do you?"

"You bet! An' you know how I like it."

She fixed up the sandwich, and I asked her how Tara and Tanya were and what Frank was up to. Things were pretty much usual, she said. "Oh, yes! Frank got a big new contract for a boat!"

"Tha's neat, Mother. I'd like to see one of his boats sometime."

"Oh, you most likely have, without knowin' it, out on the harbor. How's Fran doin', Barry?" (Mother never would call her "Gypsy.")

It'd been a while since Mom and Gypsy had got together. After Maureen divorced me, I took Gypsy to meet Mom. Mother was always kind to her, never put her down. Funny, since Mom made that change in her life, she never put anyone down, and except for calling me Moses, she never preached at me. She told me all the time how much she loved me and "how much Jesus loves you." Jesus or no, I could feel her love, and I appreciated it.

One morning I came over, and she fell into my arms, weeping, and said, "Barry, I love you so much—an' if you only knew how much God loves you!"

I asked her what was the matter, and she told me that the neighbors had been complaining about her having the Hell's Angels in her house. She had almost forbidden me to come anymore, but she just couldn't do it.

So I'd kept on bringing the brothers over, and Gypsy too, now and then, and she'd always shown them that loving concern.

Mother held her cup to her lips, waiting for me to answer.

At last, I did: "Well, Mother—Gypsy's pregnant!"

She set the cup down and leaned over and hugged my neck. "Oh, Barry, that's wonderful! But I thought . . ."

"So did we, Mother, but it happened."

"Ooh, she must be so *excited!* Barry, why didn't you bring her over?"

"Well, to be honest, Mother, her an' me not bein' married an' all . . ."

"Barry, I thought you *knew* your momma! When's the baby due?"

"I think she said March, yeah, it was March, Mother."

She counted on her fingers. "My, my, that's barely five months away! Has she got a doctor?"

"Yeah, she's got one. Mother, it's no big thing, excep' that it shouldn'of happened."

"Oh, Barry, what d'you know? I want t' call her up, Barry! Why didn't you at least call me up and tell me?"

"I didn't find out about it but a few weeks ago myself, 'cause she was scared to admit it."

Mom sat back and smiled. "Well, well! I get to be a grandma again!"

I said, "Bet you never thought you'd get another one from my end!"

"What're you gonna name it?"

"Well, we ain't decided for sure. If it's a boy, it'll be Barry, junior. If it's a girl, Gypsy wants to call her Bari-Ann. I'm tryin' to talk her out of it, but it ain't doin' no good."

"You men will never understand," she sighed. Then she turned serious. "Barry, you shouldn't bring that child into the world without a name."

I fidgeted a bit and then said, "Mother, what are you suggestin' I do about it?"

"You oughta marry Fran, of course!"

I shook my head. "I don't know, Mom, tha's pretty heavy! You know it didn't work out so good las' time!"

"Well, what you do is up to you. But that's the *right* thing to do!" She put her cup of coffee to her lips and grimaced. "Ugh! We been talkin' so much the coffee's done got cold. Can I dump yours out an' refill it?"

I got up with her and said, "No, Mother, I'm gonna be gettin' along. I'll take this san'wich with me, all right? I got t' do some thinkin' about what you said."

Mother held my arm on the way to the door. "You know, son, I can tell by the way your eyes look that you got a lot on your min'. Somethin' big's troublin' you, am I right?"

I said, "You're right, Mother. A lot o' things is happenin'. You know I can't tell you about it. But it's heavy."

"I can feel that it is, son. But I want you to know that, no matter what, I love you—an' God loves you. There's lots of people prayin' for you, Barry. God's got his hand on your life."

"Well, Mother," I smiled, "tha's all right. I can use any help I can get."

"Barry!" she said as I turned from the stairs. I looked up at her. "You promise me you'll tell Fran to call me, y'hear? A woman needs a momma when she's got a baby on the way. Promise?"

"I promise, Mother!"

"You take care now, son! I love you!"

"I love you, too, Mother!" I shouted as I waved a last time and rounded the carport.

As soon as I got on my bike and rode away, I felt the weight of my situation come down again, full force. And now I had an added thing to think about: whether or not to marry Gypsy.

I hashed this out in my head. I loved Gypsy in my way. And

she had my respect. Lately especially she was a good companion. I wanted the kid. And by the joy she was taking in carrying the baby, I knew she still had some love for me. I just didn't want the piece of paper to get in the way of my freedom—I had precious little of that left the way it was!

But I figured there was no reason why it should, provided she agreed that nothing was going to change. So why not? That's how I reasoned things out—if it felt all right, do it.

Gypsy was home when I got back, taking a nap. I turned on the TV and waited for her to wake up. I was doing a lot of hanging around home in those days, just using Gypsy's being pregnant as an excuse for not traveling around for the Hell's Angels. I realized the rest of the charter disapproved of what I was doing. I was losing the respect I once had. It used to be that when I told somebody to do something, they jumped. Nobody followed my orders anymore. And I didn't bother following up to make sure they did. As far as I was concerned, everyone could mind his own business, and I'd take care of mine.

I paid my ten percent of what I made to the club regularly. They sent their portion of that on to New York. It was as much backscratching as I cared to do anymore.

Gypsy yawned and turned over on the bed. She opened her eyes and saw me. "Hey, Barry-Barry," she said, yawning again. "I didn't know you was here."

"I wasn't until a little while ago. You know it's four o'clock? You got to be gettin' your tail to work."

She sat on the edge of the bed, collecting herself.

"Guess what!" I said.

"Tell me," she said.

"You an' I are gettin' married."

She opened her eyes wide and said, "What'd I hear you say? I mus' be dreamin'!"

"I said we're gettin' married. I want t' give the kid a name an' all that . . ."

I didn't get any further. She jumped up and raced over and into my lap. "Whooooah!" I said. "You're gonna jumble that kid all up!"

"Barry-Barry, you sure I ain't dreamin'?"

"Well, *you* may be dreamin', but *I'm* wide awake!"

She started kissing my face all over. I said, "Wait a minute! This ain't gonna mean you got a ball an' chain on me. This ain't gonna change nothin'! I'm still gonna have my freedom."

She held my face at arm's length and said, "Well, you can jus' take your ol' freedom—I'll take the marriage license!"

I did my best to try to make clear to her that this didn't mean that I was suddenly going to be "property of Gypsy." I even had her write out a suicide note and told her she had to carry it with her everywhere. That way, if she ever got in my way and I eliminated her, she'd have that note on her when they found her body. I don't think I ever could have done it. This was another con, like a lot of what I told her, but I did my best to make it persuasive.

But in spite of all my tough talk, I knew that deep inside, she thought she had me. Even knowing that, I went through with it. Again, nobody was more surprised about it than I was.

Mom was, of course, delighted. I asked her if her minister would do the wedding. When she answered that he'd do it if we both "accepted the Lord," I told her to forget it. But she said she did want to come—and to make the wedding cake, and I thought that was cool.

I found a lawyer in the phone book who said he'd be willing to perform a wedding ceremony on a stage in a bar. So late afternoon on the date we'd picked, but two days before Christmas, I biked over to the bar, the Joker Lounge, which I used to run, and Gypsy and I drove over to the lawyer's office. The nameplate read "James B. Jasper."

Now, I had a sport jacket and a shirt on and Gypsy was dressed nicely. The lawyer was just a straight young guy in a tweed suit, and he had no way of knowing what he was in for! He just looked us over, signed the marriage certificate, and followed us in his car to the Joker Lounge.

He parked behind me, got out, and started walking across the street, away from the long row of motorcycles at the curb. "Hey, Jasper!" I hollered, pointing to the Joker Lounge, "This is the place!"

His mouth dropped open, but on he came. He got to my side, swallowed hard and said weakly, "What's going on here?"

I said, "You're here to do a weddin', man! Le's do it!"

Jasper was in some state of shock as we walked past the bikes, but I could see him tremble as he caught sight of what was inside the door: thirty or more bikers, all high as kites, wall to wall, raising hell! All the Charleston charter was there, of course, and Stud, Fox, Mustang, and a couple of others from Durham, some of Heaven's Own from Beaufort, and a few Jokers Wild.

The jukebox was booming, but the screaming and roaring when we came in completely overwhelmed it. I could tell Jasper was ready to turn and run. I grabbed his arm and half dragged him toward the stage.

I was a little disturbed because I didn't see my mom. She was supposed to bring the cake in her hatchback, with Moose helping her load it up. Well, he wasn't there either, so I knew they must be on the way.

Jasper coughed as we ran the gauntlet of hugs and cheers to the stage. The place was stifling with beer and pot smoke. Jasper tripped on the stairs a bit on the way up, but he was holding his own pretty well considering the state he was in.

The girls had decorated the place nicely, I thought. They had put up streamers and wedding bells, which looked kind of nice around the Christmas wreaths. Somebody had spray-painted "Good Luck Barry-Barry and Gypsy" next to a big nude poster.

We stood there, the jukebox still going, and Jasper took out a fluttering booklet and held it up to the light. As he opened his mouth, Rattler yelled, "You're just makin' it legal, that's all!" Looking past him to the front of the bar, I saw Moose by the door, motioning to a couple of brothers for help.

"This here's a shotgun weddin' for sure!" hollered Stud. I saw my mother come in, her now silver hair standing out from the dark walls.

"Hey, Barry-Barry!" yelled a Heaven's Own. "You sure puttin' on the leg chain now!"

I smiled to Mom, and a few guys looked back to see who was there. Moose elbowed through the door just then with a four-tiered cake, white, with brightly colored icing and words all over it that I couldn't read from where I was.

Mom's presence quieted things down a bit. Most of the cursing stopped. The jukebox was still going full blast, and I yelled, "Hey! Shut that thing off!" Mom had them set the cake on the end of the bar, and she sat down on a stool beside it.

A guy pulled the plug on the jukebox. I said, "Tha's the way! Man, I wouldn't be able to hear this guy! Y'all know this don't happen every day—'specially for me!"

The whole place was laughing, and I snapped to Jasper, "Go 'head!" He jumped a little and whimpered, "Okay!" As he was starting to read in a thin, shaky voice, bikers began to blurt out things like, "You better do it right, man!" and "No mistakes at this weddin'!" That poor lawyer would stop, trembling, and I turned and called back, "Hey! Cool it! Leave the guy alone to do what he's gotta do!" Then I said again, "Go on!"

And that way, with me egging him on, he managed to get through it. He finally pronounced us man and wife, and everybody started yelling, "Whoo-oo-ooh!" I kissed Gypsy and handed Jasper two tens and a five, and off he took. I'm not sure his feet touched the floor between the stage and the door, he went so fast!

The brothers were yelling, "Way to go!" and "Nice work, man!" at him, but I'm sure he didn't care what they thought. He probably went and had a few stiff ones at another bar.

I noticed as he went out that Mom was gone. I guessed she had left right after the vows were said. Gypsy and I came offstage and got smothered with hugs and kisses. But I wished Mom had stuck around for a little.

Gypsy wanted to go back and see the cake, the makings of which Mom had kept a deep, dark secret. It was a mind-blower for sure, especially for a Hell's Angel wedding. It was done lavishly in red, green, and blue, and the words on it read "Love," "Peace," "Patience," "Joy," "Meekness," "Goodness," and the like, with doves and hearts all around. I didn't know what it all meant, but it sure was pretty! She had a lot of courage, that little lady, just coming there.

Gypsy started to cut the cake and give it out. Somebody plugged the jukebox back in, and the party was on! It was all on

me, but for the snacks some of the guys and their old ladies had
brought along. Everybody just hung around and got messed up.

Hours later, I couldn't even get on my motorcycle. But somebody loaded it up and drove us back to the clubhouse. We had a
big cookout and all kinds of drugs came out, and I can't remember
beyond halfway through the night.

But Gypsy and I were hooked, and I had to admit to myself
that it was satisfying in a weird sort of way, seeing her being just
like a regular bride, putting the piece of wedding cake with the little bride and groom into the freezer, looking proudly at the wedding band I'd got her—with her big belly and all! I really looked
forward to seeing the baby inside her. I felt a love for it already; it
represented something real at least, growing in the middle of a life
that was running away from me. I was losing control of everything
I knew, but I was glad there was something in the world I still
wanted to live for.

20

The Dynamite Knot

I continued to make Gypsy's pregnancy an excuse to avoid doing some of the Hell's Angels' business. Fear was growing in me as rumors kept coming down of people getting killed, in and out of the organization. There was talk of training me to be an eliminator, and that jarred me most of all—it was the one thing I didn't want to be asked to do.

I felt tied up in knots, strapped in. Freedom had been the longing of my life. My road to it had led me into slavery. The few good times left had a harsh edge, as I felt myself slipping away into powerlessness.

Then Ice Man got busted. He got into a gun battle, shot some guy and got one of his own fingers shot off. The fight was over drugs, and no one was killed, but Ice had been up the river too many times before. He had to jump bail and split for Durham to hide out.

So I suddenly became president. A few years before, I would have blown up with pride over the honor. Now I couldn't have wanted anything less. I didn't have any authority, I didn't want any. As far as I was concerned, the whole club could slide.

I didn't tell that to anyone. But a lot of pressure began to come down on me. Everybody'd come to me and say, "What're we gonna

do?" about this thing or that. And I said, "I don't know! Do what
you wanna do—tha's the way it's always been! Do your own thing."

Other charters began to call up: "What're you guys doin' down
there? Come on up an' see us!" They came down, but I didn't go
up. I said, "You wanna come here? Fine! But I ain't comin' there!
I got things to do!" I wanted no more of where I was at—and yet I
was there! I didn't know how to get out.

In March, Bari-Ann came. When I first saw her, I came close
to crying. She was so beautiful to me, so perfect in her tiny way,
with her brown cloud of hair and thrusting arms and legs. Everything in me wanted to raise that child, to see her grow up. I felt her
soft little hand around my finger. It was like I'd never seen a baby
before. What had I missed? She was newness, she was life, and all I
had looked like death around me.

I'd look at her and sometimes feel like a knife was twisting in
my heart, because I knew I'd never see her go off to school and be a
pretty teenager and see her married. She'd probably never even
know her dad—and what would her mother be able to tell her
about me? "He was a gambler, a drunk, he liked to hit people, he
beat women, he did drugs, he ran bars." What a bunch of memories
to leave behind!

I did what I could to kill these feelings, to try to make myself
forget the despair. I drank and drank, a quart of vodka every night.
Every time I hit a bar, I'd be blind drunk. I fought and yelled. I
snorted crank and coke, was out of my head a lot of the time.

I did do some business with the Cleveland charter, paying
them for titles to cars and motorcycles. And I found that they'd
cheat you if they could. If they could get a guy to pay two hundred
dollars for a title, that was what he paid. Another guy might be getting the same kind of title for twenty-five dollars or thirty dollars.
Greed was everything, and in self-defense, you'd turn around and
do the same to the next guy.

They had to keep absorbing smaller clubs, because sooner or
later, they'd "burn out" a territory. Take Charleston: You've got six
men there dealing drugs, and every one of them's got something
going, people working for him. Well, if somebody gets too prosper-
ous, the police move in and bust him, and all his money goes to get-

ting his "help" out of jail, paying lawyers, court fees, and the dealer himself to keep his mouth shut. When this starts to happen all over an area, users won't take any more action, and you can't do business there anymore. So the area is "burned out," and you have to move elsewhere. Until that place is burned out.

Some Angel business came down that I couldn't dodge. A feud developed with a powerful club called the Pagans, involving the Jokers Wild, who were now prospecting for Hell's Angels. The Jokers were at a concert, and two of them got jumped and whipped badly with ax handles. So a lot of pressure came down on the North and South Carolina charters of the Hell's Angels to get revenge on the Pagans.

The Angels sent people down from Cleveland to train us in demolition and poisons, for this war against the Pagans—and others. I was trained first to make silencers for automatic weapons. They brought down plastic explosives as well, with firing pins and caps.

I learned to take mousetraps, or devices like them, and attach firing pins and plastic explosives to them. Then this apparatus would be placed under something like a gas can in a garage. And when that thing was picked up— Blam! That was all she wrote.

There were electrical devices also, which could be hooked up to a firing cap and the explosives and set off at will to blow up buildings. For a while, my backyard was full of plastics, buried in a big trunk.

We had a feud going with the Outlaws, too, down in Atlanta. Since I knew that town, I was sent on a mission to blow up the Outlaws' clubhouse.

I spent a week down there scouting the job, all expenses paid by the Hell's Angels, luxury accommodations. I found out where the Outlaws' clubhouse was, when they had their meetings, did a lot of detective work, and got to know pretty well what they were up to.

Then it was back to Charleston to collect my "works" and back to Atlanta again, where I took a motel room for the weekend. Sunday was my target day for blowing the place up.

It was a rainy night, but I knew that wouldn't affect the explosives as they did their work. I drove over in my car, fully expecting the place to be empty so I could do my job.

I drove down the street the clubhouse was on—and the place was crawling with police cars and fire trucks. The clubhouse I had come to blow up was a shambles of hissing flame and rubble. And here I was, coming down the street with a trunkful of explosives!

Boy, if they stop me an' ask me to get out of the car, an' they check that thing, I'm done for, I thought. *Tha's five years automatically, jus' for havin' it!*

Plus, I had a sawed-off shotgun for close range, and that was five years, too! Federal.

Right then, I didn't care a hoot what had happened to the Outlaws. Good riddance! But how was I going to get out of this jam?

There wasn't room to turn around. I just headed straight for a roadblock up ahead. When I reached it, I stopped and asked a cop there in his rainslick what was happening.

"Oh, it's just a little fire," he said, his eyes fixed on the blaze.

I thought fast. What was I going to tell him? Something came to mind. "I got off the main road some way or other—can you tell me how to get back on I-85?"

He kept looking at the fire. Then he stopped and turned to me as if he finally realized that I really did want to know. He said, "I'm sorry! What was that you were asking?"

I said, "How do I get back t' I-85?"

"Sure," he said. "Just turn around, rather, back on down the way you came in, and turn left."

"Thank you," I said, "thanks a lot!"

I tried to back out of there slowly enough so as not to attract attention, but I made fast tracks in the wet street once I was out of sight.

I made my way back to the motel and called Rattler in Charleston.

"Man, you won't believe this," I said, "but when I got to the place, it was burned down!"

Rattler said, "You better call Cleveland and let them know."

I got hold of Cleveland president Jumbo Jim, and told him this news.

He said, "Before you leave, fin' out what happened. Send us a newspaper clipping or somethin' to show it."

So the next morning, I picked up a paper and spotted the item: The Outlaws' landlord had evicted them from the premises, with police help. He found the place in such bad shape, with bullet holes all over the floors and walls, that he decided it wasn't worth it to fix it up. He got the fire department down there, and they lit it up and supervised the blaze. I had happened along near the tail end of things.

I went back to Charleston and showed them the article and then mailed it on to Cleveland. I took the works and buried them back in the trunk in my yard. I was relieved not to have gotten caught, but at the same time, I was still worried that I hadn't been able to prove myself with that job to the Hell's Angels. I didn't know what they were going to ask me to do next. All there was to do was hang in there and wait.

Around that time, Bushy got into a bike wreck and was laid up in the hospital. I went down to see him a lot, and now and then, I'd take him out in a wheelchair to the bars to get drunk.

One day, he was feeling pretty good, so I took him out to the clubhouse, and we sat on the front porch, drinking. Nobody else was there; they were all out of town. Only Bushy and I weren't traveling.

This afternoon, I was feeling lousy, and I started to spill my mind about how we were getting used and were becoming helpless ourselves. He seemed to agree with me. He said he'd been ripped off by brothers in other charters. But I didn't feel like we were really communicating. His attitude seemed to be, so what? The heck with it. It was all part of the game.

It occurred to me later that I might have made a mistake in telling him how I felt. Who was to say he wouldn't relay it to someone else? It was too late now, though—it was out, and I just had to hope he'd keep quiet. At least I had never talked to him about wanting to get out.

I began to have more and more trouble covering up the anguish I felt, so I drank and drank and drank. I never drank at home. But the minute I got out of the house, I opened a bottle. Sometimes I lost consciousness of where I was. Sometimes I was away from home for two or three days. And I felt bad about that because I wanted to be close to the baby—and yet, all the time I was thinking, *Wha's the use? What difference does it make? There's no hope anyway.*

Sometimes I'd pick up a girl to try to ease my mind. Sometimes I'd go for long rides on my bike. But after a while, I didn't even want to ride my motorcycle anymore. A couple of people took shots at me as I rode by. I felt like I couldn't even ride on the street without someone maybe coming up alongside me and drilling a bullet in me.

I went aimlessly from bar to bar, or to see Bushy, or over to the clubhouse. Nobody ever came to my house anymore.

I took on a prospect, thinking maybe watching over him might snap me out of how I felt. Bally was a big guy, pretty mean. I had him running around, doing things for me.

But what relief I was getting didn't last long. Bally and I and another guy were in a bar drinking. I got up and left, but right after that, somebody pulled a gun. Bally tried to take it from him and got shot in the stomach.

Then I rode up to Fayetteville, North Carolina, taking Bushy, who was now on crutches, to meet with some members of a club called the Third Reich.

Bushy and I went to a bar to talk with four Third Reichers. But it was too loud in there, so we all hit the street for another bar about fifty paces away, a quiet little place, where we figured we could do business in peace. One Third Reicher had gone out first, and suddenly we saw him under a street light, swinging a chain at a citizen armed with a lead pipe.

In a few seconds, they were going at it hot and heavy. All of a sudden, it seemed like both bars emptied. As a lot of people just stood around and watched, the Third Reich began to attack this bunch of citizens.

Bushy and I stood there, near the little bar. I had started to draw out a 9-mm automatic I had on me when somebody behind me clobbered me over the head with what felt like a bottle.

I whipped around. About five or six people were standing there, and I just reached out with the pistol butt and cold-cocked the nearest one to me. He hit the sidewalk, and the rest of them started coming at me. I stood there and said, "Come on, let's get it on!"

To my right, I saw a guy wielding a big old board. Bushy said, "Come on over here, Barry-Barry! Get your back against this wall! We'll do it!"

Bushy had on a cast and his two crutches. But he also had a 9-mm! The first thing that came to my mind was just to fire away. I cocked my pistol back and got ready to blow some bodies. "Hol' it!" Bushy shouted. "Don't kill 'em!"

As soon as they saw those guns leveled, the citizens started backing away. I said, "I'll tell you what, I'll start blowin' some of you away before you get here!"

All of a sudden, Donny, who was with the Third Reich, came running to my side and grunted, "Man, check me out quick—somebody stabbed me!"

We sidled to the door of the little bar and slipped in. I said, "Bushy, you watch that door, an' if anyone puts his head in, start shootin'!"

Bushy leaned against the bar with a bead on the door, and Donny laid himself across a table. "It's in my back!" he gasped. So I turned him over. I picked up his cutoff and T-shirt, but I didn't see anything, no blood or cut, no rip in his shirt, nothing.

I said, "There's nothin' wrong with you, Donny!"

He said, "Man, there's somethin'! Somebody stuck me with somethin'—look good!" I looked again and found a little pinhole—somebody'd stuck him with an icepick!

Sirens wailed outside. I told one of the people standing slack-jawed in the bar to call an ambulance. Bushy and I took our guns and stashed them behind the bar with the bartender. I said to him, "Listen: We'll be askin' for these guns later. If you say anythin' when the cops get here, we'll burn this place down, an' you in it!"

I told Donny, "Jus' hang in there!" Then Bushy and I sat ourselves at the bar. The ambulance people came in, the police came in and started asking us questions. I said, "I don't know nothin'. I jus' heard a lot of noise outside, but it weren't none o' my business. Me an' my buddy here jus' passin' through, settin' here drinkin'."

"Yeah," the bartender nodded, "they weren't doin' nothin'." All around, they were locking people into cuffs. But the bartender kept his mouth shut, and we got off. We stepped outside after a while, and the ambulances were still cleaning up: A bald-headed GI (Fayetteville was an army town) lay there with his side split open. Beer bottles were all over the place, half of them smashed. Only then did I start thinking about how close a brush I'd had with injury or death.

I hardly had my brains settled from that run-in when another one happened. I was drinking in a Reynolds Avenue bar in Charleston, trying unsuccessfully to put a make on some girl. After about an hour, I gave up and decided to take my trade elsewhere.

I stepped out into the street, and about that time, a car pulled around the corner and stopped across from me. Out of it poked the head of a guy I'd bounced from one of my bars a long time ago for wearing a phony tattoo of the Hell's Angels insignia. He wasn't a Hell's Angel, and I knew it and gave him a crack on the head with my pistol as he hit the street. I warned him not to show his face around again or I'd do him in.

But here he was! He shouted, "Hey! Barry-Barry!"

I was anxious to take off, and I said, "Whatta you want?"

He said, "Come over here, I wanna talk t' you!"

I started to walk over cautiously. I reached into my cutoff for my 9-mm—and suddenly realized that I'd left it at home! I had no choice, I had to bluff him. I kept my hand in there as though I had the gun at my fingertips.

He suddenly said, "You sonuvabitch, I'll show you!" and laid this gun up on his windowsill.

Just then, a big car sped around the bend, and I bolted for it, stopping it in its tracks and ducking down behind it. I looked into the window—and who should be driving it but Bushy!

He opened his door on my side, and I said, "Bushy, you got your gun?" He said, "Yeah." I said, "Give it to me, man!" He handed it over. It was a Browning 14-shot repeater!

I stood and aimed it over the top of Bushy's Caddy. I said to the phony Hell's Angel, "Okay, man! I don't want no trouble! The bes' thing you can do is put that gun away and get on down the road! If you're not, then go ahead an' start poppin' them caps, 'cause I got me one, too!"

He started shooting, "Pow-pow-pow-pow!" I ducked down in front of the hood of Bushy's car. I peeked up over the hood and aimed that automatic right for the other car's door. I knew he was laying there; I'd seen the top of his head just as he fired. I emptied six shots in pattern into that door.

I thought, *Wow, that shoulda got 'im!* But just to be safe, I yelled out, "You got any more bullets, Bushy?" I knew I had those eight additional shots in there.

He poked his head up once more, and I started shooting in earnest. I shot all over that car, putting his right side tires out in the flurry. He got his crippled car started and wobbled down the road.

I knew the police were on their way. I said to Bushy, "Man, I got to get all the evidence!" I picked up all the shells and gave the gun to Bushy. I said, "You head on back to the clubhouse, an' I'll meet you over there!"

By this time, there were a few people rubbernecking out of nearby bars. I spied the manager of the place I'd been in and said, "Hey! You didn't see nothin'!"

He knew me well and answered, "Yeah, Barry-Barry! I didn't see nothin'!"

I left then, still wondering why the guy I'd shot at wasn't dead. When I got to the clubhouse, I found out. Bushy's gun, he told me, was loaded with dum-dums, which are designed to spread out on impact—they must have just busted into pieces when they hit the side of the dude's car, although they had penetrated enough to put out his tires.

The guy I'd shot at was picked up down the road. The cops went back to the scene to investigate, but naturally, "nobody knew nothin'."

We had fun rehashing this around the club, but I kept thinking to myself, *What is goin' on with me? All of a sudden it seems like death is gettin' closer—is this a signal my time is gettin' short?* I wondered about it a lot, while I did my best to keep what was left of my head in one piece.

21

Winged by Light

Gypsy and my mom got together often before and after little Bari-Ann was born. Gypsy didn't tell me much about their conversations, but I could tell she was starting to have a real love for Mom. When she didn't visit Mother, she'd call—every day—and talk, from what snatches I could pick up, about anything and everything.

I had to turn some business down in Beaufort and was gone for several days. I got back home on a midafternoon and found Gypsy rocking Bari-Ann and crying softly.

I said, "Wha's upsettin' you, babe?"

She said, "It ain't really nothin' bad, Barry-Barry. It was jus' somethin' your mom had me listen to."

"Well, hell, woman, it serves you right! You know better than to let her go to work on you! Han' me over that little one—I ain't seen her in seems like ever so long."

Gypsy held out the light, cooing bundle I loved. My hands grasped her tiny body, and I held her out in front of me and did my best to coax a smile from her.

"Barry-Barry, lemme tell you about this record," Gypsy said.

"What record was that?"

"The one your mom played for me! Don't you never listen t' me?"

"Sure, babe, I hear every word! Blub-a-lub-a-lub-a-lub!" I worked my tongue at Bari-Ann, who finally gave a little laugh.

Finally, in exasperation, Gypsy said, "Oh, you don't never wanna hear nothin' I have t' say!"

I said, "Hey! I'm all ears! Shoot! Make with it! I might disappear any secon'!"

"Well," she huffed, "I'm gonna tell it, an' I don't care if you hear it or not. But it was jus' yesterday . . ."

"This thing at Mother's?" I interrupted.

"Yeah—now Barry-Barry, ain't you gonna let me tell you this?"

"Sure, babe, I was jus' showin' you I was listenin'!"

"Well, all *right!*" She kind of preened herself for a second or two before launching into her story. Then she got to it. "All along, your mom has been tellin' me about this record she's been wantin' me to listen to. She said, 'I jus' want you to hear this—it's about people who do drugs an' everythin'.' So finally yesterday, I said I'd hear it.

"Well, she put the record on an' took Bari-Ann from me an' went outa the room. I started listenin' as she was pitty-pattin' in her kitchen.

"It was a singin' record, but there was more. The choir singin' was all drug addic's, an' they were singin' this song 'To God be the Glory.'"

My ears kind of perked up. "Drug addic's, you say?"

"Tha's right, Barry-Barry."

"Well, what the hell were drug addic's doin' singin' hymns?"

Gypsy flustered a little and then said, "No, silly, they use t' *be* drug addic's! They wasn't drug addic's now!"

"Well, why didn't you say that?"

"You didn't give me enough time! Now jus' lemme get it all out, an' I guarantee you you'll unnerstan' everythin'."

"Okay," I chuckled.

She went on, "Some of these people *use t' be* addic's an' thieves an' hookers, guys an' gals. An' they'd sing a verse of the song, an' then one of 'em would tell their story of how they got off drugs . . ."

"While the others was still singin'?"

"No, Barry-Barry! They'd stop singin', an' one of 'em would talk!"

"Oh!"

"Well, they all said it was Jesus that got 'em off of drugs an' outa crime an' everythin'. An' Barry-Barry, while I was listenin', somethin' come on me, an' I started cryin' an' I could not *quit*. An' afterward, Mom come in, an' she hugged me, an' she tol' me that she loved me an' Jesus loved me, an' that was it. But, Barry-Barry, I could not quit cryin'!"

I said, "You look like you're workin' yourself up to a good fit right now!"

"Well, I jus' can't help it. It was so beautiful," she sniffed. "I bet even you woulda got choked up."

That riled me. "It'll be a long day before you see *me* blubberin'! Tha's why I don't let her lay none of 'er trips on me."

"It weren't no trip, Barry-Barry! These folks tellin' their stories was *real*. You could tell they *been* through what they were talkin' about."

"Well, jus' the same," I said, "it don't do you no good. You oughta lay offa that stuff."

But I was having a hard time laying off of it myself: at least the love and peace I found over at Mother's. She'd ask me sometimes, "Son, are you plannin' to be a biker all your life? Don't you ever think about gettin' out?"

I told her, "No, I'm jus' gonna keep on the way I'm doin'." But in reality, I thought a lot about getting out—and the more I thought about it, the more I knew there was no way.

I remembered Ice Man saying to me before he split, "You gettin' too ol' for this, man! You ever think about gettin' out?" He gave me that sneering grin of his. "You're an ol' man!"

Of course, right away, I wanted to fight! I said, "Hey! Whatch'you mean ol' man? Ain't nobody puttin' *me* out!"

It was crazy, but I struggled to stay in. I mean, even if I could get away scot-free, what in the world would I do with the rest of my life? So I fought—for what I didn't want!

It stuck in my mind, my mom always saying, "You're no angel

from hell, son." I remembered a thing that happened right after I got my Hell's Angel patch.

A dude came down from New York who was the main drug connection for the whole East Coast. They called him the Cobra. I never saw anyone do more drugs himself than this guy—and yet he never seemed to lose control.

One night at a party over at the clubhouse, I was sitting with him, smoking some grass. And he said, "Barry-Barry, there's two kinds of Hell's Angels: There's a Hell's *Angel*—an' then there's a *Hell's* Angel. There's a difference!"

At first I thought he was questioning my right to wear the patch. But he didn't follow up on it, and I left the room. But what *did* he mean by that? I thought about it now and then.

One day when times were rough, I went over to my mother's and began to open up some. I didn't tell her much but that I was confused and miserable. "I jus' don't know wha's goin' on in my life anymore."

She said, "Son, you know you got to give up this kin' of life. Fran tells me how you've beat her an' been drunk all the time. You know that ain't right. Why don't you give your life to the Lord an' start servin' Him?"

"No, no, Mother," I said, "don't talk about it no more; you know I can't do that!"

"Well, look," she said, "I got a ticket for a dinner. It's gonna be lots of people I know there, an' I'd like you to go."

"Is it more of your Christians, Mother?"

"Yes, but, son, this isn't like church."

"Oh no? You're tryin' to tell me these people would accep' me the way I am?"

She said, "Yes, they would."

I'd have to see that to believe it, I thought. And the whole idea began to appeal to me as a challenge. Maybe I should go, and show everybody there up once and for all, and then Mom would shut up about this Jesus business.

So I said, "Okay, I'll go!" She started to get excited, but I held up one finger and added, "On one condition: That I can wear what I wanta wear, that I can jus' be me. Then I'll go!"

Half to my surprise, she said, "Okay, here's your ticket!"

I took it; it read for the following Saturday, 7 P.M., at the Francis Marion Motel, in downtown Charleston.

I got up and said, "All right, Mother. I'll be there."

"Okay, son, any way you wanta look!"

The parting twinkle in her eye made me want all the more to show up at that thing looking as outrageous as possible. As I waited for the elevator in the motel lobby, I gave myself a final checkout in the mirror: I had on my patch, spiked wristbands, high boots, the whole nine yards, topped off by my hat. My hair and beard showered all down the front and back, and I could see a lot of worried stares passing behind me.

The elevator door opened. A couple who had been waiting when I got there strolled off to the side, and I got on alone. *Man,* I thought, *I'm gonna really blow these people away!* My mind was made up to make a scene and show them all that they were a bunch of phonies.

I got off the elevator. All kinds of middle-class-looking people were milling around. I had purposely come late and missed the dinner, but it smelled like roast beef in the room. Tables had been nicely set with colored napkins. It looked like a class affair. All the better for what I was going to do!

My mom was there, talking to a few people. I put on my toughest walk to the place where she'd be able to see me. So far, nobody seemed to be paying me much attention. I was going to change all that in a hurry.

Mom spied me. "Oh, there's Barry!" She rushed over and hugged me. "Son, I'm so glad you came!"

I said roughly, "Wha's goin' on, Mother?"

She said, "Come on over here, son, there's all kinds of people I want you to meet."

I let her lead me over to some folks, all straight-looking. "Bill, Betty, this is my son, Barry!"

"Pleased to meet you," said Bill.

I turned his hand over in a biker shake and boomed, "Wha's shakin', man?"

He looked startled for a second, but threw back a reply that startled *me:* "Everything's shaking. The Bible says everything that *can* be shaken *will* be shaken!"

"Amen, brother!" said a voice right behind me. I turned my head to see a fiftyish guy in a light blue suit. Before I could move, he threw an arm around me and said, "God bless you, young man. Glad to have you here!"

My whole body just stiffened up. I said to myself, *Who is this guy? I can love my brothers, but this ol' man with his arms around me?* I felt chills running all through me.

He never did introduce himself, but he said, "Come on in, and sit down. You're sure welcome to be with us!" He indicated a part of the large room where folding chairs had been set up with a podium facing them. "Let's go in, Barry," said Mother. "You can meet the rest of the folks later!"

My mother and I went in along with everybody else and sat down. I was really uneasy, thrown off guard by the friendliness of the mood around me. A lot of people were greeting each other, men hugging men, women kissing each other; I didn't know what to make of all that. In my gaping around, I forgot about the scene I was going to make. They were making enough of one by themselves!

The older guy who had hugged me stepped to the podium and after saying a little prayer, began leading the people in some songs. I was glad for that—I was feeling so uneasy, it was a relief not to have to meet anybody else just then.

I glanced around me, and here and there, people were staring at me. Well, I glared right back, with my worst scowl on. I muttered, "Wow, what a bunch of yoyos!"

All of a sudden, in the middle of a song, the people stood up— and I stood up, too. I felt like a dummy in all these goings-on: The song proper ended, but the people kept on singing, in a rising and falling chant they were making up themselves. Their voices blended in a music that sounded something like what came in your head on a motorcycle at top speed, but weaving together high and low notes—if a rainbow could sing, that's what it would sound like.

I looked around and people had their hands lifted into the air. They sang out, "We praise you, oh Lord," "Lord I love you," "You're so wonderful, Jesus!" all at once. I saw tears streaming down from people's tight-shut eyes, and I said to myself, *Man, I ain't never saw nothin' like this before!* Whatever was going on, it was real to these people.

Suddenly, a wave of feeling struck me, a mixture of terror and grief and loneliness. I felt tears dammed up at the roots of my eyes and as if sobs were trying to gush out of me. I held back with a great effort. I didn't want anybody to see me cry. Not tough Barry-Barry!

I got up and walked quickly out into the lobby and lit a cigarette. It seemed almost as if I'd been driven away. I was twenty million miles away from all that was going on in there, yet it was cutting right through my hardness, even deeper than Bari-Ann's being born had.

I went over by the big window looking out over the city. What was happening to me? Everything was falling apart around me. I couldn't even keep up my front with this bunch of citizens! What was going on with these people anyway?

A voice that sounded like preaching came from the room I'd left. I just stayed where I was and smoked cigarette after cigarette, trying to pound down the flood of emotion this night had stirred up.

As I was standing there by the window, another gray-haired man came to me and said, "Friend, I want you to know that Jesus loves you, and I love you too!"

What could I say? I wanted to fight back, to smash his head through the window. I wanted to at least say, "Oh, man, leave me alone!" But I just stood there.

My mother came back to me, and he walked away. I said, "Mother, le's go!"

She said, "All right, Barry."

I went over and pushed the elevator button. I could see a few people looking at us. I said, "Those people seem like they're serious."

"Yes," she said with tears in her eyes, "that they are, son."

"An' they seem like good people, Mother. But I ain't ready for nothin' like that, Mother. I can't give up what I got."

"Well, the Lord's got all kinds of time, Barry!"

The elevator came, and I was glad to be gone from there, and to hell with my blown scene.

Later I told Bushy and Hair about that night—but a much different version of what happened. I told them my mother was trying to get me to go to church. They all laughed and I laughed. I said, "I can see me goin' to some church—the place'd fall down!"

I told them about this meeting I'd been to, wearing all my colors and gear. I bragged about how I'd shown them all up, put on a scene and scared everybody half to death.

In truth, it was I who'd been scared and I who'd been shown something. I knew those people were leveling. I knew that they really cared—in the same way my mother did.

One day, after this, I was sitting home with Bari-Ann, or Bam, as we nicknamed her. I called her my "little Angel," and I'd carry her around the house, showing her all the pictures of death's heads and winged snakes. I just got a bang out of being a daddy to her.

I had just put her away for a nap when I heard a knock on the door. The voices outside told me it was Mother and my sister Tanya, dropping in to visit the baby.

As I did every time Mom came over, I quickly scooped up all the joints and rolling papers and lumps of hashish and pushed them under the easy chair. Then I went to the door and asked them in.

"Where's li'l Bam?" Tanya asked.

"Oh, you missed her," I said. "She's done sacked out already—an' don't you dare go in there an' wake 'er up!"

"Aw, come on, Barry!" Tanya tugged at my hand.

But I said, "No way! She needs her res'—an' I need mine!"

"Well!" huffed Mother. "I can tell where we ain't wanted!"

"Mother, you know it ain't like that! I jus' had a hard night las' night, an' I was fixin' t' take a nap myself."

"Well, I guess if you can't stan' the sight of us— Come on, Tanya," Mother said, smiling. She turned as if to go.

"Wait, Mother," said Tanya. "The book!"

"Well, it's in your hand, girl," Mom said. "Give it to your brother!"

Tanya handed me a good-sized paperback. Its title: *666—The Mark of the Beast.*

I looked it over and said, "Wha's this about?"

"I'm not gonna tell you," Tanya said. "That would spoil it! But it's a real good book an' I'd like for you t' read it."

I said, "Yeah, okay." I just set it down on the floor near my easy chair. And they said so long and left.

And that book sat there for a few days, unopened. Gypsy noticed it and asked what it was. I said, "I dunno, babe, jus' some book my sister lef'."

She said, "Oh." And that was that.

But one night, I was sitting at home, smoking some pot and watching TV. I couldn't find anything good on, so I picked up the book and started reading. Soon I was fascinated—and amused!

It talked about modern society, in fact, the world of the not-too-distant future, with fabulous inventions and a one-world government over all the nations.

I got about that far and then went out to do some of my "business." I came back and read some more. And during a week's time, off and on, I was able to get through it.

In it, I read about an evil world ruler known as the anti-Christ, smooth and suave, who pretended to be good. He had a sidekick who was a minister, who was lumping all the world's religions into one church. In the book, Christians were coming under persecution by this big church and finally all just disappeared into the clouds one day. A lot of verses from the Bible, especially the book of Revelation, were placed into the story and as captions to the pictures.

After the Christians split to the clouds, the reporter who was telling the story began to see what was really going on and got into a pack of trouble. It seemed this world ruler gave a command that everybody had to have the number 666 on their forehead or their right hand—or they couldn't buy or sell anything. And soon, everybody in the world was being forced to bow down to this ruler, who was known as the Beast, or be killed.

The story had an exciting ending, where Jesus came back and mopped up all the evil forces, and the reporter hero and some of his friends' lives were saved. And as I put the book down, I thought, as I had several times while reading it, that there was something in it that seemed familiar to me.

I was in the middle of a coke deal later that night when it suddenly occurred to me: "Six six six!" I said aloud.

The dude who was buying said, "What's that?"

I mumbled, "Nothin' man, jus' some number I was rememberin'."

Six six six! That was it! The Cobra Man, the main dope man from New York City—he wore a patch with that number on his cutoff! All of a sudden I was scared. I'd said all through the book, "Naw, naw, this can't be real! This is stupid!" trying to keep that fear at bay. Now it was on me—I knew somebody who used that number and might even know what it meant!

Well, I said to myself, *I'm sure even if he does know what it means, it's just a joke to him!* But then some other things began to pop into my mind, like when an important get-together of Hell's Angels was going to take place, you'd hear guys saying, "We gonna *have church* next week." That was probably all fun, too, just trying to mock straight society.

There couldn't be anything at all to it, I kept telling myself. But another side of myself kept whispering to me. *How can you be so sure?*

22

Funeral in San Diego

About a week after I'd finished *666*, Black told me at the clubhouse that Cleveland had called saying they wanted somebody from our charter to be representative at a funeral being held in San Diego, California, for a brother Angel who'd been shot in the back.

I said, "So?"

And he said, "Man, you got to go to Nebraska in just a few days for that presidents' meeting—you could go to the funeral an' then catch a ride from there out to Omaha."

I said, "That makes sense."

He said, "The club could pay your way to fly out there, an' you could probably get a lif' back from Omaha."

"That soun's likely 'nough," I said. So we made reservations for me, one way, to fly to San Diego.

For a Southern California morning, it was cloudy as I stepped off the plane carrying my small suitcase. A prospect, who said his name was Mick, met me, and we rode on his bike to a patch member's house on the outskirts of San Diego.

This seemed to be one of several gathering points for the many Hell's Angels who were attending the funeral. Angels from all over were mixing in and around the house, drinking, smoking, snorting crank, coke, mescaline, getting revved up for the event to come. Bikes were all over the area, and Angels were wandering up and down the alleys, cursing and breaking beer bottles.

A lot of them, I found out, had partied there the night before and hadn't even slept that off. I quickly got in on the drug action, speeding up pretty well. But for some reason, I didn't want to do any drinking. I guess it was mainly fear: I didn't know a lot of these people, most of whom were from California, and I felt like it'd be best for me to keep my head together.

The bikers here weren't friendly. I felt they were looking at me with contempt: After all, they were old-timers, California Angels, and—South Carolina? What was that? All of a sudden, I felt the way I had the first time I came up that driveway in Durham: a big test, starting all over again for the first time.

A few guys talked to me. "Whadda you got in South Carolina?" "What's goin' on in the South?" "Got any Southern belles down there?" "Sen' me a rebel flag when you get back!"

I tried my best to please everybody, to stay on the good side. I didn't feel like any hassles with guys who were messed up, so I just grinned and agreed and kept on the up-and-up.

But inside, I felt lonely and frightened. I said to myself, *There's got to be somebody from Cleveland or New York or someplace I know.*

And after a while, a few began to show up. I found Red from Connecticut, who had a big bag of crank. We went around behind a tree and snorted up. Some other guys saw us and got in on it, but that's how it was: Nobody was offering anything to anyone. You couldn't turn down a brother if he asked you, but I noticed that everyone was sneaking and hiding what he had.

Little groups formed here and there, and except for the brother or two I knew, I felt shunned by these "brothers." I walked around, looking for at least a friendly face, but I couldn't find any. After a while, I just felt all by myself, an onlooker, but not really a part of what was happening.

I asked myself, *Why is everyone doin' this to me? Wha's goin' on? Why don't these people accep' me?* But the more I flashed my clean (maybe *too* clean) South Carolina patch, the more it seemed people turned their backs on me.

There was about enough time for me to go down the alley to a Jack's and get a hamburger and then everyone started piling into cars or on bikes and making along the interstate toward the city and the funeral home. I rode in a car with a San Diego patch member whose name I never did get, and his old lady, and another patch member. The prospect who had picked me up at the airport followed close behind us.

A police escort joined us before long, and as we rode along the interstate, we were joined by other streams of bikers and police, filling in a long line ahead of and behind us. By the time we got to the funeral home, there must have been well over two hundred and fifty bikes and a fourth that many cars, with motorcycle police in "shades," four cycles each at the head and tail, interspersed all along the line, all roaring along the stuccoed city streets. In spite of my fear and sense of apartness, I felt some pride at this display of power in motion.

Bikers were soon careening all around the grounds of the funeral home, the cops keeping a guarded distance from the scene. I made my way to the steps in front of the place and surveyed the goings-on.

To me, it seemed like a stampede of wild animals spread out in front of me, like a herd of gorillas gone berserk. Guys were roaring and grabbing one another by the hair and shaking and pushing each other, while the old ladies stayed still, off to themselves.

Right out in the open, joints were lit up, beers popped, bottles and cans were flying around. I remember saying to myself, *There's no respec' here—no respec' for nothin'!*

The grounds began to empty after a while, as bikers started to file into the funeral home. The line was being let in a side door, and I joined it, wondering more and more why I was there. What was I going to see? I didn't even know this guy. He didn't mean anything to me.

But I went through the door and into what looked like a little chapel. The line turned left into a smaller, closed-in chapel, and up ahead, I saw the open casket. People I guessed were the guy's mother and father were sitting on a bench in front of the casket, along with a few other relatives. All of them were in dark clothes, and crying. A lot of flowers surrounded the scene. As we approached, I could read the names of the various charters from around the country.

The room was filled with noise. Bikers were hooting and yelling, and I heard somebody holler scornfully, "That stupid sonuvabitch never should of got shot in the back!" Somebody else said, "Yeah, man, what a dumbshit!" Here were all this guy's relatives, and his patch brothers were cutting him down!

I started thinking, *What happened to this guy? Who shot 'im?* I knew that if somebody had gotten shot in our charter in South Carolina, I would *know* who did it—we would find out. Here, I had asked around, and nobody would tell me anything.

One guy said, "He got shot. Somebody shot him in the back three times. He was in his van, and somebody was in the back and shot him." That was one version. Another guy told me the police did it and left him on the side of the road. Someone else told me the guy had tried to get out—and you just didn't *get* out.

I kept on thinking, *Why doesn't somebody know for sure who killed 'im?* Then I thought, *Maybe nobody'll admit it because his own people did kill 'im! There's no real brotherhood here—it's jus' a bunch of selfish, glory-seekin', ambitious animals that are after their own thing, an' it don't matter who gets hurt!* I felt a terror, almost like a vibration running up my backbone, that dizzied my head. I had to hold onto myself to keep from breaking into a run.

I looked up. Hell's Angels were pouring beer over the body as they passed by, and stuffing things in the casket. As I got to the coffin, I saw the body, its makeup dripping garishly in streaks, beer foam all over its clothes. Where the color had splashed off, the skin was pale and waxy-looking. Any illusion that he wasn't dead was blown all to hell.

Joints were stuffed between his lips and jammed in his fingers. All of a sudden, I started to taste my hamburger again and turned away, swallowing hard.

I walked out again to the steps and looked at the savage scene below. The same kind of cursing and screaming was going on, the shoving and can-throwing, but something else struck me now: the ugliness of the faces, the twisted sneers of pride and gnarled-up lust, the hard-bent grins curving under busted noses and eyes filled with hatred, the missing teeth, the chewed-up ears, the fresh and hardened scars, all spitting curses, flecked with foam, and inhuman noises, like monsters set loose from jails under the earth.

And I was an animal, too! I had done just as much as they had, and I was just as much a wild beast as they were. My past began to go through my mind. I wondered, *Where in the world have I come from?* I saw myself again as a little kid, five years old, sitting in Sunday School, singing, "Je-esus loves me, this I kno-o-w, for the Bi-i-ble tells me so-o-o . . ." My childhood rolled by me, my army days, the Ford plant years, then all the drugs, all the nightclubs, all the rushing around—and where had I come to? Just standing here looking out on a bunch of *beasts,* and me nothing but a part of them! And what was ahead? Being slaughtered like an animal, just like that guy back there in the pine box, and having droves of animals growling and yapping around me, too!

I froze into the steps as a huge, grizzled shape trudged up toward me. He stopped two steps down and leaned his face in, eye to eye. He opened his mouth, and his sour belch said, "We're *glad* to see ya *here*—South Carolina!" His tone was hard and filled with sarcasm. His eyes didn't look bloodshot, they seemed solid red to me. He said, "I just want you t' know—we *love* ya!"

His arms reached out suddenly, and he pulled my body into his and nuzzled his head into my cheek. I made a half-hearted attempt to return his hug. When he drew his head back, the dark hair over his brow had shifted, and in the center of his forehead was a clear blue tattoo: the number 666.

In that instant scenes from the book I had just read flashed in my mind's eye: the Last Days, the Rapture, the anti-Christ, the Mark of the Beast! My whole body felt like one shrill cry. I clamped my mouth shut so as not to let it out. But I shuddered with thoughts of horror: What *was* this whole biker thing really all about? Had the Rapture happened already and left me in the middle of this hell swirling around me?

The Angel took his hands off me. I mumbled, "Yeah, man, yeah." His lips sputtered a few times and he lumbered off, showing me his California rocker.

My head was spinning. I began to wander around, trying to find more evidence of that number 666. And all over those funeral parlor grounds, I saw it: 666 embroidered on cutoffs; 666 tattooed on foreheads. Each one I spied sent a fresh wave of fright through me.

I wanted away from there. I wanted to get away from *them*, but I was stuck. I thought to myself, *How do I walk away from them? A guy's layin' in a box back there tha's been blowed away for tryin' t' get out—an' I ain't about t' tell no one I'm thinkin' about it!*

The gathering began to break up before long. Some Hell's Angels went on with the funeral procession to the cemetery; most just went their separate ways. I found the people I'd come with and rode back to the clubhouse.

Almost immediately upon our arrival there, I ran into Shades, a charter president from Rochester, New York. He said, "Man, you're just in time. You gotta be heading for Nebraska, right? You can ride up north with me and get a lift easier from around Frisco." I said, "That soun's all right." He said, "We're leaving right now, so come on!"

I grabbed my suitcase, and went out and, along with a California Angel, got into an odd-looking foreign compact and made for the freeway.

Shades and I sat in front. I kept getting strange sensations about the guy in the rear seat, seeing myself getting shot in the back of the head by this silent dude.

As we were riding along, Shades took a gun out of his cutoff and handed it to me. "This gun's hot," he said. "I want you to hold it for me."

I said, "All right," but I kept wondering, *Why did he give me this gun? My fingerprints is on it now!* I looked it over: a .32 revolver. Shades said, "Put it someplace where you can get to it quick and throw it out, maybe." So I used the corner of my cutoff to wipe the prints off it and set it in a little hollow under the dash.

All the way up to Los Angeles, Shades kept asking me what was going on in Charleston. I filled him in to what I knew. He also ran on about the guy who'd been buried in San Diego. He said, "The word is out some Pagans did him in. We found a couple of 'em hanging out near where he was killed."

The Pagans were a growing Carolinas club; I knew of a charter down in Jacksonville, S.C. I heard Shades say, "Something's gotta be done about these guys." He looked over to me. "You guys in South Carolina got to take care of it."

I said, "Okay, we'll handle it."

He glared over at me again. "You're gonna take care of it all right. No more playing around. We're gonna have some action from you!"

To me, this sounded like, "You better do it or else!" I was being threatened.

He said, "You're the leader down there—can't you get your guys to do nothing?"

I said, "Yeah, at times I can, sometimes I can't. They got a will of their own."

"Oh yeah? Maybe we oughta get somebody down there who can handle it."

All of a sudden it was clear to me that I was being put on the line. I said, "Yeah, I could probably use a li'l help down there. It'd be good for you t' come down an' check on the way things're goin'."

He said, "I'll have to make a note of that and get on it."

We started talking about drugs, and I told him I was having a rough time making any money in our area. He said, "Oh, yeah? I'm getting three, four ounces of coke—I'll front you an ounce to take with you. Won't even cut it once—you can do that. But you gotta take the whole four to Omaha."

He even suggested I might fly it out there, instead of riding with him. That sounded good to me until I thought about the possibility of getting caught in an airline inspection with four ounces of cocaine and the ten or fifteen years in jail *that* could mean.

This alternating threat and friendliness swing made me more uneasy. Fear was mounting up in me. I tried to keep up a hard front, but I heard a lot of excuses coming out of my mouth: "Times are rough, the cops are heavy down on us, we can't do nothin' here, can't do nothin' there—" Actually, I wasn't doing what they wanted me to do—and I knew that they knew it. The hammer was coming down.

Shades kept dropping hints about how something needed to get stirred up down in my area. He knew I was in charge. In a roundabout way, he was saying the finger was on me.

In silent moments, my mind reeled with thoughts of 666 and

anti-Christ and the last days. A conviction was forming in me that I was on the wrong side of things. Frightening as the idea was, I had to think about taking a chance if I got one—and trying to get away!

It was early evening, still light, when we wound through Los Angeles. Shades pulled into the driveway of what he said was the clubhouse of a local charter and went in. I stayed in the car, as Shades said he'd only be ten or fifteen minutes. The other Angel had leaned his seat back and seemed to be sleeping, with his head in the luggage area.

For a second I thought, maybe now was the time. But how did I know that guy was really sleeping? Maybe they were trying to make me run for it, putting me in this situation just to see how I'd react. I decided I'd better stay put.

Shades came out and we headed north again toward San Francisco. It was a long ride, not marked much by conversation. We stopped a few times for coffee and food, but never for long. Shades seemed anxious to push ahead. I kept hyper-alert for his every move—and the quiet dude in back.

Somewhere in the middle of the night, we pulled into San Mateo. We stopped at the home of an Angel named Jackal. Shades said, "This is where you're gonna be staying."

As he took me inside, I saw a garage next to the house with a sign on it saying JIVIN' JACK'S MOTOR CYCLE SHOP.

Jackal was a young guy, blond, lived there with his old lady. The house had all the usual pictures and things to be found in a Hell's Angel's place. Shades said he had to split to shack up with some chick, and he'd get back to me later.

Jackal seemed all right, didn't say much. His old lady offered me a sandwich and Jackal rolled us a joint. There was some booze around, but I was still leery of doing any drinking.

We finished the joint and the phone rang in the kitchen. Jackal went in and got it, and I heard him say a few "Yeahs" and "Got its" and hang up.

He came back in and said, "Think you'd like to know—Slim's in town from North Carolina, Rattler's in town from South Carolina. They say they're pissed off at you, want to see you. Say you've been running your mouth too much about something."

I said, keeping up my front, "Sure man, tha's fine. I'll talk to 'em, whenever they want."

A call came a few minutes later. "For you," Jackal said. I picked it up.

A voice said, "Are you Barry-Barry?"

I said, "Yeah, who's this?"

"It don't matter who I am. I jus' wanted to tell ya that Slim an' Rattler's here in a motel room."

I said, "I heard that—where 'bouts is it?"

"That don't mean nothin' to you, man. Don't you worry about it. You jus' hang loose. They wanna see you."

I said, "Okay, they know where I'm at."

The phone clicked to a dial tone. *What're they doin' t' me?* I thought. *Are they settin' me up for the kill—or jus' testin' me to see if I scare?* One thing I couldn't let them do was see the fear in me. I had to keep battling to be the man they were looking to see. It was beginning to look more and more like my life depended on it.

Inside, I was screaming. My brain was shouting, "Keep calm! Keep cool, man!" When Jackal wasn't looking, I snuck deep breaths and shifted my body around, struggling to stay relaxed. I went to the bathroom and whispered to my reflection in the mirror, "Hold on! Keep it together! Firs' chance you get, go!" Looking at myself, I could see the terror in my own eyes. I worked at narrowing them so that it didn't show and fixing my expression so there wouldn't be any emotion in it.

Jackal and I didn't sleep that night. We did some crank, and he asked me some things about Charleston, and I gave him the line of bull I'd been throwing everybody else.

When it got light, his old lady Sue offered to make us some breakfast. I had no appetite at all, but I bolted down some scrambled eggs just to keep up the front that I was feeling fine. I asked Jackal about his cycle shop, but he didn't have much to say. I spent the day leafing through old *Playboys* and cycle magazines, doing my best to keep from jumping up the walls.

Late afternoon, Shades came by and said he wanted me to meet some more brothers. He took me on a forty-five-minute drive to a clubhouse out of San Mateo, in a hilly section that might have been the outskirts of San Francisco.

It was getting dark when we got there. Two patch members were in the place, one a California man Shades introduced to me as Wolf, the other a guy all the way from Australia who said his name was Wilson. A prospect lurked around who was never identified. All three patch members, it turned out, were presidents of their charters, as I was.

We sat around, talking about nothing in particular for a while, and then Wolf told the prospect to go out and get some beer and stuff for sandwiches. I volunteered to go along with him. I was churning with fear inside; having to sit still and play it cool was making it worse. I jumped at the chance just to move. Besides, I thought, this just might be the chance for me to make the break.

It wasn't. The prospect seemed to be under orders to keep a close watch on me. Even on the way out to the car, he kept slightly behind me, ready to react to any move I made.

I tried to get him into conversation on the way to the store, to no avail. To my distress, the trip didn't seem to be any more relief than sitting back in the clubhouse. That Wolf made me especially uncomfortable. He was a scrawny runt of a guy with a sharp voice. He had huge eyes that burned out from under matted, filthy hair. He seemed like a steel bar of solid meanness.

All too soon we had picked up some beer, bread, and lunch meat and driven back to the clubhouse. Wolf set the prospect to putting together some kind of sandwiches and then said to me, "Come with me—I want to show you some things."

I followed him into a small sparsely furnished back room. In the middle was a large wooden chest, whose lid Wolf lifted. In it were medallions, chains, loose patches, and other biker gear.

Wolf began fingering these as I stood watching, and he said, "This all belonged to Shazam, the guy whose funeral you were at. All of it was our brother's." He shined his fierce eyes on me. "All of this means nothing. It's all just a bunch of junk. *It* shouldn't be here —*he* should be here! What happened, there was no cause for it."

I didn't answer, and he went on: "You know we got two Pagans captive."

"I heard that," I said.

"We don't know exactly what to do with them yet, but, believe me, we'll do something!"

I wondered whether I was really getting the truth now or this story just for my benefit. Maybe they were playing head games with me. I didn't know.

But he said, "You got some Pagans back in South Carolina that need to be taken care of. When you go back, you've got to do the job."

He dropped a medal into the chest and shut the lid.

"I want them all dead," he snapped with authority. "Every one of them—dead! I want every Pagan who's got a patch in South Carolina out—dead!" He began tapping his forefinger rapidly on the lid of the trunk as he said, "You are in charge of this, you are the leader of the South Carolina charter, and you're responsible to take care of it."

Here it is at last! I thought. *The Big Order!* And there was no way around it. Coming from this guy, and backed up, I was sure, by Shades and a bunch of other higher-ups, it had to be obeyed. And yet I knew that there was no way I could obey it.

I sat down on a narrow cot that was over against one wall. As I did, Shades and the Australian, Wilson, came to the doorway. In Shades's hand was an ax handle.

Shades entered and stood between me and the door. Wilson sat in a chair by the side of the door. Wolf let himself down into a chair at the side of the trunk and fingered a bowie knife, sliding it in and out of its sheath at his side. Shades swung the ax handle back and forth at eye level in front of me. All of them stared intently my way. Nobody spoke for some seconds.

Wolf broke the silence. "You know what you got to do, don't you?" I felt like I was dissolving under the three pairs of eyes. I was fading away suddenly to a great distance, like I wasn't even there. The fear was so intense I went numb.

Wolf slowly drew a gun from inside his cutoff. *This is it,* I said to myself.

Words came from my mouth then, not as I formed them, but as if someone else were moving my lips: "I'm a Hell's Angel. An' I'll do what I have to do. But I'm not a murderer. I'm not gonna kill nobody senseless, for no reason."

Wolf turned red, and I could see him begin to tremble with

anger. Shades stood still, only his ax handle moving. Wilson didn't move a muscle.

I said again, "I'm jus' as much a Hell's Angel as one a you guys. But I'm not a murderer!"

Wolf leaped suddenly into the air and landed crouched on the chair he'd been sitting on. His back hunched like his namesake, a wolf, ready to spring.

He screamed, "YOU'RE NOT *WHAT!!!*" His lips peeled back, showing the yellow of his teeth. He crouched, still poised and quivering, and shouted, "You're not one of us!"

I said, "Yeah, I am—I'm jus' as much a Hell's Angel as you are . . ."

"NO YOU'RE NOT!!!" He shrieked, "If you were, you'd kill, you'd maim, you'd cut your own child's throat!"

Shades's ax handle swayed. Wilson didn't move. An instant of calm suddenly hit me. I said, "You're crazy, man—you're crazy!"

At that very instant, a head appeared at the door. Jackal! He stepped around and said, "What's going on?"

Nobody said anything. The tension reached a peak. When were they going to strike? When was that ax handle going to slice my face?

Then it all seemed to whoosh out, like a shot tire. Shades thumped his ax handle into the floor and said, "We're just getting a few things straightened out here."

I stood up. I knew I might get met with a blade or a bullet, but I had to make a move. No blow came.

Wolf stepped off the chair. "I got something for you," he sneered. *Now! Here it comes!* He opened the lid of the chest full of dead man's things and rummaged through it. He picked out a black fountain pen and an old rusty key. He handed me the key first, saying, "This is the key to the town. You're gonna need it!" Then he handed me the pen and said, "This right here signs your way out!"

I said, "All right!" and stuck them in a pocket. Jackal said, "You about ready to go? I'm heading back to the house."

I said, "Yeah, man. I'm ready to ride."

And I stepped past Shades and out into the hall. I felt ready to get plugged with a bullet from the back. But nobody shot. Nobody even followed.

I didn't understand why they let me go. But I was glad to be out of there!

Jackal's old lady Sue was in the car, waiting. Jackal said, "Let's go get something to eat."

I said, "It's okay with me." What had prompted him to come by just then? Or was he *told* to break right into the middle of things? He had sure asked the right question: What was going on here?

My head was straining with possibilities: Were they just trying to test me? Or were they planning to break me and then snuff me? Why hadn't they done it then? I had said I would disobey an order given in the presence of three powerful presidents. I had signed my death warrant! Or were they giving me a chance to change my mind? It was almost too painful not knowing.

We went to a chain restaurant and sat at a booth. A waitress brought us some water and silverware and Jackal asked, "What was going on back there?"

He didn't seem to know. Or did he? I had to be careful what I told him.

I said, "Jus' a few disagreements."

But during the meal, I found myself breaking down. I asked him, "Can you tell me wha's happenin' aroun' here? Somethin' I don't feel like is right!"

He said, "Maybe you need some help."

I said, "Whatta you mean?"

He said, "They got this place where a lot of us go and we get counseling and relieved."

"You mean a headshrinker?"

"No, not a shrink, it's called Higher Meditation. We got a guy in charge of it. It'll really broaden your mind, and you'll be relaxed and at peace, and you'll be okay."

I shook his suggestion off angrily. I didn't know what he was talking about, but I didn't want to hear it. I said, "Man, I don't need no headshrinker, I don't need nothin' like that. Ain't nothin' wrong with me!"

Jackal shrugged and fell silent.

We finished eating and went back to Jackal's house. He showed me to a room. "You can sleep here," he said.

As if there was any chance of it! I never took my clothes off. I lay in darkness, rigid on the bed. I saw shadows walking in the dim light the window cast on the wall, I kept hearing the sounds of people tramping around outside. I leaped up, time after time, and craned my neck out the window and saw no one. I heard nothing. But as soon as I got back in bed, the noises would start up again, the shadows would pick up their march, hour after hour.

The whole bed shook underneath me with my fear. I kept staring at the open door, certain at any moment someone was going to burst through and blow me to bits. I had to be on the death list. I'd refused to do what I was told.

Down the road from the house, I had seen a big landfill. They could bury me out there and nobody would ever find me! If anybody asked about me they could just say I up and left and that was the last they'd seen of me.

I battled with everything in me to stay awake as long as it was still dark. Somehow I felt that if I could just hold out till daylight, I'd have a chance.

But there was a crack in a closet door I couldn't open. I was sure someone was looking through it, just waiting for me to close my eyes and start breathing heavily. Only my terror was strong enough to keep me awake.

23

Loose on a Chain

I strained to see what I thought was a lightening just over a housetop nearby. Could that really be the dawn? I couldn't tell whether it was, or only my exhausted eyes playing tricks on me. Not until a mild pink tinted a small cloud and I saw the first wash of blue did I let myself believe day had finally come. I collapsed onto the bed and let myself fall into a kind of stupor that must have lasted an hour or so.

I didn't move again until I heard Jackal and Sue talking and chairs scuffling in the kitchen. Finally I dragged myself out of bed and walked as straight as I could toward the smell of fresh coffee.

All day, I did my best to pretend I was all right. But I kept moving to keep alert, sitting down and getting up, walking from one room to another, as people came in and out to drop off and sell drugs to Jackal. I rang up Gypsy in Charleston, just to hear a familiar voice.

With her, I tried to play it cool, too. But I called her several times during the day. "Sen' me some money, I need to get a ticket," was the main thrust of what I kept telling her. I didn't say a thing to her about the ordeal I was going through, for fear somebody was listening in on my conversation.

She said once, "When you comin' home?" I said, "Soon as you sen' me some money—aroun' two hundred dollars."

She said, "Well, I ain't made much . . ."

"Well, *get* some! I'll call you later an' tell you where t' sen' it!"

One time during the day, Jackal was talking to a citizen who'd come in, and I thought, here's my chance! I went into the living room, where they were sitting, and said, "Sorry to interrupt, man, but I wanna borrow your car an' go down to that greasy spoon we passed on the way home."

He said, "Okay," and tossed me the keys.

I took off my cutoff and left it on the bed in the room of my uneasy night, along with my suitcase. I figured if I was going to make the break, I was at least not going to look like a Hell's Angel. I had no intention of stealing Jackal's car; I just wanted to drive it far enough so that I could get transportation to somewhere else, preferably San Francisco, where I could get lost in the crowds.

I drove to the diner and ordered some soup, a sandwich, and a glass of milk. But once I got it, I couldn't eat. My stomach was tight, all the way up to my throat, it felt like. I knew I was famished, but I was just too wrapped up with thinking about my next move.

I didn't have much time to decide on it. I heard a motorcycle roar outside. I looked back to see a Hell's Angel and his old lady getting off. They came in and sat down at the counter. They didn't look at me, but I figured they had to have recognized Jackal's car. The thought crossed my mind: *Are they followin' me wherever I go? How can I lose 'em if I can't get outa their sight?*

I forced down half my glass of milk and left everything else on the table and walked toward the exit. The Hell's Angel glanced at me as I left and nodded slightly. I nodded back but didn't stop to talk with him. But I cursed him under my breath for costing me the chance to run for it.

Back at Jackal's, the house was empty. I found Jackal and another Hell's Angel in the cycle shop next door.

Jackal looked up and saw me. So did the other guy, who walked over to me and said, "You wanta make some money?"

I didn't know him from Adam, except that he was a brother, but I said, "Yeah."

He said, "You need some money, don't you? Well, you're gonna have to work for it!"

"I don't min' some work," I said.

"You know," he said, "my trade is a plumber."

A *plumber?* I thought. *That ain't no Hell's Angel's work!*

He went on, "I can use you. You can go with me on a job. I travel a lot, here an' there, doin' my business."

I thought, *Could this guy be an eliminator? Is that what he means?*

He said, "Yeah, I do construction work, too."

I thought, *He buries people!* Wild thoughts like this spun through my head during the whole conversation.

He said, "Tonight's the night. You come with me an' we'll make some money. I'll take care of some business; you'll help out."

I said, "Okay." Not that I wanted to go. But I had to keep this front alive. I wondered as I walked back to the house how he knew I needed money? Had Jackal overheard me talking to Gypsy? Was somebody listening on the line? I hoped they hadn't heard me tell her I was coming home as soon as I got the money. They knew I was supposed to go to Omaha!

I hung around until it got dark and Jackal said, "Pretty soon we're going out and make some money. We got some things to take care of. You just kind of ride along with us and you can help out."

All I could think of was, *They're fixin' to take me off now! This is it! Jus' like that other guy, they're gonna shoot me in the back!*

Jackal said, "Leave your patch and everything here. You won't need nothing in it."

I thought, *This is it!* I folded up my patch and put it on top of my suitcase on the bed. I took my rings and wristbands off and laid them down.

I walked outside to wait for this other dude to come. *Somehow, I've got t' get outa here! Ain't gonna be no chance in a little while!*

Just then, the guy I'd talked to that afternoon pulled up in an old sedan and hollered, "Go get Jackal an' let's go!" I yelled for Jackal and he came out. He outwalked me to the car and sat in the back seat. He said, "You sit in front."

The guy driving said, "We gotta go by an' get one more dude. It ain't but a few blocks."

Boy, they're makin' sure! I thought. *If they're gonna bump me off, they'll have plenty of help doin' it.*

He drove down the block, and I spied a phone booth. I said, "Hey! I jus' remembered I gotta call Charleston. I gotta make a report to the clubhouse about now."

It was slim, but I figured I'd try this dodge. At least it might give me a couple of minutes to think.

I was almost shocked to hear Jackal say, "Okay. We'll be back for you in a few minutes."

I got out by the booth and watched them glide down the street and turn left. The instant they were out of sight, I went into the phone booth and dialed O and the clubhouse number in Charleston.

A woman's voice came on: "Operator Assistance, may I help you?"

"Yeah, I'd like t' make this a collec' call from Barry-Barry."

"Surely."

I heard the little set of beeps and the phone ringing.

The ringing stopped. On the clear connection, I heard Bushy's voice. "Hello, who is it?"

"I have a collect call to anyone from Barry-Barry, will you accept the charges?"

"Nope!" Bushy's voice was stern and hard.

"You won't accept the charges, sir?"

Again Bushy's voice snapped, "Nope! I sure won't!"

"Sir," the operator began to drone, "your party will not accept . . ."

I had heard enough. I banged the phone onto the hook. I reached down and clutched the phone book, twisting it in my hands. I gritted my teeth. My head felt ready to explode. *My own people wouldn't accept my call! I knew then that it hadn't all been my imagination. I was on the list. No more a part of the family! Junk to be got rid of!*

I felt a scream racing out of my throat. The booth seemed to be closing in on me. I threw open the door and flew down the street, blindly running, hurling myself down street after street in sheer terror. My heart was pounding and pounding, my breath ripped in and out of me, but I drove myself against the pain. Only one thought possessed me: *Get away, get away from here! They gonna kill you!*

Car lights turned a corner ahead of me. They would be combing the streets for me by now! I saw some bushes in front of a house. I dived into the middle of them and hoped I hadn't been seen. I glued my eyes to the headlights until they passed. I heard my aching breath and heart race like a floored car engine.

As soon as the car was out of sight, I took off again, running; huddling behind trees; running; trying to catch my breath behind the corner of a house; running; spreadeagled on the ground behind a low shrub—and headlights everywhere slicing through the night.

I have no idea how far or where I ran, or how long I'd been running when the thought came to me: *Gypsy! Now they know I'm on the run, they'll try to pick up Gypsy an' the baby an' hol' 'em an' do God knows what to 'em!*

I knew I had to warn Gypsy before they got to her—if they hadn't got to her already! I had come to a hilly residential area, and I was at the top of an incline with wooden houses slanting down it. Near the bottom of the hill I spotted a place with a yellow porch light on and lighted windows. A car sat in the driveway next to it.

I thought, *Maybe there's somebody there—maybe I can talk 'em into lettin' me call Gypsy collec'!*

I tried to catch my breath as I turned off the sidewalk and paused at the lowest step to the porch of the house. *I got to get outa here an' back home! Gotta get me some money!*

I went up the few stairs and knocked on the door. A middle-aged woman opened it and peered out. "Yes?" she said.

Behind her I could see her husband and some children sitting in a dining room with some supper things still on it.

"Ma'am, my car is broke down, up the road here. An' I was wonderin' if I could jus' use your telephone for a minute an' get a taxi?" That was the best I could do.

I might have looked a fright, but she didn't hesitate. She said, "Sure, come on in!"

She opened up the door and led me to the kitchen, right off the dining area. I mumbled some words of apology for interrupting their evening and repeated to the husband my tale about the car breaking down. I said I had to get a taxi, I was supposed to be some place at a certain time, I had to call my mother, my mother and my wife were expecting me, and so on. I was even scared of these folks—who knew but they might be friends of the Hell's Angels?

The husband said, "I understand. Feel free."

I thanked him and went to the phone. I talked in a low voice, hoping they couldn't hear me. I got the operator to ring up my mother's number collect. After she accepted the call I said, "Mother, I want you to get Gypsy. I want you to go over to that nightclub an' get 'er out of there an' get 'er home with you!"

She said, "What's the matter, son?"

I said, "I can't talk right now. I can't tell you a lot a things right now, but you gotta get 'er outa there, because I jus' quit the Hell's Angels, an' . . ."

"PRAISE THE LORD!" she shouted across the miles. "THANK YOU, JESUS!"

I said, "Mother, calm down! You don't understan'—these people are out to *kill* me! They're tryin' to *kill* me! I gotta get outa here —an' I'm worried about Gypsy. Get 'er home with you, an' I'll call you later an' let you know where I'm at."

She started to say something, but I interrupted: "I need some money, Mother—you gotta wire me some money, Western Union, San Francisco!"

"Okay, son," she said quickly, "don't you worry about nothin', 'cause, see, you're in God's hands—God's gonna help you, God's gonna take care of you! You're gonna be all right!"

I said, "Sure, sure, Mother, but you gotta wire me enough money to get me back home—an' quick! Jus' get me that money!"

"All right, son, we'll get it! You jus' look to God!"

I hung up and asked the lady of the house if she could look me up the number of a taxi. She picked one out of a phone book and also told me the address there. I called for the cab.

The people in that house did a lot for me. Maybe they could tell I was in some real trouble. The husband kept asking me, "Are you okay?"

I said, "Oh, yeah, I'm all right!" But I was trembling like a leaf with dread, worn out from lack of sleep and full-tilt running. I asked, "Can I sit down on the front porch an' wait for the cab?"

The wife said, "Well, you can sit right here and wait for it!"

She was just being nice, but in my frame of mind, I got suspicious. *They're tryin' t' hol' me here*, I thought. I said, "Tha's okay, thanks, I'll jus' stay outside." I didn't want to be in a cooped-up place; I wanted to be ready to run.

They must have thought I was strange, but they didn't say anything but "Fine, make yourself at home!"

"Thanks for lettin' me use your phone an' everythin'."

"That's all right," the husband said smiling. "Glad to be able to help."

I went outside and down the steps and began pacing back and forth, waiting for the taxi. Every time a car came by, I ducked out of sight behind the steps, checking it over.

I was huddling back there when I heard the wife's voice: "Yoo hoo!"

I stepped into sight and said, "Yeah?"

"I brought you a cup of coffee."

"Thanks," I said, and she went back inside.

I sipped it, on and off of the steps, until the taxi pulled up. I knocked on the door of the house. The lady answered and I handed her the cup and said, "Thank you."

She said, "Good-bye!" and I walked to the cab and got into the back seat.

The driver had opened the front door on the passenger side. He said, "Come on up front!" I said, "No, man, I wanta sit in the back!"

He said, "You can sit up here with me." I said, with more force, "No, I tol' you I'm gonna sit in the *back!* I'm payin' for this ride, an' I'll sit where I wanta sit!" I was paranoid; I didn't know who he was.

He said, "Oh, okay, man! Don't get all uptight!" He was a young guy, dark hair, mustache, wearing a light windbreaker.

I settled in, and he said, "Where to?"

"The airport."

He smiled and said, "Man, you're talking about thirty-some miles! That's twenty, twenty-something bucks!"

I had just less than twenty left on me. He said, "It'd be a lot cheaper if you took the train to San Francisco and got you a subway and then a taxi to the airport."

I said, "Okay, take me to the train station. An' don't you ride me all over the place, man! You take me straight where I wanta go!"

He started the car moving and said, "Okay, man! All right! Be cool! I ain't gonna rip you off! What's the matter with you, anyway?"

I kept thinking as we drove along that somebody was following us. I looked back every few seconds to see.

The driver stopped once outside a restaurant. "I gotta get something," he said. All the while he was in there, I was stewing. Was he tipping somebody off that he had me in the car? What was he up to? He came back out, and I said, "You ain't chargin' me for this!" He said, "No, man, I turned it off." I leaned over and looked into the front seat. He had a clipboard with paper in it and a pencil on a string attached. I was looking to see if he had a gun or some other weapon. If he had, I'd have probably hit him or jumped out, I was so nervous.

Soon he said, "There's the station." The fare was three dollars and fifteen cents. I paid the cabbie, and he wasted no time taking off. I was just about as glad to see *him* go.

I saw Railroad printed on walls and steel pillars, as I went down some stairs. I put two dollar bills into a changer to get some extra coins and a token, which I used to go through the turnstile and down to the San Francisco platform, out in the open air. Against a wall I saw a coffee machine and used some of my change to get a cup.

As I waited for the train, a guy came onto the platform with a military-style overcoat on, carrying a blue duffel bag. He wore an old stocking cap. I kept looking over at him and catching his eye. I'm not sure whether he wasn't just as scared of me as I was suspicious of him.

Just before the train came, a few other people came down. I didn't pay them much attention, just this guy. When the train rolled in, I got on, and walked several cars down, looking back through the glass door, keeping an eye on him.

When the train got moving, I looked out the dark window and

saw myself. Around my waist was my death's head belt buckle! My light leather jacket didn't come down far enough to cover it up! So I pulled my shirt out and let it hang down over the buckle so no one could see it. I saw the chain to which my billfold was attached. I took it off the wallet and put both chain and wallet in my pocket. I was determined to alter anything about me that made me even look like a biker.

The train soon went down below the ground. At every stop, as all the doors opened, I got off, walked down a couple of cars, and stepped on just as the doors were closing again. If anybody was following me, I was going to shake him off.

I had to transfer to another train to get to downtown San Francisco, and on it I kept up my same evasive tactics. As I got off the train, I hesitated. I thought, *They'll know I'm comin' down here to Frisco! They know I need money, they know I can't get out of town without it. They'll know I got no frien's in town. They know somebody's got to wire me that dough!* Had Mom wired it already?

Still below the street, I found a phone booth and looked up Western Union. I called up and found out that they closed at midnight. I still had a couple of hours—if Mom and Gypsy had already wired the money!

I rang up my mom's house and Mom answered. My first question was, "Mother, did you get Gypsy an' little Bari-Ann there?"

She said, "Yes, son, Fran's here. You want to talk to her?"

I said, "Put 'er on, Mother."

"Son, it's so good to hear your voice."

"Sure thing, Mother, now lemme talk to Gypsy."

She put Gypsy on, and I said, "Are you all right?"

"Yeah, I'm all right, Barry-Barry. What 'bout you?"

"I'm all right—an' I'm gonna *be* all right, don't you worry." Even at that moment, I had to show her my superiority, that I had it all under control. Whistling in the dark!

She said Mother had called her at work and she'd caught a taxi home and Mom was getting a friend of Gypsy's to take her to get Bari-Ann from the baby-sitter's and bring them over.

I said, "All that soun's fine, babe. Now did you wire me that money yet? I gotta have it t' get me outa town!"

"Barry-Barry, we got the money together between us, an' we're gonna wire it tonight. You'll get it tomorrow mornin'.'"

"Well, I'll have t' hole up somewhere till then. I don't know wha's gonna happen to me, Gypsy. I believe these guys is out to get me. But you get that money to me, an' I'll fly home. You jus' stay where you're at. I'm gonna be okay. I'm gonna get me a room someplace, an' I'll call you tomorrow. You jus' stay there, don't go back t' work. When I get there, we'll fin' someplace, we'll get outa town, we'll move on."

"Okay, okay!" Gypsy said. I must have sounded mighty upset in spite of myself.

Mother, who was on the extension phone, piped in, "It's gonna be all right, son; we'll take care of her here. Nobody's gonna mess with her." She had no real idea what kind of people I was dealing with!

I hung up and looked through the phone book for some cheap hotel nearby. Then I realized I didn't know where I was. I walked up to street level, and my eyes were splashed with neon and movie marquees. The whole area was porno flicks and topless dives, head shops, strip and live sex joints, barkers yelling to passersby, "Come on in! Acts beyond your wildest dreams!"

The nearest signpost said "Turk Street," and I spied another phone booth on a corner. I ducked in and found there were quite a few hotels along this strip. I put a few names in my memory and went looking.

My funds were touching close to the ten-dollar mark: Whatever place I found, it had to be cheap! I wound my way through gawking businessmen, drunks and whores, shook off a pimp who tried to grab my arm, always looking around me for anyone who might be a biker. I stopped at two hotels—too expensive. I finally found a place with a room for only six dollars a night.

As I was at the desk, half-tight men passed in and out with hookers, a few of them black. I signed a phony name to the register, and the guy at the desk looked up suspiciously when I mumbled something about just being drunk and needing a place to sleep. He gave me a key to a second-floor room.

An elevator was to the left, a stairway to the right. I decided on the elevator, seeing the lobby was empty at that moment. I

looked to see if anybody was getting in behind me as the door
closed. I pushed the third-floor button, and the old elevator
wheezed its way up there. I pushed the lobby button and stepped
out. When the door closed, I went to the stairway and walked
down to the second floor, still hoping to shake off any follower.

The hall was dimly lit and narrow. I heard voices laughing
behind the closed doors here and there. I turned the key in my
door and cut the light on. I shut the door, put on the chain lock,
and immediately checked the closet and the bathrooms to make
sure nobody was hiding in them. I cut the light off and took the
bed, a double, and pushed it up against the door, and the dresser
against that. Anybody below me must have thought the person
above was crazy, with all the scraping I made on the wood floor.

I took the pillows and blankets into the bathroom. I dropped
them onto the floor and opened the bathroom window and looked
down to see how far it was in case I had to make a quick exit.
Right underneath was an open, half-full dumpster. Good.

I left the window open, closed the bathroom door, and locked
it. I spread the pillows and blankets on the floor, curled between
the tub and toilet, and tried to stay calm.

Another long, sleepless night began. My mind raced with anxious thoughts: What was going on back home? What was going to
happen to me? What would happen if the Hell's Angels found
me? Was I going to be able to escape town?

I kept getting up and staring out the window into the alley.
From lack of rest and very little food, my head felt light, floating,
like a helium balloon, attached to me only by the steady churning
of my stomach. And through that lightness whirled visions of
Gypsy and the baby being held hostage and tortured, Mom and the
family being blown away, the door crashing open and me being
shotgunned to pieces.

But somehow, I held on, I had to hold out, till dawn . . .

24
Sprung Free!

One look by morning light in the mirror told me there was nothing I'd be able to do about my eyes. They gaped out at me cracked with red, bleary, the pupils wide and wild. My hair was greasy and strewn every which way. My beard! That I could shave off. I could get me a razor and a bunch of blades and change my appearance!

I had the room until noon, time to buy what I needed and get this shagginess off. I washed my face and tried to straighten my hair out as well as I could. I went into the room and dragged the bed and dresser back into place. I took off my belt with the death's-head buckle and stuffed it under the mattress. I threw the pillows and blankets on the bed, opened the door and peered down the hall. Nothing moved, so I headed for the stairway.

Down the stairs, out a side door, I said nothing to anyone. I walked across the street to a drugstore, through all the hustle of cars and people revving up the business of the day. I found a seat at the drugstore counter and bought a cup of coffee. It was scorching hot, but weak. I glanced over at a guy reading a World Series wrap-up in the morning newspaper.

But what was next for me? Get a razor, shave. *Wait a minute,* I thought. *What're you doin'? You know better than ever to back-*

track! You gotta keep movin'. To hell with even bringin' the key back! It's the fleabag's key, it's your life!

I sipped some of my coffee, then left a quarter on top of the check and hit the street. It probably wouldn't be too early now to go to the Western Union office. Market Street, the phone book said. I had no idea where that was, so I began asking directions from people on the street: "Follow these cable car tracks down until they intersect with two more lines, and that wide street will be Market Street," said my last guide, a Chinese-looking fellow.

Where I hit Market Street, there were Army-Navy stores, pawnshops, and movie theaters within sight. Trolleys clicked along as well as buses, cars, trucks; and everywhere there were people bustling. I got my bearings and headed toward the number I was after, just looking around at faces floating in the sea of people around me. There were more different types of people than I had ever seen in one place: black folks, Mexican-looking women, Chinese, an Indian guy with a beard and turban, white people of all ages and descriptions, a red-headed girl (nice-looking), a guy with wavy, Italian-looking hair, hippies, a big guy with blond hair but a red beard . . . *my God! That face!* Looking at me from over by the leather store! I had seen him in San Diego, I could swear it! *Hell's Angel!*

Two other guys, dressed rough, no patches, stood by him. I saw him nudge one of them and point at me, saying something. The three of them started pushing my way, through the crowd.

I walked fast, then faster. I lurched across the wide street and looked back. They were still coming along behind me. They had crossed the street after me!

Up ahead on the corner, two more faces glared out at me. One of them clicked into my memory—scrawny beard, balding head—the other one—a wallet chain hanging from a belt—Hell's Angels! I saw them look past me, signaling to the guys behind.

A big clump of people waited for a stoplight a few yards away. I elbowed my way into the middle of it, trying to find protection in the crowd.

The light changed, and the mass of people started crossing. A big, bearded dude stood on the next corner, saying something into a walkie-talkie. *Jesus! Another one!* I saw him look over at a car—

full of rough-looking faces—wasn't that driver a guy I had seen on one of the runs? He lifted a walkie-talkie over the steering wheel and said something. As I passed him, the guy on the corner nodded. I bumped into a lady as I craned my neck to look back. "Watch where you're going!"

"Sorry!"

The three behind me were still coming, closer now—and the guy on the corner joined them! And halfway up the block stood another guy—with a death's-head ring on. A Hell's Angel may take his patch off—but not his ring. I'd been right, figuring they'd come down here. They knew I'd have to come here for money!

All I could picture was Hell's Angels everywhere, all over the place. *There's no escape for me! There's no way!* I forced through the crowds and kept looking back, seeing the Angels elbowing past people, waving each other on in my direction.

Through the automatic sound of my own breathing, mixed with the grating of auto gears, the hiss of bus brakes, and the clang of trolley bells, the curses of people I shoved past, I heard a shout, or a thought, call out to me, "CALL HOME! CALL HOME! TALK TO GYPSY!"

I saw a sign above an open space in a building by a corner: Wayne's Cafeteria. Over the heads of people sitting in there I saw open, pocked-metal telephone booths. "CALL HOME!" the voice in me shouted. I turned into the cafeteria. The tables were fairly crowded, but the line wasn't long. I drew myself a cup of coffee from the machine, trying as best I could not to act scared. *Let 'em come in here after me,* I thought. *At least if they drag me out, it'll have t' be in front of all these people!*

Holding my shaking cup and saucer with both hands, I went over to the phones. Over my shoulder, I saw two Hell's Angels in the food line, by the coffee urns. More Angels collected outside on the sidewalk, talking.

There was no hope for me, I thought. All I wanted to do was call home once more before, one way or another, they got me. There were about ten phone booths, five in a row across an aisle from one another. I picked one out, set my cup down, and found a dime in my pocket. I put it in and called my mother's, collect. Gypsy picked up. I said, "Hey, baby"—and choked up.

Gypsy said, "Where you at? Wha's goin' on? I been so worried about you!"

There was a lump in my throat so bad, I almost whispered. "Baby, I just wanted to . . . call you an' . . . an' tell you . . . how much I love you!" Sobs were welling up in me, I could tell. I tried hard to hold them back.

"Wha's the matter, Barry-Barry?" she pleaded. "Tell me somethin'!"

The first sob wrenched from my throat, and I began to feel tears trickle from my eyes. "Gypsy, I . . . I want you to know . . . oh, Gypsy, the way I been treatin' you . . . I don't know how t' say it all, but I'm sorry . . ."

"What for, Barry-Barry?"

All of a sudden, I saw it all, and with the seeing came the words. "Ooh, Gypsy, the beatin's, all the busted teeth an' black eyes, the bruises I done put on your body! The thin's I made you do, the hookin' an' standin' there while I shot at you! I could of got you killed or hurt so bad! I'm so sorry, babe, so sorry . . ."

I couldn't hold back the tears then, and I heard Gypsy begin crying on the other end, "Oh, Barry-Barry, it's all right, it's jus' all right!"

"No it ain't, babe, it's awful what I done t' you. The way I worked you like some animal, the way I cut you, all the lies, all the women . . ." Reeling in my mind were all the blows, all the harsh words—"I care about you so much, an' little Bari-Ann . . . Can you forgive me, babe, can you tell me you'll forgive me?"

All I heard for some seconds was Gypsy weeping. Then she said faintly, "Yeah, Barry-Barry! Yeah, I forgive you!"

"Oh, girl, I been so bad to you . . ."

"Barry-Barry, wha's the matter? You in bad trouble?"

I said, "Sweetie, they're all aroun' me . . ." I looked behind me —and the two Hell's Angels who had come in the restaurant were standing over my either shoulder, just a few feet away. A girl who seemed to be with them sat in a booth across, facing me and smirking. I went on, "I'm in this little restaurant, an' they're right here an' standin' outside." Just then I saw the girl get up, walk outside, and start talking to the guys on the sidewalk. I said, "I can't get by 'em, babe."

She said, "We sent you money, we sent you money—the money's in the Western Union. If you can jus' get down there an' get your money, you can get outa there, an' we'll meet you at the airport, an' . . ."

"Sweetie, there's no way, they're all aroun' me. I'm tellin' you good-bye!"

"No, Barry-Barry, it can't be that way! I love you, man! You gonna be all right . . ."

"Gypsy . . ."

"You *can't* die, Barry-Barry! You know that night I tol' you that we were gonna die together—I ain't dyin', an' nothin's gonna happen to you!"

I looked around, and the two guys were still standing right there. I felt a rush of anger, and I said to them, "Whatta you want?"

One sneered and said, "We want to use the phone!"

I said, "You got plenty o' phones aroun' here—use one o' them!"

The other guy said, "We wanna use *that* phone, man!"

I said, "You ain't gonna get on *this* phone, 'cause *I'm* usin' it!" I felt as long as I kept hold of that phone, I was safe. I turned around and kept talking. And they just kept standing there.

My mom spoke up then. "Son, I been on the extension. I heard everythin'. Listen, everythin's gonna be okay, everythin's gonna be all right . . ."

"Mother, you don't understan'—these guys is all aroun' me, two's standin' behin' me, an' these guys are out to *kill* me! Mother, this is *it!* I jus' wanta tell you I'm sorry for the disgrace I done brought on the family, bein' in an' out o' jail, the neighbors talkin' 'bout me. I'm sorry I hurt you so many times . . . I'm jus' sorry!"

I heard her say, through my tears and hers, "Son, it's nothin' to be sorry about. I love you, son, an' it's all forgiven.

"Son, listen: There *is* hope for you!"

I said, "Whatyou mean, Mother—what kin' of hope is there for me?"

She said, "Son, your hope is in Jesus Christ!"

"Mother, Jesus Chris' couldn't care for me! When Dad died of malaria, I *cursed* God! An' Mother, you don't know all the things I done since then."

"He cares for you because two thousand years ago, He gave His life for you. He shed every drop of His blood—so you could *live!* An' be with Him!"

And I said, "Not *me!* He can't love me!" I was battling now, fighting *her*—I didn't believe.

She said, "John 3:16 says, 'For God so loved the *world*, that He gave His only begotten Son, that whosoever *believes* in Him should not perish, but have everlasting *life.*' Son, He loves *you*, and He died for *your* sins! Every evil thing, every bad thing you ever did, He took it on Himself, an' He shed His blood for it!"

I wrestled with myself. In inner vision, I saw Jesus as long ago I'd seen Him in pictures, nailed on the cross with blood flowing from His hands and feet and His side, streaming from the crown of thorns on His head. And I saw myself, kicking a fallen, writhing body in a bar, stabbing Gypsy in a drunk rage through the car seat, slicing faces with my wristband. And suddenly it was as if I was doing it all to Jesus, and He wasn't a picture anymore, but the one getting kicked, stabbed, knifed, cheated on, cursed, covered with blood streaming from His wounds. It was Him as much as it was them, and it was wrong, evil, and I knew that I was in the presence of God with no excuse, no hope—but that what my mother said was true!

I heard her say again, "He died for your sins. All you have to do is ask God to forgive you, and He will, and take all that sin away!"

Would He? How could He? Something sprang up in me then—and I *wanted* to believe, I *wanted* what she was telling me. At that instant, something in me, faith, whatever it's called, came alive.

I said, "Mother, I don't even know how to pray—I don't know how to talk to God!"

"It doesn't matter what you say," she said, "He'll hear you!"

I broke into a sweat as I thought and thought and couldn't come up with words. "Mother," I cried, "I don't know what to say!" I heard Gypsy's soft sobbing into the phone then, and I knew that she was struggling, as I was, to somehow believe.

"Son," Mom said, "I'll pray, an' you pray with me. An' all you have to do is repeat after me."

I said, "All right!" I didn't know anything else to do.

She said, and I heard Gypsy's voice trembling along with mine as we spoke after Mom, "Lord Jesus . . . I know I'm a sinner . . . I know I've sinned . . . I jus' ask if you'll forgive me of my sins . . . and that you come into my heart . . . an' help me live for you!"

I felt the tears break from me like a well springing from deep in hard, cracked ground. I heaved sobs so deep it seemed like they were torn out of me by a huge hand reaching inside me and pulling all of me out of my body. I felt a rush of love, of peace, of warmth, and in my mind's eye, it was like I was an ocean shore with ugly shells and dead fish and dried-up seaweed and soggy papers and broken bottles and wave after wave of rolling sea crashed over me and dug deep and carried away the filth and trash and left clean sand with fresh, bright shells and pebbles, all trickling with eddies of coolness as the ocean drew back from where it came. I *knew* Jesus Christ *had* forgiven me, I knew He *had* come into my heart. I could feel Him put His arms around me, and I could hear His voice say, "I love you, I love you, I forgive you everything!" And I *knew*, without a shadow of a doubt, that I was going to be with Him forever. I knew for the first time—that I had *life!*

In those moments, what people around me, even the Hell's Angels, thought, I didn't care. I savored the joy, knowing it might be the last thing I ever felt. Maybe when I was first on the phone, the Angels thought I was calling the cops; later, they might have thought I was crazy. But as my tears began to ebb away, I wiped my eyes and looked around cautiously to see what they were doing.

Their heads were cocked in puzzlement. I still had tears flowing out, and that must have amazed them. Hell's Angels didn't cry—I myself hadn't cried in many years. But they stood their ground, and a glance past them told me that their companions were still stationed outside.

I knew what was waiting for me when I got off that phone. And I still felt the fear of it. Yet I knew I was *free*, even with death hanging over my head, for the first time in my life. I could see that through drugs and women and drink and weapons, I had been struggling for the peace of some kind of acceptance. I'd never found it until now, moments before what might be my death. Everything that had weighed on me was lifted away. The only sorrow I could feel was that I had finally found what I had been struggling for all my life, and I was going to lose it so quickly. Now, with my time almost up, how I began to ache to live!

I wanted to see my mother, I wanted to see Gypsy and the baby again. I said, "Mother, I jus' know God loves me, I know I'm gonna be with the Lord. But boy, I jus' wish I could get home! I want t' be with y'all an' love you an' . . ."

Mom said, "Listen, son! I want you to open up the phone book. I want you t' hang up an' call a minister . . ."

I said, "Mother, if I hang up this phone, these guys are gonna jump me—they're standin' right behin' me!"

She said, "Son, God can make a way where there is no way! Yes, hold that telephone. But open the phone book to where it says 'churches.' An' I want you to look up under Assembly of God or Full Gospel churches, an' you give me a number of a minister."

So I put the phone against my shoulder and started looking. Meanwhile, the two Hell's Angels began walking around. One of them got on the phone and called someone. My mind started flashing strange things: The phone was bugged, the FBI was listening, the CIA was on the line, good and evil forces were wrestling for me.

One Angel stayed on the phone. The other came back and stood behind me. I found the number of a Full Gospel minister named Reverend Browner and gave it to my mother.

"Okay," she said. "I'm givin' the phone back to Fran. You jus' stay right there until that man comes! Don't hang up!"

There was no chance of that! As far as I was concerned, once I hung up, that was it! I'd never hear their voices again.

Gypsy and I talked for some time: I continued to tell her how much I wanted to see her, how much I loved her, and she gave me what encouragement she could. At one point, she told me, Black came to the house, but Mom sent him away.

Suddenly my mother came back on the line. "Fran, I want you to go over there an' talk to the man. He's a little leery 'bout goin'. Come by me an' get the number!"

Mom stayed on with me while Gypsy went to the neighbors'

and called up this reverend. It wasn't long before she came back. When I heard her voice, I asked her, "What'd he say?"

Gypsy said, "Well, I cussed him out some, tol' 'im, 'You call yourself a man o' God, an' here this guy's in trouble an' you won't go out an' see 'im!' He finally said he'd go."

"So you jus' stay put, son," Mom put in. "He's on the way!"

Just then, the two men who'd been standing behind me walked off. My eyes followed them outside, where they joined the other Angels and put their heads together. There were two entrances to the cafeteria, and I knew they had me cornered both ways. It was just a matter of time; sooner or later I'd have to come out. It occurred to me once to call the police. But to me that was as fearful a prospect as the Hell's Angels outside. I couldn't imagine that I'd have any friends in the police!

A tall, husky man came in the side door not long afterward and looked around. He was dressed in a navy blue suit, white shirt and tie, looked to be in his early forties. He walked over and loomed above me. "Are you Barry Mayson?" he asked.

I snapped at him, "Who are you?"

"I'm Reverend Browner," he said. "Your mother and wife asked me to come down here and talk to you. They said you needed some help." His voice was gentle—but I was suspicious.

I asked my mother and the reverend a host of questions, trying to make sure he really was who he said. I even asked him what my mother's name was. For all I knew, he was a Hell's Angel incognito, ready to take me out and blow my head off.

Finally, my mother said, "Listen, son, you've given your life to Jesus. He's your Lord, He's your Savior—an' you're gonna have t' *trust* in Him now. There's times when not all your questions is answered, an' you jus' have to *trust*. God's gonna take care of you, everythin's gonna be fine. Now I want you to hang up an' go with this minister."

I said, "Mother, listen: I'm jus' afraid I'll never hear your voice again, you know, I'm afraid I'll never . . ."

"Trust the Lord, son! Jus' trust the Lord! An' if you don't, I'll hang up on you!"

I didn't know what "trust" meant, but I knew I had to do it then. I said, "All right, Mother. Good-bye!" It was like I crumpled all my fear into a tight ball, just gritted my teeth, and forced the phone into the receiver. I looked up at Reverend Browner and said, "Well, le's go!"

I got to my feet and felt a touch of dizziness, whether from the fear in me, or from having sat there for nigh on three hours, I don't know. But I righted myself, and the reverend and I headed for the door.

As we stepped into clear sight, the Hell's Angels outside straightened up and watched us, startled. I saw them back up to near the curb. Reverend Browner was a big man, with no sign of the preacher about him. I believe the Angels thought he was a cop.

We stepped outside and stood right in front of the restaurant. Reverend Browner asked me, "What seems to be the problem?"

I said, "Man, I used to be a Hell's Angel, an' I jus' quit 'em. An' these guys are out t' kill me!"

"Where?" he said, looking around.

"They're all aroun' me!" I didn't point them out because I didn't want them to hear me talking about them.

He looked here and there and said, "I don't see any."

I insisted, "Man, they're not flyin' no patch! They're incognito —I know these guys! They're all aroun' here, an' they're set t' get me!"

He said, "What do you want me to do?"

I said, "Well, all I want you to do is walk down to Western Union with me so I can get my money an' get outa here."

"I can't do that," he said after a pause.

"Wait a minute! Ain't you a man o' God?"

"Yes."

"Well, I always thought you guys was supposed t' help somebody when they was in trouble!"

He said, "Yes—but this is something you've got to do yourself!"

I was stunned and frightened. He wasn't going to go with me! I could tell there was no use arguing with him. But one thing I knew—I had to get to that telegraph office!

The Hell's Angels skulked now by the curb, against the wall of the cafeteria, waiting. But the time had come. There was no other way. Where the courage came from, I didn't know then, but I turned from the preacher and started down the street. Out of the

corners of my eyes, I saw the Hell's Angels signal one another and
start to move with me.

It was like walking in a dream. Step by step I said to myself,
"God, help me! Lemme get that money, God! Jus' lemme get
home!"

I walked faster and faster, trying to mix with the crowds. Over
my shoulders, I could see the Hell's Angels following. I saw the
sign just ahead: WESTERN UNION! I cut in toward it, sifting the
crowd, and opened the door.

The office was narrow, with two windows, stamp machines,
and Western Union and postal posters on the walls. A woman
waited for service at one window; the other was empty.

I walked up to it. Behind the glass was a young black woman.
She said, "May I help you?" And I said, "Do you have a Moneygram for Charles Barry Mayson?" She said, "I'll look and see."

She riffled through the papers behind the counter and said,
"Yes, sir. Where is it from? . . ."

As she started to give me the third degree, I saw two Hell's
Angels, reflected in the glass, come into the office. As they came
right up behind me, I spied three more standing outside. The two
stood, arms folded, with smirks on their faces.

"How much is the Moneygram for?" the woman broke into my
fear.

"I don't know how much, lady," I said impatiently. "Lady,
look—gimme my money!"

"Do you have any ID, sir?"

I said, "Yes." I pulled it out. "See?"

She said, "Would you slide it under here, please?"

I started thinking, *She's in on it, too! They're gonna strip me of
my ID before they do me in!* I said, "Look, tha's my ID, tha's me!
Tha's my money! My mother sent me that money! Gimme my
money—I gotta go!"

She hesitated, then said, "Okay." And she counted it out. "A
hundred sixty bucks," she said. She looked up and said angrily,
"You think I'm gonna steal your ID or somethin'? What's the matter with you?"

I said, "I *know* you're not—because I ain't gonna let you have
it!" I held up the driver's license. "There it is, you can see it."

She pushed the money under the glass, and right away a thought hit me: *They're gonna get you* an' *your money now!*

I stuck the money in my pocket and turned around. The Hell's Angels backed away a little bit. I thought, *This is it! They're gonna escort me outa here, an' tha's all, brother! But I'm gonna go kickin', screamin', fightin', whatever I have to do!*

They were crowding outside the door. I was heading right for them. I stepped through, and they came around me. *Here goes!*

Just then, over one of the Angels' shoulders, I saw Reverend Browner, heading straight toward me. I turned to him in desperation and shouted, "Man, I'm glad t' see you!" The Angels all turned, and when they saw him, they backed off again and went to the corner and watched.

I grabbed that reverend by the arms and said, "Man, they were jus' fixin' t' get me!"

He said, "You know, I was standing there after you left, and the Lord told me, 'That man is in real trouble and needs some help!' I came right down then."

And I said, "Boy, I'm sure glad God was talkin' t' you—these guys were ready to take me!"

He said, "I could see you were in trouble."

The Hell's Angels stood at bay while Reverend Browner hailed me a taxi. As I got in, I said, "Man, I don't know how t' thank you!"

He said, "You're surely welcome—and don't forget to thank the Lord, too!"

"I sure won't!"

"God keep you, now!" he said as I shut the door.

"Where to, mister?" We were already going as the cabbie glanced back.

"Airport." I noticed then a little old lady sitting in the front seat.

"Fine," the cabbie said, "I can drop you off right after I drop her off; she's headin' the same way!"

This old lady seemed filled with pure sweetness. She talked about how nice the day was, about her children and grandchildren, just chatting on pleasantly in the front seat.

After a while, the driver said, "Bub, this old lady ain't got much money. I was wonderin', since it's on the way, if you would just pay her fare, too, as part of your trip?"

I said, "Yeah, man, I'll do it!" It was the first good deed I could ever remember doing for anyone!

And we drove on, and while that old lady was in the car, I had no fear. She talked and laughed, and I began to feel at ease just being around her.

When she got out, she said, "Thank you, young man." It was a pleasant interlude; I even forgot to think about whether I was being followed or not.

The cabbie dropped me off right in front of the airport and I paid him his five and some dollars and walked in. I went to the Delta airline counter and checked about flights to Charleston. The girl told me the fare was one hundred and forty-some dollars, stops at Dallas and Atlanta, and that I had a few hours to wait. I didn't like the length of that wait. I mumbled something and walked away, wondering about how best to kill the time.

A striped barber pole stuck out from among the shops, and it occurred to me that it might be a good idea to get a shave to change the way I looked. So I went in and told the guy to take it all off.

He started by putting hot towels all over my face, but that worried me because I couldn't see. As the barber went to work, I peered out with one eye—and saw a Hell's Angel pass by the doorway! *My God! They come out here, too!*

I growled at the barber, "Come on, hurry up, man! I ain't got all day, I got a plane to catch!"

"What time? What flight?" he asked.

"Delta. Charleston."

"Oh, you got a long time to . . ."

"Hey! Don't gimme that! Get me shaved! Le's go! I ain't got time t' mess aroun'!"

He said, "Okay, okay!"

He took off the towels and began to shave me with his straight razor. I said, "Man, if you cut me, it's gonna be the las' guy you ever cut!"

And he said, "Mister, you act just like a Hell's Angel!"

I said, "I ain't no Hell's Angel. Jus' hurry up an' get me shaved! An' leave the mustache!"

When I walked out of the barber's, my heart started pounding with fear: It looked like the whole place was full of Hell's Angels!

I ran to some phones and called home again. The line was busy! As I heard the signal, a Hell's Angel walked by carrying a box. Below the short sleeve of his T-shirt was the death's head tattoo. He turned and glared at me as he went by.

Maybe a drink would calm my nerves, I thought. I hung up the phone and headed for the lounge and sat down at the bar. I ordered a bourbon and Coke. Expensive—three dollars. I went over to a little table and just chugged the drink down.

Before these last few days, I'd been drinking a quart or more booze a day. If I wasn't an alcoholic, I don't know how much more I'd have had to drink to prove it. I felt I *needed* a drink, now like never! And once that first one was in me, I sprang up and back to the bar for another. I held out my glass.

The bartender was talking with another guy down at the end of the bar. He came over and filled me up again. As I was heading back for my table, I heard him say to the dude he'd been talking to, "You know who that is?" The guy said, "No." I looked back with the corner of my eye. The bartender was pointing at me. "That's a Hell's Angel!" he said.

My head began to reel, and I looked down at the drink in my hand. *Poison!* I thought. I'd learned poisons as part of my training as an eliminator. *If I drink this, it might kill me!* I pushed it away, got up, and walked out. That was a good thing—if I hadn't, I probably would have drunk up my whole air fare, I had such a craving.

I said to myself, *I'm gonna get this dough out of my han's right now!* I went directly over to the counter and got my ticket. With only a few bucks left in my pocket, I started to walk around, keeping in the middle of crowds as much as possible. But I could still see Hell's Angels all around. I felt like they were just waiting for an opportunity to get me someplace by myself where they could stick a knife in me and leave me lying dead. I figured if I could stay in the open, where people could see me, the Angels wouldn't attack me. I stayed away from corners and halls, keeping on the move around the lobby.

Outside, it was starting to get dark. I stood before a huge picture window looking out on the airfields. Lights had started to blink on the airplanes and the runways.

Time was dragging on. I was scared, hungry, tired, burned out, thinking constantly about getting home. I said under my breath, "God! I wanta make a deal with you!" I was so used to wheeling and dealing, I couldn't think of any other approach to Him. "God, if you get me home again, where I can be with my family again, my wife an' kid—I'll *give* you my *life* totally, an' I'll raise my family, an' my kid the way you want me to!"

I wiped tears from my eyes and saw, as a reflection in that picture window, five figures standing with folded arms, in an arc behind me. *Cops!* I thought to myself. *My mother's done called the cops on me! The FBI's here!* After twelve years of sneaking and hiding from the police, they were the enemy! So my first instinct was to get away!

I turned and started heading for the bathroom. The "cops" followed me. I got to the bathroom and went into one of the stalls and locked the door. I sat down on the stool and pulled out all my ID. I took all the pieces of paper that had Hell's Angel phone numbers or addresses on them and tore them up and threw them into the toilet. I looked through the cracks at the sides of the stall door: Two of the "cops" had followed me into the bathroom, three were still outside. These two were straight-looking guys, one in a brown windbreaker, the other in a suit.

They stayed in there the whole time, about half an hour, while I tore up everything I had that connected me with the Hell's Angels. My thinking was that if they arrested me, I might be able to con them into thinking they'd got the wrong guy!

When I'd finished flushing all this down, I said to myself, *Well, I can't sit in here forever. I'll jus' get up an' walk out, an' if they get me, they get me!* I flushed the toilet a last time and opened the door. I started out the door in a hurry, and I heard one of them say, "Boy, he's hard to keep up with!"

They came out after me, and I saw the other three nearby. I thought, *Maybe they're gonna haul me in an' try t' get me t' give 'em information! Well, I ain't doin' it!*

I found my way over to the phones and called home again.

When my mother answered, I said, "Mother, did you call the police?"

She said, "No, son, I didn't call any police. I only tol' about this to my pastor an' my prayer group."

I said, "Well, there's cops all aroun' me!"

"Well, son, if it's the Lord's will that those police be there, an' they arrest you, you go with 'em. Jus' believe God that's your way home!"

I said, "No! I'll fight 'em! I'll go down swingin'! Ain't no cops gonna get me, I ain't goin' t' jail!"

"Son, that ain't the Lord's way! You just try and do it His way an' trust Him, y'hear?"

I said, "Mother, I got no idea what I'm gonna do if they try t' pick me up. I'll try an' do it the Lord's way if I can figure out what that is!"

She said, "Good! If you ask Him, He'll show you! Now, listen, son! You got your ticket yet?"

"Yeah, all the way to Charleston!"

"Well, son, don't you go to Charleston, all right? We're gonna do everythin' safe—we'll meet you in Atlanta!"

"But the extra money, Mother . . ."

"Don't you worry about it, son! Let anybody who's tryin' to check on you think you're goin' all the way to Charleston. That way they won't try to get you in Atlanta, okay?"

I said, "All right, Mother, that soun's good!"

While I was still on the phone, I saw a couple of Hell's Angels go for the phones, and near me I heard one of them say, "We can't touch 'im! There's cops all aroun' 'im, we'll have t' get 'im at the other end!"

I hung the phone up, walked to the restaurant, and ordered a cup of coffee. The five "cops" stood outside the windows like bodyguards. They never spoke to me, tried to corner me, or laid a hand on me. They just followed me, watched me, and somehow seemed to be there only to keep the Hell's Angels away.

I sat in the restaurant booth for a long time and watched through the windows as, to my amazement, the Hell's Angels, one by one it seemed, began to walk away. Before long, there wasn't one in sight. I felt a faint sense of peace come over me. I knew the ordeal was almost over somehow. At last I got up and walked back out into the lobby.

And everywhere I went, these five "cops" walked behind me, watching me closely. I sat down for a while in the waiting room, reading a magazine I'd found on a seat. A girl came by with a handful of little white flowers. "Would you like one?" she asked.

I said, "Wha's it for?" I looked around and saw a lot of people wearing them on their lapels or dresses.

I heard her say, "A Hell's Angel just died!"

I said, "No, I don't want one!"

She said, "No, I didn't think you did!" And she turned around and walked off.

I shook my head and went back to my magazine—and when I looked up, the "cops" were gone! I didn't see any Hell's Angels, either, but because my "guardians" had vanished I was almost ready to worry again. But at that moment, I heard the PA system crackle, "Flight 78 now loading for Dallas, Atlanta, Charleston, at gate 17." I breathed a sigh of relief and got up and started hoofing it for that gate.

I saw the metal detector up ahead and found that encouraging, because I knew no Hell's Angels could get by there with weapons on them! I went through it and down to my gate and got in line.

It wasn't moving yet, but the flight that had been on the plane was unloading and people were pouring off and coming toward me. For some reason, these people looked strange to me. I heard various ones saying: "You going to the party tonight?" and the answer, "Yeah, a Hell's Angel just died! We're gonna celebrate his moving on!" I said to myself, *What is all this! It's all tryin' t' make me go crazy!*

Then a man got on a phone across from me, dropped his money in, dialed, and started laughing. He said, "Hello! Is this the devil? Can you believe that a Hell's Angel just quit and joined up with Jesus?" And he looked at me and just grinned.

I looked at him and said, "Man, you ain't stoppin' *me!*" I shook my fist at him—and about that time, my line started moving forward!

I was almost on now and looking nervously around at everybody. The ones wearing the little white flowers—maybe *they* were in with the Hell's Angels! Maybe *all* these people were Hell's Angels incognito! Maybe Jesus *had* come, and I'd been left behind! In my panic, I muttered to God again, "Hey, God! Please lemme get on that plane, an' take me t' heaven! Jus' don't leave me down here on this earth—take me t' heaven! I don't wanta live here no more!" If I had any nerves left, they were all fried by now: I hadn't had any sleep in days, I'd hardly eaten anything, I'd been going through heavy spiritual battles, been running for my life, hadn't done any drugs, scarcely fueled my alcohol habit, cried my eyes out for the first time in years—I was just a frightened child, longing for home, heaven, anywhere out of the agony I'd been through.

And when I got on that plane and sat down, I felt it all snap. For an instant, I felt fear, as I questioned what was going to take the place of the me I had known. Then I knew: At the center of my being was a core of peace that would never be shaken loose again. And I knew who had put it there, who had led me through all of this, into His love: no one else but God.

With my napkin, I wiped the corners of my mouth. I had wolfed down everything the stewardess had put in front of me and could have eaten a lot more. I looked over at the little man sitting next to me, who was examining the plastic cup on his tray.

Like a faint shadow of my ordeal, a thought tried to crowd in: that he was going to break that cup, and, if I fell asleep, cut my throat with it! I let the thought drift through and then said to him, as if to let him know for sure he couldn't hurt me, "You know why they put plastic utensils on airplanes?"

He said, "No, why?"

I said, "In case this plane crashes, all the plastic flyin' aroun' ain't gonna hurt nobody!"

He smiled and said, "Yes, you're probably right. But I see something in this cup. This cup was made a certain way, and it's been this shape for some time. It's kind of ugly, it's dull-looking, it's not worth too much. But you know, you can take this cup and melt it down to nothing. And you can take some fire and mold it into anything you want, even something beautiful."

I didn't know what to make of that. It irked me a little, then upset me, and I excused myself. I went back to the bathroom and locked myself in. I started talking to God again: "Listen, God. Will you let me stay in here for the rest of this flight? Everythin's weird, that guy, this whole day—jus' let me be alone!"

I guess the Lord didn't want it that way, because people kept knocking on the door. So I finally opened it, and there was a line of people waiting. Near the seat I'd been occupying, I spotted two empties. All of a sudden, I felt like I couldn't keep my eyes open another minute. I got a blanket from above the seats and stretched out in the empties. I said to myself, *If anybody wants these, they're jus' gonna have t' roll me out, 'cause I can't go any farther!* And nobody did; I slept like a rock until we reached Dallas.

25

The "Haunted House"

We touched down in Atlanta, and I got off and walked toward the terminal. I felt a bit stronger for the food and sleep I'd had, and I scanned the windows eagerly for my family.

Nobody was there! I expected Mom and Gypsy, the whole family to be waiting. I softened my discouragement with the thought that maybe they were waiting down at the luggage pickup. Of course, I didn't have any luggage, but they might have thought that was the place to be.

So I headed down that way, and a full-bearded man wearing a cross stepped toward me. Light flashed from his glasses into my eyes as he reached me and said, "Are you Barry Mayson?"

I looked at him, still walking, and said, "Who wants to know?" I didn't know this guy; he may have had on a cross, but I had never seen any preacher with a long beard!

He said, "My name is Dan McFarland; I'm a United Methodist pastor from East Point. Your mother called me from Charleston and asked me to come out to the airport to pick you up."

"I wonder why she didn't call my brother—he lives in East Point," I answered. "Wait a minute, I gotta make a few phone calls before I go with you."

"Okay," said McFarland.

First of all, I tried to call my mother. The phone rang and rang —no answer. I got frightened then: Had someone come and killed them all? What was happening?

I found my brother Rick's number in the book and called there. Now, this was five-thirty in the morning. So I roused him out of sleep and tried to tell him what was going on.

He thought I was messed up on something or drunk. I said, "Listen, you come out here! I don't know wha's goin' on—people been tryin' t' kill me . . ."

"Ain't nobody tryin' to kill you," he said.

"Look," I said, "jus' come out to the airport. I'm out here an' I'm . . ."

"Okay," he said wearily, "I'll come out."

I hung up and waited for him. I told Dan McFarland, "I ain't goin' nowhere till my brother gets here!" I didn't say much else to him until Rick got there.

When he came, Rick and I and the preacher went into an airport restaurant and ate breakfast. I shared some of what had gone down, and I'm sure Rick thought I was crazy. He said, "It ain't that bad, it ain't as bad as you think it is. Maybe you jus' imagined a lot of it."

I said, "Listen, Rick, I ain't imaginin' nothin'! I know wha's happenin', I know wha's goin' on!" *He thinks I'm loony*, I thought. *He thinks I los' my min'!*

Then Dan McFarland said, "Why don't you come home with me, Barry?" And somehow I knew he could understand where I was at better than Rick could, even though Rick was flesh and blood with me. So I said, "All right, preacher, I'm with you!"

We parted company with Rick, and Dan drove me out to his home, where we had a second breakfast, served up by his wife, Lois. And it was one good meal: eggs, bacon, toast and jelly, big glass of milk—more than I'd had in two days put together!

Then I took a shower, and they gave me some pajamas. I think they threw my raggedy old clothes away! My brother brought some over for me later.

That morning, before I went to bed, Dan reassured me of my salvation. He sat down with me in a little room in the basement and read the Bible to me. I cried again, as he told me that I was indeed saved, that the Lord had done it in me. How wonderful it was to hear again that I'd been given a new life, that I'd been, as he read, "translated from the kingdom of darkness into the kingdom of God's dear Son"!

Dan said, "Go to sleep now and get some rest." And I sacked out peacefully and slept like a baby until about two that afternoon.

I went over to my brother's house and spent the next night there. He still thought I was crazy, that I'd imagined everything, but it didn't bother me now. My mother called my brother's, and I talked with her. She told me, "We're just about to leave to come up. Everythin's gonna be fine, son. We got a house for you an' Fran t' stay in out in Alabama."

At first I thought, *She believes I'm crazy, too! She's gonna put me in a nuthouse!* And I said, "Mother, I ain't crazy, I didn't imagine nothin'!"

She said, "I know that, son, but you need to be with people who really care so you can get you some rest."

I said, "Lemme speak t' Gypsy!" She said, "Fran can't come to the phone . . ." I said, "Listen, I jus' wanta talk to my wife. If she's home, okay. If not, don't bother talkin' t' me." I wanted to make sure nobody was going to sneak me off to any insane asylum!

I hung up and Mom soon called back. This time Gypsy was on the phone. She told me she and Bari-Ann been staying with Doug Phillips, another minister. I asked her if she was okay; she said she was. Then I said, "Does Mother an' them think I'm crazy? D'you think I'm crazy?"

She said, "No, I don't think you're crazy!"

"Well, wha's this house about?"

She said, "It's jus' a place for us t' stay."

I started to believe her then, but I asked, "Y'all ain't tryin' t' con me an' get me into no nuthouse or nothin'?"

She laughed and said, "No, Barry, we wouldn't do that!"

"Well, all right," I said. "When am I gonna see you?"

"We'll be there tomorrow mornin'."

Early next morning, Rick drove me out to a private airport near Atlanta. He didn't tell me a thing about what was going on; it all seemed to be top secret! All the way, though, he seemed in a hurry, checking his watch as if we had to be there at a particular time.

Which we did! And when we pulled onto this strip, things began to move like clockwork. Just after we got there, my mother's husband, Frank Carder, drove up in his car with Gypsy, Bari-Ann, and Mom. There was hardly time for hugs, kisses, and a few words when "ROOOWRRR!"—a light plane landed right near us and out walked two men.

Only one introduced himself, as Jack McCulloch. Mom introduced us, Frank, and Rick. McCulloch said to me, "Okay, you ready?" I nodded, and in a few seconds we were waving to everybody and soaring over the treetops! Gypsy and I didn't have but a few dollars in our pockets. I had the clothes on my back, plus an extra pair of pants and some shirts Rick had given me. Gypsy had a few of her clothes and some for little Bari-Ann in a small suitcase. There we were in the back of that four-seater, headed for exactly where and what we had no idea!

Gypsy and I kissed there in the back seat, and I took my baby girl in my arms. I felt a joy so deep I hardly cared where I was going. Gypsy told me how different I looked without my beard and biker's clothes. She looked different, too, in a way I couldn't put into words just then. Her eyes were softer, the glaze and wildness were gone from them. It was like looking at the same face, but with a different person behind it.

She sort of commented on that when she said, "You know, I can't call you Barry-Barry no more."

I said, "Why not?"

"An' you shouldn't call me Gypsy, neither," she continued. "Your momma says that with Jesus in us, we're new people now, an' ol' thin's are all done away with. So you ain't Barry-Barry no more—an' I ain't Gypsy."

I gave that a few moments' thought. "You know somethin'?" I said at last. "If tha's true, then in a way, Barry-Barry's *dead*—an' Gypsy's *dead*, an' what you said come true!"

"What was that, Barry-Bar—jus' Barry!"

"Well, you said that when I died, you was gonna die, too.

Think about this: If the ol' *me's* gone an' the ol' *you's* gone, then we mus' of died together when Jesus came in!"

"Gee! I ain't thought o' that, *Barry!*" Fran said, laughing. She poked me and said, "See? Don't say I never get nothin' right!"

I shared with her some of what I'd been through during those heavy nights, and then she began to tell me her version of things as they'd happened on the other end:

"You know, I was on the way t' work that las' night, an' the muffler fell off the sports car! A couple guys rigged it up, sort of, but I drove it over to your mom's house an' asked her if Tanya could drive me over t' work, 'cause I was scared t' drive with the muffler off.

"Well, Mom says, 'No, sweetie, *I'll* take you!' I tried t' talk 'er out of it, but she had her way, an' we drove along an' jus' talked the usual stuff on the way over there.

"But when we pulled up in front, she says, 'You know, sweetie, I just don't believe you're gonna be comin' back to work here any-more after tonight. I believe this is gonna be your las' night.' An' I said, 'Well, that'd be great!'

"Later on she called me an' tol' me that you had quit the Hell's Angels, an' I was so scared! When I got off the phone an' tol' Ron-nie that I had to leave, Black was sittin' in the bar jus' lookin' at me. You know, I was always scared for him even t' talk t' me!

"So I went an' called me a cab, an' you know, it mus' of been God, because this guy come walkin' in the door, I mean, he was *huge, big, real* tall! An' it was like, I knew that was the cab driver, an' I jus' walked up to 'im an' looked up an' said, 'Are you the taxi?' An' he said, 'Yeah.' An' he tol' me t' get up in the front seat with him, an' he took me to your mom's.

"Well, she got me in the house an' tol' me what was goin' on. I wasn't speedin' my brains out, but when she tol' me t' go in the bed (this was after twelve o'clock at night), I tol' 'er, 'Ma, I took a diet pill!' But she said, 'Lemme pray for you.' An' she did, and do you know? I laid down an' I went t' sleep!

"That really did somethin' t' me, her prayin' for me. An' before I slep', she tol' me, 'Don't you worry about li'l Bari-Ann—I'm goin' t' get 'er. You jus' res'—I'll take care of everythin'!"

And as Fran went on, it became clear that that was what Mom

could see out: looked like solid hills and trees. "Man, this is the boonies!" I said.

McCulloch laughed and righted the plane. Before long we were leaning past a small town and heading downward. We landed at a little airport outside of Jacksonville, got off, and McCulloch said so long to Floyd, the other guy who'd flown with us. Floyd drove off in his car, and the rest of us piled into McCulloch's big Ford.

We soon skirted the town and headed for woods. "Where we goin'?" I asked McCulloch. "My place," said McCulloch. I asked him how he had managed to get connected with us, and he explained briefly how my mother had heard of him through connections with the Full Gospel Business Men.

Full Gospel . . . That was the kind of church Reverend Browner was from. And also, I remembered, that strange dinner I had gone to with my mother.

"What we gonna do up here?" I wondered aloud.

"Rest, keep out of sight, learn," McCulloch said. "And I have a deliverance ministry."

"Wha's that?"

"You'll find out!"

Before McCulloch pointed it out, I could see the house through an opening in the trees, way up on a hill. It looked big from where we were just then—and it got nothing but bigger as we got closer.

We turned left onto a narrow road and then made another left onto a gravel driveway. A couple of S-curves took us right into the front yard.

"Here we are!" McCulloch announced.

The house loomed above us, old, white, with pointed arches. As McCulloch got out, Fran whispered to me, "Looks jus' like one o' them ol' haunted houses in a horror flick!" I nodded agreement and stood up, taking in the surroundings.

There were trees everywhere in sight, a large pasture and horses to my left. From somewhere I could hear the clucking of chickens and a bleating sound that turned out to be goats. I took a big breath of the air, fresh with all kinds of smells, and thought to myself, *Boy, this is a perfec' hidin' place! They'll never fin' me!*

A pretty woman, obviously pregnant, who I guessed was McCulloch's wife, came onto the porch, and a small boy of four or so stuck by her side looking at us shyly. McCulloch introduced us to June and little Tommy, and then they showed us inside. The house was decorated bright but woodsy, early American style. In the living room, I noticed shelves of books with titles like *The Holy Spirit and You,* and *How to Release Your Faith.* Through a door, I could see a huge wooden table half-filling the kitchen.

McCulloch was a big, powerful-looking man with a personality to match. Everything about him spoke authority. It seemed clear without his even saying it that he was in charge there and would put up with no nonsense. I didn't know quite how to deal with him; authority had always been something I either ran from or fought tooth and nail. I found both those impulses doing flip-flops in me as he spoke.

"And this is the kitchen," he said. "June's in charge here, and she'll let you know about mealtimes and all the rest." Out the window I saw some stables that looked like they needed some repair and chickens pecking around a pen and eight or so goats wandering around a small pasture. The kitchen looked well stocked—and I still had some catching up to do on my eating!

Leading us out of the kitchen, McCulloch said to his wife, "Dear, I'm seeing to the goats; you see to our guests!"

"All right," she smiled pleasantly. June was certainly a good opposite to McCulloch: She had a quiet sweetness about her, but also a strength and a loyalty to her husband—and to his orders.

She showed us to a pleasant, slant-ceilinged room on the second floor. She'd fixed up a crib there for Bari-Ann, and a big bed for Fran and me, with plenty of towels and linens for our use. I noticed a cassette tape recorder below the lamp on a night table.

June left us to ourselves to settle in, telling us lunch would be in half an hour. She added that meals were served promptly at 7 A.M., 12 noon, and 6 P.M., and if we wanted to eat, we'd best be there on time.

As she went down the stairs, I groaned at the early hour of breakfast. It was clear we were going to have to do some adjusting.

I sat down on the bed and held Bari-Ann as Fran unpacked our few belongings, enjoying the broad view of the pastures and the woods beyond. "This is sure one great place to hide out," I said. Fran looked up from the baby things and said, "I got me a feeling it's gonna be more to it than that!"

How right she was! I got one of my first tastes of that fact after dinner. That had been all right, though I felt a little like I used to at my mother's, with the saying of the blessing before. Jack (as he insisted we call him) and June heard a lot of our story, nodding seriously throughout, and spoke to us for some time afterward about the Lord.

I can't say I understood much of it. Most of my conversation all these years had been about bikes and dope and loose women; the only time God or a church had been mentioned was in curse or in jest. But I found myself attracted to this talk about God. Here was a whole new world, and I was in it, so they told me, and I had a curiosity to learn all about it.

I said so at last, and Jack replied, "That's good, because tomorrow morning you'll get started."

"How do y' mean?" I asked.

He looked me straight in the eye and said, "Barry, I'd like you to go with me tomorrow morning to a breakfast!"

"Breakfas'?" I said. "What kin'? Where's it at?"

He said, "It's a Full Gospel Business Men's breakfast down in Jacksonville—at 7 A.M."

Seven A.M.? I thought. *I ain't used t' goin' t' bed before seven* A.M.! I stiffened up and said, "I ain't goin' t' breakfas' with no businessmen! I don't know nothin' about those kin' o' people!"

Jack leaned slightly in my direction and said quietly but commandingly, "Well, I'll tell you something: As long as you live in *my* house, you're going to do what I tell you to do, or you can hit the road!"

Well, I grumbled some, but he said, "It's not what you might think it is. It's just a bunch of men who love the Lord, and we have some fellowship and have breakfast, and we pray, and sometimes we have someone share."

Jack was a pretty demanding man, and I thank God for him. Plus, he was bigger than I was! He said, "You're going, whether you like it or not!" He had a grin on his face, but it didn't mean he meant any less business!

Being that I had no place to go and no money and couldn't imagine a better hideout, I figured I had to play along. "Okay," I said, "you win!"

Next morning found me in the car on the way to this breakfast, yawning all the way. Fran and June and the kids were in the back seat: There was a women's version of the same thing going on called Women's Aglow.

We got to this motel and went our ways. Jack took me to a dining room, and the smells of breakfast as the door opened encouraged me. There were some forty men there, shaking hands and hugging one another. One interesting thing I noticed as Jack introduced me to one guy and another: The men called each other "brother"—"Brother Jones" or "Brother Marsh"—almost the way we did as Hell's Angels.

But we soon settled down to a good breakfast, and afterward, various men began sharing about what Jesus had done in their lives. A lot of "Praise the Lords" and "Hallelujahs" came forth, and then the men sang some choruses about Jesus and raised hands and sang spontaneously, just as they had at the dinner I'd gone to with Mom.

But how different I felt about it! All this was still unfamiliar to me, but I no longer felt like a total stranger. I even tried raising my hands once myself.

And I found out that although these guys wore suits and looked straight, a lot of them had had problems in their lives, too. There were guys who had been nearly done in by alcohol and pills; guys who had made their life's work or money their god and then found it didn't satisfy; guys who had cheated on their wives and neglected their families; guys whose businesses had flopped, who'd gone bankrupt and started again; guys who had known fear and torment, who had struggled to find the meaning of manhood and failed.

So although they looked different from me, in a lot of ways, I could feel we were brothers under the skin. And we had something else in common, too: Jesus had come into our lives and saved us out of our trouble.

Then one guy got up and told how he had been a religious man all his life, a churchgoer, but he just didn't feel like God was real in his life until he got "baptized with the Holy Ghost."

I listened and I said to myself, *Holy Ghos'! Only ghos' I ever thought about is Casper the frien'ly ghos' or some spooks out in a graveyard. An' I don't believe in that stuff.*

But he began to talk then about the power of God, how when you received Jesus Christ as your Lord and Savior, you needed power from on high. "You need the Holy Spirit," he said, "to fill you with the fullness of God, so that you can walk the daily walk with Christ Jesus."

Now I began to get excited: I had always been power-hungry, and this guy was talking my language! I turned to Jack and said, "What is this he's talkin' about, this Holy Ghos' power?"

He said, "Well, it's a gift from God, and all you have to do is receive Him, and He'll come within you. And He'll fill you. And He has a lot of other gifts for you, too."

Just then the man speaking said, "Anyone who wants to be baptized by Jesus, come on up here!"

I stood up and told Jack, "I'm goin'!" He just smiled at me and said, "Go on!"

I went to the front, and the man said, "Friend, you want to be filled with the Holy Spirit?"

"You bet, man! I want that *power!*"

He said, "Well, you can have Him! All you have to do is just raise your hands up to God and just begin to praise Him and worship Him and ask Him to fill you, and He will!"

And I started to do that, the way I'd seen the men around me do it, and I heard them worshiping along with me. As I did, I felt a heat come all through me, like I was burning from inside! Then I felt a trembling that started in my feet and moved up my ankles to my knees. My legs began to wobble and shake, and all of a sudden, they just felt like rubber. A proud biker found himself sinking to his knees.

And when I touched the floor, I began to laugh, I began to cry, and I began to speak out words I couldn't understand. Waves of this heat and joy passed all through me. And I don't know how long I stayed in that state.

But when I came back to myself, I heard myself talking away in this strange language—and I said, "What in the worl' is this?" Nobody had told me anything about "speaking in tongues"! It freaked me out!

And this brother said, "Hey! Don't you know what's happening?"

I said, "I don't know—what was that?"

He said, "Friend, that was the Holy Spirit speaking through you—and that's a direct line to your Father! You can use that as a prayer language. You get off by yourself and any time Satan tries to attack you, you start praying in the Spirit, and the devils *flee!*"

I said, "Hey, tha's all right!" And I went right back to praising and worshiping God in the Spirit!

I was never quite the same after that. When we went back to Jack's, I opened up the Bible, and the Holy Spirit began to teach me, and I was like a sponge.

God began to show me things, too. One of the first was about that funny little man on the airplane and what he'd said about the plastic cup. God showed me that *I* was that cup, hard, ugly, and that way for a long time. And I got reduced to nothing. And then Jesus Christ came into my life and the Holy Spirit filled me, and that *fire* began to do a work on me, molding and shaping me, taking all the old out of me, and putting newness in, renewing my mind daily! It wasn't all going to happen overnight—but the work had started, and was never going to stop!

Next God showed me that those "cops" back at the airport weren't FBI men. I read in the Bible, Genesis 18 and 19, that angels of the Lord came down to visit Abraham, and they didn't have wings and fly around; they looked just like ordinary men. They left Abraham and went to Sodom and Gomorrah, and they still looked like men. And in Hebrews 13:2 it said that we should be careful how we treat strangers, because we "might be entertaining angels unaware." And I became convinced that those five "cops" were angels sent by God to protect me from those Hell's Angels. I believe it to this day.

When I shared this with Fran, she told me something my mother had related to her the day I met Jesus: While I was still at the airport, my mother got a call from her sister, who told her she'd had a vision, but didn't know what it was all about and thought Mom could help explain it. She said, "Mary, I saw a burnin' bush. And inside the bush was a figure tryin' to get out, but he couldn't! An' on the outside of the burnin' bush was a whole lot of other figures tryin' to get in, an' they couldn't." And the Lord had used that to encourage Mom about the trouble I was in.

Fran said, "Mom showed me a Bible verse that said somethin' like, 'The angels of the Lord camp aroun' those who fear 'im, an' He delivers them!'"

And I said, "Tha's it! Tha's what was happenin' right then!" I gave God special thanks that night for what he had done. Mom knew that that vision was of me and those Hell's Angels all around me there in California!

Fran, it turned out, had gotten filled with the Holy Spirit that same morning at the Women's Aglow. And after that, we wanted all we could get of teaching and the Bible. Jack and June proceeded to feed us well, with cassette teaching tapes of men like Houston Miles, Gerald Derstine, Bob Mumford, Kenneth Hagin, and we really began to learn! At first, for example, I had only known that Jesus was the Way; now I learned that he was God, that He had risen from the dead and brought me into life when He rose! I learned how His blood had washed away my sins, and that He had the power to deliver me, though I didn't know yet what *that* meant.

When Fran and I weren't eating, we spent most of the time off to ourselves, listening to the tapes and reading up in our room, or taking walks around the countryside. I slept a lot, sometimes almost all day, building myself up with rest from all I'd been through.

Jack and June didn't put up with any nonsense, though we tried some. Fran hadn't brought any cigarettes with her, and mine had disappeared with my old clothes. Both of us had been heavy smokers and still felt a need for them. So one day on a drive with Jack, I got him to let me out at a store, and I snuck a can of Prince Albert and some cigarette papers under my coat. Fran and I would roll makeshift smokes and blow them out the open window. That sneaky ruse didn't last too long—but I'll get to that by and by.

Our tape education continued as we learned about faith and the thousands of promises of God to His people, and who we were in Christ. I began to catch a glimpse of the richness that God had for me.

And I came to a grudging appreciation of Jack McCulloch. I still rankled at his authority, but I could also recognize his love for the both of us. Jack was no candy Christian; he meant every word he said and loved God with all his heart and did exactly what he thought was best for us. Every morning, I remember, when Fran and I would come down the stairs for breakfast, he would say, "Fran, have you got something to tell Barry?" And she'd have to tell me she loved me. And she'd have to tell *Jack* she loved *him!* He could sense, I guess, some of the lingering resentment Fran felt for his authority.

I couldn't see it at first, because I was thinking so much about what a great hideout it was and how and when I was going to move somewhere and get a job and start life over, but I was just like a little baby, listening to tapes, falling asleep, eating, being told what to do. I was just taking, without realizing anything about maturing in the things of God or growing up. Nevertheless, I was learning and growing quickly. And it was like that for about a week and a half.

Fran and I weren't used to being told what to do, and we spent some of our time in the room talking about Jack and June. "Boy, they sure are mean, ain't they?" Fran said. I said, "Yeah, but it won't be long till we're outa here! We'll get it all together an' be gone."

But before we left, we found out what "deliverance" meant! Not long after we'd been baptized with the Holy Spirit, Jack came to me and told me I needed "deliverance from demons." Now, I knew nothing from here to there about demons! But he shared with me that these were invisible, evil spirits, who manifested themselves in people in the form of lying and hatred and lust and a whole bunch of other spirits. Jack was very much into the whole thing—and not much else. If he saw something in you, he'd say, "There it is! A spirit of hate!" or whatever.

Now, I thought he was crazy, but God used him in that area of my life. I asked him if he was playing some sort of head game with me. He assured me he wasn't. He opened the Bible and read to me about how Jesus drove out evil spirits. And he told me that Jesus said some deliverance needed prayer and fasting. Jack wanted me to fast for three days and pray—and I didn't know what fasting was! But I said, "Yeah, okay!"

I didn't find out till later that I wasn't supposed to eat. I just ate away, and three days later, Jack came to me again and said, "Are you ready for some deliverance?"

I said, "Yeah!"

He said, "Have you been fasting and praying up?"

I just wanted to be cooperative, partly in hopes that Fran and I could "pass the course" and hit the road soon, and I said, "I sure have." I had no idea what was going on.

"Okay," he said. "Tonight!"

After supper, June and Fran cleared off the big oak table and stood nearby in the kitchen. Jack sat down across from me and began to tell me more about demon manifestations. He described one lady who had a demon that made her feet swell up like pig's feet and her face like a pig's face.

I thought, *Boy, this guy's stupid! This is crazy!*

He said some people puked the demons out, some spit them out, some coughed them out; there were all kinds of ways devils came out! Sometimes they came out screaming and fighting.

I couldn't begin to imagine what he was talking about, but I knew I wanted to get the whole thing over with. So I said, "All right, le's do it!"

So Jack got me a big paper bag and set it on the floor to my right. He said, "If you have to throw up, do it into that bag right there. Or just spit 'em out!" I shrugged and thought nothing of it.

Suddenly he shouted, "I come against you, spirit of Lust! Come out of this man in the name of Jesus!" I just sat there, and he yelled, "Spit it out, Barry, spit it out!"

To make him happy, I faked a cough and a spit into the bag. In my own mind I thought, *Either this guy thinks* I'm *a turkey—or* he's *a turkey!*

But I played the game as he came against a spirit of Lying and a spirit of Homosexuality, coughing and spitting them out. Then Jack began to get more intense. He shouted, "The blood of Jesus, the blood of Jesus! Barry, you've got to come against these yourself! Don't beg the devil, command him to come out!" I did my best to follow along. In between spirits, he kept telling Fran that she was next!

He came then to what he called the spirit of Hate. He began to pray, and I prayed along, and I thought, *Well, I'll jus' spit this ol' hate right out!*

But all of a sudden, my body started shaking all over. I had no control over myself. Jack came around behind me and put his hands on my shoulders. He said, "You foul spirit of Hate, you have to leave! You can't hurt this man; he's a child of God! Now you get out and leave this room, this house, and go back to the pit you came from!"

As my body continued to shake, this voice came from me, screaming, "NO! NO!" At that moment I knew that this thing was real! And it seemed as if the part of me that was the real me leaped straight out of my body, and I was looking down from the ceiling at what was going on!

The strange voice kept shrieking out of me, "NO! NO! NO!" and Fran ran out of the room, terrified. At that moment, my body picked up that huge table and shook it like it was a feather! Jack never let go of me. He shouted, "In Jesus' name, you have to leave him! You have to go! Be gone right now!"

And at that "Now!" I felt myself whooshing earthward. I felt as though I was crashing back into my own body, then I was inside it, and the impact knocked me over! I heard the heavy table thud as I fell right out of the chair onto the floor. I tried to get up, but I couldn't I was so weak.

Jack said, "Just stay there, Barry! Just lay there and rest! That was a battle going on in you—and you're free!"

I had felt the love of Jesus when I got saved, and I had felt some of His cleansing fire and power when I was filled with the Holy Ghost. But now I knew the tremendous force of His power to deliver!

Fran got some deliverance, too, but this incident frightened her so much, she didn't go through all of it that Jack had in mind for her. But I went on, and Jack over two nights went through the dictionary and called more out: the spirits of Unforgiveness, Envy, Rebellion, and on and on, though that Hate was the last really violent manifestation.

All of this impressed me so much that for a while, I was really bent out of shape on a demon kick! I got so one-sided, all I wanted to do was read about demons. Jack warned me not to get wrapped up with Satan, to concentrate on Jesus. But I reasoned that the more I knew about devils, the better I could fight them. It took me a while to discover that it works just the other way: The more you learn about Jesus, the more you learn the authority you have in Him!

This deliverance thing served to throw a good measure of the fear of God into me—and the fear of the devil! Fran had told me that wasn't my voice coming out of my mouth when I was shaking head to toe. And after that, I clung closer to Jesus. I said, "Lord, I don't want no part o' that other guy; I'm stickin' with *you!*" It got me communicating with the Lord constantly and buried in His Word.

It also got me looking around for devils! I'd see something in Fran that wasn't good, and I'd say, "You need some deliverance!" And she'd holler back at me, "No, it's you that need the deliverance!" And after some back-and-forth like this, we'd sometimes end up laughing!

Fran didn't like my Prince Albert smokes too much, so she somehow did without. But I kept it up for a while, undiscovered. But one morning while Fran and I were out for a walk, June was cleaning up the room, and she found some butts that I'd left around. To her, they looked like they might be pot, and later she confronted us.

I kind of laughed and told her what they were, just Prince Albert out of the can. But the incident put a bit of a strain in our relationship, and Fran and I began to feel maybe it was time to move on.

So later that day, we sat down and wrote my mother a letter, telling her we wanted to leave and maybe stay with Aunt Helen in Augusta, as the whole family was supposed to meet there for

Thanksgiving anyway. The same day we mailed the letter, we received a letter from Mom, saying that she felt we should be leaving there and moving to Augusta. I took this as confirmation of my feelings and shared it with Jack and June.

They thought we needed to stay longer, but I said, "I think we need to leave. We prayed about it, an' we feel God wants us to go." Jack said, "Well, if you feel it's God's will, we can't keep you here."

And I know it *was* God's will: If we'd stayed much longer, all we'd have been doing was casting out devils everyplace we went! Not that I think there's anything wrong with casting out devils; I'm glad some were cast out of me! But God had other things in store for us.

My sister Tanya and her fiancé, Randy Foret, stopped by and picked us up. They were in Bible school down in Pensacola, Florida, now, and on their way to Augusta for the Thanksgiving holiday.

With some extra bags of Bibles, books, and tapes in hand, we said our good-byes and gave heartfelt thanks to the McCullochs for all their kindness to us. As we drove down the road, I cast one last glance at the old "Haunted House," as we called it ever after. It *had* had one Ghost in it—the Holy Ghost! And were we ever glad He'd been haunting there!

26

"Sugar Shack" and Beyond

My grandma had lived in the little "Sugar Shack," as we called that furnished shed at Aunt Helen's backyard, before she passed on. And it proved sweet to us, too, as we learned to grow in the Lord.

After the joyous family reunion at Thanksgiving, Fran and I and Bari-Ann stayed on there until New Year's. I worked around the yard and the house—and for a week and a half with my Uncle Marcus on a painting job.

That was the first work I'd done in years (honest work, at least!), and to my amazement, it felt good!

Fran stayed around the house, talking with Aunt Helen. That woman ministered a lot to both of us. She was strong in the Lord and really knew the Word of God. And each night she'd come back to the Sugar Shack and hold a little Bible study with us. We'd sit there and read, and I called Job "job" and pronounced all the kings' names wrong, but through it all, I kept studying. A hunger for God's Word grew in me. I just couldn't get enough.

Before long, I felt as though the Lord was nudging me to go to Liberty Bible College down where Tanya was in Pensacola. So I wrote the school a letter telling them of my wish. They sent me application forms, which I filled out as well as I could and sent along.

In another letter I shared my testimony about the Hell's Angels and how God delivered me from them, and the school sent back a letter asking whether I thought my coming down would present any risk to my sister Tanya's life. I wrote back telling them that I believed God would protect me, my family, and my sister from all harm, that His angels were encamped around me, and that I feared nothing from the Hell's Angels. They finally told me to come on down.

About all I had to my name was my Harley-Davidson (which Mom and her husband had brought down with them at Thanksgiving), a hundred dollars saved from my painting job with Uncle Marcus, and the few clothes and belongings we had carted with us from the McCullochs'. How we were going to get to Florida was a mystery that was solved when Frank Carder gave us a '63 Ford van. All he promised us was that it ran! I decided to rent a trailer and tow my bike down with us.

It was cold when we set out just before New Year's. That old van had no heater, and we nearly froze to death! It was the middle of the night, and rain came pouring down—and the windshield wipers didn't work! The taillights went out, and I had to get out and fix them. We worked on that old van more than we drove it!

But all through the trip, we were praying and praising God, bundled up in blankets, our teeth chattering away! "Praise God! Praise you, Lord! We're gonna hit some warm weather soon!"

High as our spirits were, we never did get that warm weather! But we drove on that whole night, stopping off and on, keeping the old van going as best we could.

My sister Tanya had given us directions to the house we were going to live in, and when we rolled into Pensacola about ten that morning, the van began to overheat. It sputtered along for a block or so and just stopped!

We went across the street and knocked on the door. I asked the people there which house was the one we were supposed to live in, because I knew it was in that area somewhere. "Why, you're parked right in front of it!" the neighbor said.

It turned out they were the people who were holding the keys to the house for us!

The place was being rented by a minister friend of my sister who had to go back to school for a few months. It was roomy and nicely furnished, with a big backyard, and the first month's rent was paid in advance.

And it's a good thing it was! For about two months, we lived on the about twenty-five dollars a week my mother sent us to "help out."

I couldn't get a job. Nobody would hire me because of my past. I learned that the Christian life wasn't going to be all goodies, and I'd have to undergo some real tests of my faith.

I wouldn't lie, and everyplace I went (and I went to bunches of them), I'd look over the application: How much experience have you had? Where was your last employment? Dates for this and that going back ten years?

And I'd put down, "United States Army, discharged 1966, Ford plant until 1968, from then on, just a bum! Rode Harley-Davidsons and worked in nightclubs, etc." At the end I always wrote that I'd given my life to Jesus Christ, I knew my past was messed up, but I wanted to serve the Lord, and I needed this job!

You can imagine the response, time after time: "Well, uh, Mr. Mayson, uh, that is . . . uh, if we need you, you know, well, we'll definitely get in touch with you! Uh, we'll, uh, keep your application on file in case, you know, anything comes up!"

Nothing ever did, though I always had an opportunity to share and give a witness to what Jesus had done in my life.

After a while, this routine got to be a battle for me. I loved the Lord. I really loved Him. I had enough in me to know that God would be faithful to me. I knew people wouldn't understand, but at first I was pressing on, excited to tell people what God had done for me, regardless of the outcome.

Eventually, though, I began to get discouraged. On the one hand, the Bible said that if any man didn't provide for his own household, he was worse than an unbeliever. On the other, I'd sit there holding my application, waiting for an interview, thinking, *I'll jus' go in there an' tell them the same ol' story, an' they're not gonna hire a guy like me! Who's gonna hire an* ex-Hell's Angel? *Who's gonna trus' 'im? Who's gonna give* him *a chance?*

And I finally got so depressed I just quit going out. When I started to get down, Fran got down. She began to worry, and soon we were arguing, at each other's throats all the time, accusing each other of needing to be resaved or "needing deliverance," and on and on!

At last, I just told God, "I quit!" I went into the bedroom and lay across the bed, and I just cried, completely broken. I said, "God, I don't know what I'm gonna do! I jus' quit! If I can't get a job, how in the hell am I gonna take care o' this family You give me?" I cussed God out and argued with Him.

Being three months or more old in the Lord, I still didn't have my mouth cleaned up. And I was more than hopping mad!

But it was then that my mom came down to visit my sister Tanya, and we put her up at our house. She heard me going on like this with God one Sunday morning. She came in and started telling me, "You need to go before the Lord about this job business."

I said, "Whatta you think I *been* doin'?" And soon I was arguing with *her!* I ran down my whole list of gripes against God, employers, and everyone else.

She said, "Well, we can talk some more about it after church this mornin'."

I said, "I ain't never goin' back t' no church! I quit! I don't care! God ain't listenin' t' me anyway! I don't even know why He's got me here!" And I went on in my self-pity until she walked out.

But it wasn't a few minutes before she was back. She said, "God hasn't forgotten you, son. These trials and troubles come on us t' build us up, not tear us down! Let me tell you somethin': Most of the time, all God's waitin' for is just for us to quit strugglin' to make good things happen on our own an' just give up! He don't want *us* to solve our problems; *He* wants to be the solution to our problems.

"Barry, you may of done the right thing in givin' up. 'Cause now, if you'll just turn to Him, you might be really willin' to give Him a chance to fix things up."

I said, "Mother, are you sure about all that?"

She said, "Son, have I ever steered you wrong about the Lord?"

"No, Mother."

"Well, I ain't about to start now. You come on and get offa

that bed and come with your family to church. You been a tough
man out in the world—now be a tough man for God!"

I said, "You know, it's a lot harder t' be a man for God,
Mother."

"I ain't a man, but I imagine that's so, son," she said. "But a
man's what God saved you to be, so it's time to get up and *be* it!"

I said, "You know, Mother, it's good to be able to look at you
with tears in my eyes."

She dabbed at her own and said, "That's one of the joys a
Christian man can have, son. God don't min' it."

I sat there for a minute and then said, "All right, I'll go!"

Mom said, "Thank God! We'll all be waitin' outside!"

Quickly, I got cleaned up. She was right; I ought to go to
church. I had been, all along since we'd been in Pensacola. And I'd
talked with the pastor and my elder there about my need for a job,
even filled out an (other!) application at the church's job-placement
service. It hadn't done any good.

I went to the church service, then, but with my grudge against
God pretty well intact. I hadn't really understood what Mom had
said to me about giving up. But as far as God was concerned, I
guess I showed Him just enough faith by getting up and going to
His house that morning.

I don't remember most of that service; I cried through almost
all of it. I felt the love of Jesus all around me, and I realized I'd
been a fool. My fury at Him had been so wrong—I had shut myself
from His love, I hadn't been truly thankful to Him for the way He
had provided for my family, I was so wrapped up in bitterness over
not being the instrument He was using to do it. He tenderly assured me that I *had* been providing for my family, just by being
obedient to Him in seeking work. Where I'd gone wrong was in
quitting. But getting a job itself was in His hands, not mine.

My tears now weren't for myself, but for the grief I had caused
Him in doubting His love and His wisdom to know best for me. An
altar call was given for anyone with needs to be prayed for, at the
end of the service, and I went forward.

Liberty College chapel was a big fellowship. Twenty elders
were there waiting to pray for the people. I don't remember which
one I talked with, but I laid the whole story out to him. I finished,

"I jus' need a job, I don't care what it is, washin' dishes, or what, I don't care what it is, I need a job." And he said, "We're gonna pray!"

After the prayer was done, I turned back to my seat, and a Bible student I knew named Mike Cassidy reached out and grabbed my arm and said, "Hey, Barry!"

I said, "Yeah!"

And he said, "You need a job, man?"

My grin was about as wide as the church door. "Yeah, I sure do!"

"Well, I think I know where you can get one!" he said. "Tomorrow morning I'm gonna check on a job myself—they need some painters. You done any painting?"

Well, I had done that little bit with Uncle Marcus; outside of that, my experience was limited to pointing spray cans at my Harley-Davidsons.

But I was willing! I said, "Yeah, a little."

"Well, come on out with me tomorrow morning, and we'll see if we can't get a job. I'll drop by at seven-thirty and pick you up."

"Okay, man."

My enthusiasm wasn't sky-high. Part of my mind figured, "Here I go, I'll truck out there again, fill out another application, same ol' routine!"

Mom and Fran were a lot more excited than I was, but I did know I *had* given up and really laid it all in God's hands this time. If it was His will that I get a job, He'd see to it.

The next morning, Mike and I walked onto this huge apartment-complex construction site and found the painting foreman. He looked us up and down and said, "You guys wanta work?"

"Yeah," said Mike, "we sure do!"

I said, "You bet, mister!"

The foreman said, "Okay, start tomorrow morning. I need for you to fill out an application—just for our records—but you be here tomorrow morning at seven o'clock, and we're gonna start you out painting." He waved a hand around. "We need all these complexes painted."

We went over to the office trailer, filled out applications, and that's all there was to it. It was just that simple! And how Mike and I rejoiced on the way home!

But that was nothing to the jumping up and down that started when I *got* home. I told Fran, "God answered my prayer, an' He taught me a lesson. He wanted t' show me that it wasn't no *man* that held the key! Mike didn't hear me talkin' 'bout a job there in church. *God* put it on his heart. An' God showed me I can trus' *Him t'* take care o' this family's business!"

The real thrill was the way God had worked it all out. It wasn't the job so much—I was glad I had a job (though I didn't yet *like* work apart from knowing I needed it). The exciting part was how God answered that prayer just like that, from Sunday to Monday morning! Bam! The whole thing was directly from God! No middleman: It was straight from my prayer to the throne of God and straight from there to Mike Cassidy! The whole thing just blew my mind!

I spilled a lot of paint learning how, and I was slow at first. But Mike had done a lot of painting, and he was a real encouragement to me. He wasn't the kind of guy who got down on you. He was always praying in the Spirit, singing to the Lord, full of love and compassion.

Mike was a single guy, about twenty-five, who'd been going to Liberty for about two years. God really put him and me together for that time in my life. We'd work side by side, and I came to share everything in my life with him: problems at home with Fran, disagreements with my bosses and neighbors, wrestlings I was having with the Lord. He'd just laugh and tell me what the Bible had to say about my situations and frustrations—never condemning me for my feelings or shortcomings.

What a difference this was from my relationships with my "brothers" in the biking world! I had thought then that I had a closeness with those guys. But it was really shallow compared with what I came to have with Mike. Among bikers, I could only show a tiny part of myself: To admit I was weak or had problems was to court danger or humiliation, at least. I always had to be tough, on top of things. There was no love or concern for "brothers" as people: It was only, could they turn me on, did being with them make me feel good, did they add to my power, could they do anything for old number one—me!

But I had nothing to offer Mike but a mass of confusion and problems that needed God's help to sort out. Not that Mike had it all together; he had problems in his life that he shared with me. And we'd pray together and laugh and cry together and work out these problems together.

That old tough guy I used to be began to look more and more like a cardboard dummy, just a one-sided shell of a man. I could start to *feel* now, let myself *love*, let myself *care* about others, let myself sympathize with others' weaknesses without condemning them. It was glorious to begin to feel the joy of being a whole person!

Mike taught me a lot of Scriptures through the songs he sang as we worked along. And not too much time passed before I began to give back to him, mostly by accident at first, things that blessed him! I'd say something sort of stupid, but he'd brighten up and say, "Yeah! Yeah! That's right!"

We had to climb up these high scaffolds, and I remember once going up and I was saying, "Praise God for this climbin'!"

Mike said, "What're you praising God for? Up and down on these scaffolds all day?"

But I said, "Not only is God feedin' me spiritually on this job, an' He's renewin' my min', but He's makin' me strong an' healthy, too, workin' me out with this climbin'!"

And that ministered to Mike. I went on, "Everybody in the Hell's Angels was always pumpin' iron, tryin' t' get strong an' healthy! Man, it's jus' as easy to *work*, to climb up this thing an' get pumped up! An' you do somethin' useful to boot!"

Mike'd get excited about that kind of thought I'd share. It helped make the work go better for him, too. All in all, the six months we spent together made for a lot of growth in both of us.

I started going to Bible school at night a month after this job started. That was quite an experience! I felt like an old man sitting in with a bunch of kids! The first class I took was called Family Relationships, and I took it with Fran, which was a real comfort in helping me get started.

But I felt uncomfortable, like everyone was looking at me. And the instructor—I thought he could read my mind, his insights were so on target. When he hit home about some mistake I knew I was making in my marriage, tears would come to my eyes. I could never look him in the eye, I was convinced he knew me so well! He was an older man, a pastor, and he just had too much authority.

Next came Genesis. I sat right in front—I knew if I sat in the back, I'd probably fall asleep or my mind would drift! Now, I looked around a lot, and I saw a lot of people sleeping. And after a while, I couldn't understand how anybody could be bored—what I was hearing was so exciting!

I had always cheated on the books back in high school, and I never did crack one during my brief stay at college. So I had all kinds of trouble writing and trying to take notes. But I didn't really feel out of place. In fact, I felt I belonged there more than some of the goof-offs! And yet they were making A's and B's and I was getting D's!

But God was getting my heart prepared a lot quicker than He was my head! I couldn't get much head knowledge. I couldn't remember a lot of things. But I was studying hard, even if not much sank in—and in later years, the Holy Spirit brought a lot of it to remembrance!

I'd take three-by-five cards to work and study at odd moments, and Fran and I would go over the material, and I'd go to the school on a test day, the teacher would slap down that test, and I'd draw a blank. I'd read it over three or four times, trying to understand it. I'd sometimes glance over at another student's paper to see how to spell something.

I'd pray, "Oh, Lord, help me with this!"—all the way through. And when I did know the answer, I couldn't write it down the way the teacher wanted it. All the rest of the students would walk out in an hour and a half. At the end of three hours, there would be old Barry, still with one answer to go. The teacher'd come and tap me on the shoulder, and I'd scribble something down and hand it in.

I'd go home at night crying. Fran'd say, "How the test go?" And I'd say, "I don't understan' it, I don't know why God's got me here! I ain't no student!"

But Fran found a verse in Hebrews that gave me real encouragement. It said that in the last days, God wasn't going to write His laws on tablets of stone, like the Ten Commandments; He was going to write them on men's hearts! And right after she read that, it was like God spoke to me in my mind, saying, "Don't worry about man's tests—you just keep passing *My* tests, son! That's what counts!" That filled me with such joy, I was totally freed!

I went back to classes and just said to the teachers, "I can't listen to you an' take notes, too! I can't even read my own writin'; it's like writin' 'in tongues'! So I'm jus' gonna sit here an' let the Holy Spirit teach me. I'll listen t' you, an' what the Holy Spirit speaks in my heart, tha's what I'll write down!"

And that's how I D'd my way along through school!

27

Hauling the Weight

For a man who'd spent most of his life running from responsibility, I now found myself with piles of it. A lot of times I felt myself champing at the bit. A lot of times, I didn't know how I was going to make the bills. I was bringing home one hundred dollars a week.

But God was faithful to us. A lot of people dropped groceries at the door, often just in time! Sometimes I had to decide whether to buy food or pay the rent or pay the school bill. I'd holler over those school bills: "Don't they unnerstan'? They're supposed t' be men o' God. Here I am tryin' t' learn God's Word, an' they keep writin' me these letters askin' for money!" I didn't handle that kind of pressure very well—sometimes I felt like just telling them to stick their Bible college in their ear!

There were times when I looked back and thought about all the money I'd had in the old biker life. But then I read about how the Lord took the children of Israel out of Egypt and then they murmured against Him. And that reminded me of what I was doing, and I cut it out.

There was just too much in this life, with all the problems I had to face, to think of giving up. Sure, I could try to go back. I might even be able to throw my tattoo at somebody in Pensacola and play a con and say, "Yeah, I'm down here on business," and get some drugs fronted to me and get to know who the big shots were and start hanging around again.

But in my heart I knew I would never do it. I knew what was at the end of that road: death! Every time the Enemy came and tried to show me everything I could have, the Holy Spirit showed me where it would end up and what He'd brought me out of, and I'd praise God and press on, no matter what the trials were—even when I had to sell my bike to make a school bill.

After six months on the job, Mike left, and another brother in the Lord took his place. I wish I could say our relationship went as smoothly as things had with Mike, but they didn't.

Now, having been there all that time, I pictured myself as the man of experience, the boss. But Matt didn't see it that way, because he'd been painting for five years! But that didn't matter to me: I was there first, and that was what counted. I knew just as much as he did, I thought—I knew how to paint!

The old ego popping up again!

Well, we went together like a couple of pieces of sandpaper. I learned that just *because* a guy was a brother in the Lord, it didn't guarantee you were going to like him! God put some people in our lives so we would learn to trust Him for supernatural grace to get along with them!

He'd tell me I was painting too slowly—and I'd tell him he was painting too sloppily! I knew I was supposed to do good to a brother and overcome evil by doing good. But it seemed all he and I saw in each other was each other's faults. Next thing we knew, we were grabbing each other, fixing to duke it out, eyeball to eyeball, shirt to shirt, fist to fist!

We yelled and screamed at each other. I found myself saying words I never thought would come from my mouth again: "I'm gonna kill you! I'll punch your eyes out, I'll break your nose!" And he was yelling the same back to me.

But things didn't end up the way they would have in my biker days. All of a sudden, he and I looked at each other, and it was like an invisible wall sprang up between us, and we looked across it and saw each other as we were. I said to him, "Man, I know this ain't from God! The devil's got in here! I'm sorry, forgive me, man!"

He said the same, and we shook hands. It wasn't the last time. But every time, God intervened, and I walked away and apologized later. We sat down together and got into God's Word and resolved our differences. And this was sure evidence to me that I was indeed a new creature, this being able to step back from the edge of a fight and make it up with a brother!

Matt and I never did get really close. The job lost some of the joy it had when Mike worked with me. But at least I learned I could work with a brother I didn't like that much without getting out of hand. I was in God's hands now, and all things were indeed new!

Added to my weight was Rusty coming down just when I started Bible school in March. Rusty had been told Fran was his sister, and thought so until he was ten years old! But we wanted him, the Lord told us he was *our* responsibility, *our* son, and we were to raise him in the things of the Lord. We went to his grandparents and told them this, and they didn't want to let him go. But we went to court, and finally he was allowed to come down.

At first, his reaction was total rebellion. He hated me. I wasn't *his* daddy. Sometimes he'd tell his mother he hated her, and I'd take the belt and tear his butt up! I'd say, "You don't ever talk to your mother that way!" It was an effort, but I began to train him.

He was a big, overgrown baby when he started getting trained. He'd had no discipline at all. When he'd gotten in from school at his former home, her father and mother were working, and Rusty was used to just running out and doing his thing! Sometimes he didn't even go to school, and his grandma never knew it. So he'd failed a grade and been in a bad school to boot.

So we had some struggles coming to "unnerstan' one another"! But slowly, with a lot of "knowledge applied to the seat o' learnin'," he began to come around!

It was something as well, me changing from an "old man"—to a husband!

I had thought nothing of beating Fran up in the old days. And

you know, the Lord changes what's in you, but not your basic
shape! I still had my temper and anger, and they'd flare up occa-
sionally. I'd look at her sometimes and want to hit her. But the
Lord would shout loudly in my ear, "N-O-O-O!" And I'd look at
her and grit my teeth and say, "Woman, God needs t' do some work
on you, I ain't kiddin'! You need some deliverance!"

It was a real struggle. But God promised to give me a spirit of
power and love and a sound mind, and it was that sound mind that
gave me the self-control to keep my hands off of her. Not that she
made it easy! She'd get to yelling and screaming at me, and she had
never gotten away with that stuff before! In the old life, that was
her ticket to a black eye or broken bones. Now I couldn't!

And I'd use that! I'd say, "See? See how you are? Before I was
saved, you know I'd a hurt you! But now that I'm saved, you takin'
advantage of me 'cause you know I won't hurt you. You jus' scream
an' yell at me an' treat me like a dog!"

And she knew it! I'd say at last, "Well, I'm gonna pray for
you!"

And she'd yell some more, and I'd just get off on my own.
She'd go her way, and an hour or so later, she'd come over and say,
"I'm sorry, Barry." I'd say I was sorry, too, and we'd make up.

With all the new strains and problems, we overcame, and God
set about building a wonderful new relationship. We'd get on our
knees together and pray that God would help us to have the kind of
marriage He wanted. At times we were frustrated, with each other,
with Rusty, and we bowed down over the supper table and cried,
"God! We jus' don't know how to raise this kid! We don't know
how t' keep *ourselves* under control! Please help us! Help us love
one another and respec' one another!"

He always did. And through it, I learned, I who had prided
myself on my independence, to, like a child, be dependent on God.
God got to be the center of our home.

Then Ron and Jim came, too! The Lord led me to write
Maureen letters, telling her how sorry I was that I'd been a louse
and asking her to forgive me. I told her that I loved the kids and
wanted to help them and how much I wanted to see them again. I

asked if they could come down and stay with us for the summer, and to my surprise, she said yes!

Fran and I kept them the whole summer, and when it was over, I told Maureen that there was a good Christian school in Pensacola, and I wanted to keep them a while longer. And again, she said yes! I expect it was kind of a vacation for her; Fran and I were sure glad to have them.

Ron and Jim were nine and eleven when they came down. We piled them along with Rusty in bunkbeds, with little Bari-Ann in a room of her own.

We'd moved just before that, to a place just down the street, with chickens and goats and horses in the backyard. The next-door neighbors, Herman and Janice, were the landlords, and we soon had some run-ins with them.

They had no truck with Jesus, and one night, Herman got to wrestling with me. I was sharing the Word of God with him, and all of a sudden he grabbed me by the throat. In the old days, I would have tried to kill him on the spot. But now, I put my hands on his shoulders and started coming against the devil in him in the name of Jesus! "Devil," I cried, "you loose this man right now!" And all of a sudden, his hands just dropped. Tears ran down his cheeks, and he said, stunned, "Jesus Christ *is* Lord!" The struggles didn't end, but he was a lot more respectful after that!

And it was a lesson in responsibility just moving in there! When we opened the door, roaches jumped out on us! Swarms of ants had made the house their hotel.

So we got in there and cleaned that place up! We swept it, mopped it, sprayed it, and shoveled roaches out! We had a few pieces of furniture by then, but we used benches with boards across and telephone cable spools for tables and chairs. It was something else! But it was home! Hot in the summer, cold in the winter, but we got by!

Ron and Jim grew in body and in the Lord. They weren't used to close discipline either. They had to learn to live in a crack-the-whip situation, and it wasn't easy for them—or us! But the real change in them came in church, where I could see the tears come from their eyes as they learned about the love of Jesus! And all three of them, Rusty, Ron, and Jim learned a lot about the Lord at Christian school.

Just before Christmas, Jim wanted to go back home. He was homesick, he said, as we talked it over. He felt that in a way that I had taken him from his mother.

So both he and Ron went to be with their mother for Christmas. Jim stayed; Ron came back. Ron liked his friends and the Christian school. He said he could pretty well endure not eating steak to be with us and his friends! He stayed with us till the end of the school year and then went back to Charleston.

The stay with us wasn't just good for them; it was good for me, too. Having to discipline them taught me to be consistent and self-controlled myself. Surely, if I had to get them to toe the line, I had to toe it myself!

And again, I could see the great hand of the Lord, using all of it to shape, to mold that "old cup" into a bright, new vessel!

I wasn't the only one growing. Fran made a lot of strides, too!

As it was with me, the ability to carry responsibility didn't come to her overnight. But it began. The first help to that, of course, was that she no longer got drunk or high on pills! That made her easier to live with and more open to the Lord's molding right away.

At first, she just sat on her tail and got fat. Maybe she'd earned a little rest, after all the slave labor I'd put her through in the old days! She just sat by the hour and watched those old soap operas on TV. She took pretty good care of Bari-Ann, but the house was a mess.

One day, though, I came in and unplugged it and told her that if I ever came in again and saw her "fat butt sittin' in front o' this TV set, an' watchin' them soap operas, I'll promise you, I'll throw that TV set out the door! An' we'll never have another one!" That cured her! It may have been harsh medicine, but I knew that tube was destroying her.

And of course, all the responsibilities that came on me, she shared with me. Through it, I could soon see more love, wisdom, compassion, gentleness, and skill in being a mother and a wife.

Believe me, without her, I never would have been able to

make it! A lot of times when I was depressed and down, she came to me and hugged me and encouraged me. And I'd yell at her! But she'd just stand with me through the whole thing.

I found myself loving her ever so much more than I ever had before. She used to be just someone to make me money and sleep with. Now, it was more than sex and dough, it was companionship and respect and good counsel, too. Many times she ministered the Word of the Lord to me when I needed it most. And we both know God created all that in her!

In both of us! And believe me, that made life more exciting than I ever imagined it could be. To live with yourself is one thing. But to feel yourself changing, day by day, into someone who completely amazes and surprises you, who reacts differently to situations than you ever did—that's strange, and wonderful, and mysterious, and you know it's the work of God!

28
Light Club I

Watching Bari-Ann grow was a great joy of my life. She was still my "li'l angel"—a different kind now, of course, talking in her baby way about Jesus, when she was just past two years old. She was our miracle baby, the one Fran wasn't supposed to have been able to have, and God used her to work one of the greatest miracles we were to see in our early walk with Him.

When Bubba walked in, I didn't recognize him at first, but I knew he was a biker right away. It was just a strange place for him to be, a Christian coffee house.

The Globe was run by the college as a student ministry, and I was over there as usual every Tuesday night.

I may not have known Bubba, but he knew me. He came over and grabbed me and hollered, "Barry-Barry!" I knew I'd seen him somewhere: He had a scar across his nose, a long beard, black hair and a voice like a gravel road. He was glassy-eyed, like he'd been drinking or doing pills.

He tried to give me a "bikers' kiss," open-mouthed, but I pushed him away and said, "Hey, man! I don't do that no more!" He looked surprised.

But he quickly recovered and said, "Man, I been hopin' t' fin' you!"

I said, "Come on, man, an' set down an' tell me what brings you t' Pensacola!"

We sat at a table, and he told me a hard-luck story about how he had been pimping a couple of women down here, and they split on him, and he had no money, no place to stay, nothing.

And he said, "How 'bout you, man? Can I stay with you?"

I looked him over. I didn't really want him to, but in my spirit, the Lord said, "Yeah, bring him!" I said to myself, *Boy, I don't know how Fran's gonna take this!*

But I said, "Yeah, come on!"

So I put him in the car and started home with him. I had a lot of second thoughts. He was just as filthy-mouthed as any biker, and I really didn't want him in my house. I had a hard time drumming up any compassion for him, and I was kind of surprised not to feel it for a man in trouble. But I also had the feeling that he was conning me, that he was there for a reason he wasn't telling.

But the Scripture came to me that if your enemy's hungry, you feed him, and if he's thirsty, you give him a drink, and not to give evil for evil, but overcome evil by doing good. *So I've got to feed 'im,* I said to myself, *an' I got to bring 'im in!* So we drove home.

All the while I was pleading the blood of Jesus on my family and over my home, and I asked the Lord to have His angels encamped about us!

When we got in the door, Fran put on a show of hospitality. We set him up on the couch, made him as comfortable as our meager means could.

But when we got into our own room, Fran said, "Why did you bring him here? We don't have no food, we don't . . ."

"Baby, I *had* to," I said.

And I quoted Scriptures to her, which went over like a lead balloon!

I felt bad because she felt bad, but I was in the middle, between the Lord and her, and I knew Who had to win out!

For several days, Bubba came and went. I told him I didn't want any drinking and drugs in my house. I said, "I'm tellin' you right now, if you drink, you might as well bring your sleepin' bags right back to wherever you came from. 'Cause you gonna sleep outside, you ain't gonna sleep in my house!"

And he knew I meant what I said! We'd sit at the dinner table and pray and just live the life of the Lord in front of him. We talked to him about the Lord, too, all the time. He sloughed it off: "Oh, yeah, I know about all that!" He knew some Scripture, and he'd quote it back. But I knew it wasn't real in his heart.

But Bari-Ann was the one who did the real work on him. He'd be around, and she'd raise her little hands in the air and cry, "Praise the Lord! Thank you, Jesus!" And he'd come in from wherever he'd been, and she'd run up and put her arms around his hefty leg and look up at him with her big blue eyes and say, "I love you, Bubba! And Jesus loves you!" And he'd soak it up.

This kept on for a week, and I knew he could see the change in us. And little Bari-Ann melted his heart. I could see him fighting back tears as she told him how Jesus loved him. Here was this big tough brute with a tiny girl sitting on his knee, getting through to him with Jesus' love!

One night, he came in stinking drunk. He'd fallen off the back of a motorcycle; his whole back was just eaten up, and he could hardly walk.

I had been telling him that the devil was out to kill him, and Jesus wanted to give him life. And all he could think of now, in his stupor, was that the devil was trying to kill him!

He said to me, "I wanna tell you shomethin'!" I saw the bottle of beer in his hand.

I said, "Uh-uh! You don't come in here with that bottle!"

He set it down on the porch and staggered in the door and dropped onto the couch. He looked up at me with a pitiful look in his eyes.

He told me about his accident, and then he said, "Man, I think God'sh after me! I think the devil'sh out t' kill me, but I think God'sh after me, too!"

He put his hand to his mouth and burped. "I got a confession t' make," he went on. "You know, I didn't come down here on my own—the Hell'sh Angelsh sent me down here. There'sh a five thousan' dollar bounty on you! An' I come t' collec'! They tol' me if you wash here, I wash t' collec', an' tha'sh what I'm down here for!"

His big head began to bob up and down. He put his head in his hands, and I saw tears start to drop to the rug. "But I want you t' know that I can't do it!" he sobbed. "I don't know *what* I'm gonna do!"

I said, "Bubba, what you need to do is what I did, an' tha's give your life t' Jesus!"

And we got down on that living-room floor and prayed and Bubba asked Jesus to come into his heart!

Bubba stayed with us for six more weeks. He started going to church. But he drifted from church to church, saying he wanted to see what all the churches were like.

God supplied our needs while Bubba was there. He even began to be helpful around the house. And he'd sit around with Bari-Ann, talking about Jesus.

I wish I could say it all stayed rosy for Bubba, but soon things went awry. He got mixed up with a Christian woman, a rich gal from one of the churches he visited. She asked him to move in and they ended up in bed together.

I remember the both of them coming to me and her crying, "He took advantage of me!"

And I said, "Boy, you both a bunch of idiots! I could see that wasn't gonna work from the beginnin' when you'all started stayin' together under the same roof. All this Christian stuff an' brother an' sisterly love—it don't work that way! When you not married, an' under the same roof—boy, forget it! It's jus' a matter o' time!"

I tried to counsel them, but Bubba finally said, "Well, I guess I'm jus' gonna leave!"

And he did. I don't know where he is; I've never heard from him. But I know God has His eye on Bubba, and I have faith for his soul—because I know Jesus never lost a case yet, and if He's got His hand on a man's soul, He'll collect that bounty, more surely than any Hell's Angel ever can!

All this while, I kept plugging on with school. It would have taken eight years for me to finish, at the night pace I was going. I did get all the way from Genesis up to Second Chronicles. I took Romans, a course on cults and some others. But almost everything else I know about the Scriptures—including the Gospels, the Letters in the New Testament, Revelation, all the Prophets—the Lord's taught me, through books, tapes, sermons, and my old Bible with almost more scribbled notes in the margins than type on the pages, which I've passed on to Rusty. Put the Old and New Testaments together by themselves, though, and I guarantee you, you'll get the whole picture of God and His ways!

I remember having to read a book called *Spiritual Authority* by Watchman Nee, and write a report about it. For me, this was quite an experience! I had to plow through it three times before I could see the difference between God's plan for His people respecting and being obedient to the men He's put in authority in the church—and probating for a bike club! I kept saying, "Boy, I ain't gonna be no probate for nobody!"

But God dealt with me on that, showing me by His Word that He's established ranks of authority. He's gifted certain people with leadership, which doesn't make them *better* than everyone else, just with a different job. And God's people had to allow themselves to be guided and be led. This didn't mean some man became my dictator. But I had to be open to being advised, and at times have my will overruled, by more experienced people in the Lord and by people ordained to certain positions in the church, like pastors and elders.

It took me three months altogether to work through that—but I did get an A on the paper. And I think my marks on God's tests have gradually gotten better!

All students had to be involved in some kind of ministry, too, and I chose to go to the prisons and share with the men there. I found that my experiences and age made me able to relate to these guys on their own level, as few of the younger students could. The taste I got of this work became important to me later on, when God launched me into wider prison work.

After my painting stint was done, my next-door neighbor offered me a job making fiber-glass boats. It only lasted a month, because he went bankrupt! Interestingly, I had told him he would go bankrupt, because he was cursing God. Every time he blasphemed God, I would shout, "Praise the Lord!" We got into it

often, and I told him, "You're gonna have t' repent an' quit doin'
what you're doin'! God's gonna do somethin' awful to you!" It
wasn't two weeks later that he couldn't even sell a boat. He barely
had enough left to pay my check.

My next job was with a home builder, making cabinets, and
every night on the way home from work, I'd see teenagers hanging
around an arcade in which were pinball machines and other amuse-
ments. It was dark in there, I noticed, and kids parked outside,
drinking beer and cursing, just up to no good. I kept thinking,
"Boy, that ain't nothin' but a nightclub for kids!"

So I asked the Lord if there was something I could do about it.
At times I used to stop and walk through the crowd of kids, talking
to them about the Lord and giving them tracts to read. The owner
of the place didn't take kindly to this and told me in no uncertain
terms to bug off.

One morning on my way to work, the Lord showed me how I
could help those kids. I remembered Jesus saying, "I am the light
of the world," and another Scripture saying, "Where there is light,
there is no darkness." And I started thinking, *Light! Light! What I
need to do is open up a place!*

And a vision came to me of an arcade, with poolrooms, foose-
ball, and pinball machines—all lit up with bright light!—a place of
wholesome fellowship and recreation, with pictures all over of
Jesus and Bible verses and wise sayings. I had never seen any place
like this, but it was all as clear in my head as if I were there. I
could hear contemporary Christian music, and see young people
strong in the Lord serving there as counselors and witnesses to the
kids. And I said to myself, *Tha's what I'll do: I'll open up a Christian recreation hall! Surely God'll supply for that!*

The idea of light kept coming to me as I thought about this
new kind of ministry. I said, "I sure ran enough *night* clubs—I
think I'll open up a *Light Club!*"

So I began to pray about it and share this vision with people.
And everyone said, "Yeah, Barry, that's good!" But it seemed like
nobody would grasp hold of it in quite the same way I did. I wondered how I would ever get the support to get it started.

God chose a strange way to get the Light Club going. My
mother has experienced her share of tragedy in life, in men's eyes.

But only God knows how to portion out what's best for us. Mom was to know more sorrow now, though not unmixed with joy. Her third husband, Frank Carder, had a heart attack and went home to be with the Lord.

When Frank's will was read, we found that he'd left each child in the family two thousand dollars. I took that as from the Lord, and I rented a building, bought some equipment, got some insurance, and opened up the Light Club.

We got started the last part of my second summer in Pensacola, when school was out. That gave me some time to get things off the ground, but it was still a struggle, for both Fran and me. I'd be working all day, and Fran would open the doors and mind the place until I got off work. Then she'd go home, and I'd take over.

We began to see young people who came in saved and filled with the Holy Spirit, and soon several of them volunteered to work with us. They were especially helpful when Fran was running things.

We were joyous over the results, but the separations from one another and the family were rough on us. When I came in at night, Fran would go home and make my supper and bring it back to me, and then I'd work until closing time, ten-thirty or eleven o'clock, six days a week. During the summer, hours were longer, from nine o'clock in the morning until midnight.

Steady streams of kids came in, and the newspaper did a nice article on us, with pictures. And it was a joy to see those kids responding to the Word of God.

The machines made about enough to pay the rent and the bills for the place. But it was becoming obvious that this was a full-time job—and yet the club didn't make enough to supply my family's needs. I needed support.

But I couldn't seem to persuade people that the Light Club was a ministry. Some thought I was just a young Christian, still in school, who didn't have enough of Jesus Christ in me to start a ministry. And others thought it was just a business. I approached the church and other people in a number of ways, asking them if they would recognize the Light Club as a ministry, an outreach of Liberty. I asked if the college would direct students to it as a ministry. But the school and church never would officially endorse us, though a number of students who shared the vision came and helped out.

Gradually I grew to feel that the Bible school just didn't understand me. I didn't think they could follow my thoughts about things or see what was in my heart. In my immaturity, I thought that to them, I was just another Christian to train. They had showed a lot of patience with me, because when I first came, I was still hard. But my heart wasn't really in the school anymore, I wanted to get out and minister to those kids.

I finally went to the head of the college (after sharing with my elder) and told him I believed God was calling me to be an evangelist and that God was leading me back home to Charleston. By this time, I was already ministering in churches, sharing my testimony.

Well, the man said he thought perhaps I shouldn't leave the school—but who was he to be the judge of what God was saying to me? He said he thought it would be better for me to finish school. But I told him I was having just too much trouble trying to keep up with the bills, and my family had to come first.

I told him I was grateful to those men of God for putting up with me and for all they'd taught me. But under the circumstances I felt my decision had to stand. So I said, "I'm leavin'."

I knew it was God directing me back to Charleston, because I never would have gone back on my own. I had charges facing me there; I risked one to five years in prison. But I had no fear whatsoever of the Hell's Angels. All I wanted to do was witness to them and tell them about the Lord if I got the chance.

I wanted to get a job and get settled, open another Light Club, and just live for the Lord.

So, leaving Fran and the kids for a while, I went back to Charleston and got a job with an exterminating company. I lived in the office until I got enough money together to get an apartment and pay my school bills and move the family up.

When I had the means together, I returned to Pensacola, loaded the family and our furniture into a big U-Haul truck, and we soon settled into Charleston.

We thanked the Lord for the training we'd gotten, for the testing times we'd been through. We knew all that wasn't over; there would always be trials. But we'd really felt like strangers in Florida. It was good to be back on home turf!

29

Free—
From Both Sides
of the Law!

If anybody had ever told me a few years before this that there'd come a time in my life when I'd think one hundred and fifty dollars a week take-home was a lot of money, I'd have called for an ambulance and men in white coats to cart him off! Let's face it—if anybody'd dared to tell me I'd be happily living for Jesus, I'd have been tempted to put him out of his misery!

Yet here I was—and loving it! Why? Because I knew Jesus! I had no more temptation to go back to my old haunts or do the old things. I knew what I had in the Lord, and He always reminded me of that deal I'd made with Him on that night of terror in San Francisco!

Before Fran and the two children came up, I already had good Christian friends and a solid church family for my own to become a part of. We needed that—especially since Fran was now swelling with a little guy who turned out to be Barry, Jr.

I didn't seek people out to witness to in Charleston, the Lord just sent them my way. I witnessed and prayed with people on the job and on the street, as the opportunity came up.

Many people in church asked me about our time down in Pensacola, and I told them about the Light Club. I'd hint, "Sure would be nice if we had one of these aroun' Folly Beach or Mount Pleasant!" And I was delighted when people in Charleston backed me up! Before long, I had another Light Club going, this time on Folly Beach.

We had a wonderful time through the summer months and saw God do great things in the lives of young people. The church backed us up with financial support and people help. I felt real satisfaction in finally seeing my ministry recognized.

When the young people all went back to school, Folly Beach became like a ghost town, and we shut the doors of the Light Club. I was sure it would be resurrected again, but God had other ideas for my future.

The church had ordained me and pledged me monthly support, and I was now able to go into prisons as a minister. Since I didn't have a club going, I began to see the work in the county jails as part of Light Club Ministries, and soon my burden for men in prison began to loom large in my heart.

I could see that it wasn't enough to just go and share the Gospel with these men and get them saved individually. A lot of them still had a long way to go before they'd get out from behind bars, and they needed encouragement and help to live for Jesus the kinds of lives they'd have to endure right there in prison. Simply going to chapel every Sunday wasn't enough either. They needed to be a part of a church fellowship, just as every believer does. So I got into my mind to go into prisons and found churches *behind* the walls, to develop leaders right there in the prisons who could get fellowships and Bible studies together and become supports and faith builders to their brothers. I seriously considered whether God might be leading me into this challenging kind of ministry full time.

As far as my former brothers, the Hell's Angels, were concerned, I never went walking up to their clubhouse and said, "Hey, guys! Remember me?" But I did go by the clubhouse and put tracts in their mailbox, which was out by the road, and I mailed letters to them. I wanted them to know that I wasn't in town to bring them trouble, but to start my life over again and minister the Gospel. I told them Jesus loved them and I loved them and held no hard feelings and hoped they didn't, either.

And I meant every word of what I said. I'm not out to destroy

the Hell's Angels or put anybody from my past in jail. I'd like to
see them all get saved! Then they could change their names to
Heaven's Saints, too!

I'm not certain what their intentions are toward me. Some people have asked me why I'm still alive, in light of all my dealings
with the Hell's Angels. To tell the truth, I don't know. Perhaps they
think I'm just plumb crazy. Perhaps they're assured by this time
that I mean them no harm. Whatever the reason, I know that the
Lord still has His angels encamped around me, and I have nothing
to fear from angels, devils, or men. Nothing's going to happen to
me or my family that God doesn't allow. And you can't really take
from a Christian man what he's lost already—his life.

The only Hell's Angel I saw face to face in Charleston was a
probate I visited at a hospital. I'd read in the papers that this dude
had had a motorcycle wreck, and I brought my Bible in hopes that
he might let me share with him and pray for him.

I remember him lying on that bed, trembling with fear or
anger when he found out who I was. He screamed at me, "You better get outa here! We gonna cut you up in a million pieces!"

Well, that young man didn't get saved—at least not that day! I
did leave some books in his room, and maybe he read them.

But you know, the devil isn't stupid! I don't think he wants
those Hell's Angels to get around me because he doesn't want to
get 'em saved!

I did have the privilege of leading one of my former patch
brothers to the Lord. God allowed me to share my testimony before
many thousands on the PTL Club television program. And not long
after that, I got a call all the way from California, and who should
it be but my old fellow Tribulator, Bull Tongue, who's been living
out there for years! As we shared together, the Lord touched Bull's
heart, and he gave it to Jesus, and I trust Bull's walking with God
to this day.

But Bull wasn't the only figure from the past that God laid
hands on.

Back in Charleston, I shared my testimony early one Saturday
morning at a Full Gospel Business Men's breakfast. This time, I

didn't feel the least bit out of place! I can say truly that I shouted Hallelujahs and praised God with the best and loudest of them!

And after our time of sharing and worship was over, various men came up to talk with me. Near the end of the line was a mild-looking man with sad eyes but a slight smile across his lips. Something about his face looked familiar, but I couldn't place him.

When he reached me, this man looked me in the eyes and said, "You remember me?"

I said, "I'm sure I know you, but I can't remember!"

He said, "I'm the guy you were talking about, that you used to pay off!"

"Anderson! The ol' vice man! Mister, you done gained some weight!"

Tears came to his eyes. No wonder I hadn't recognized him: All the smugness was gone from his face, the smirk was no more, the voice was subdued. "I guess I am a little heavier. The prison food, you know!"

I said, "What was that, man?"

He said, "Barry, they caught me at my game. I lost my job with the police. And I served time. But praise God"—and here his tears started to fall—"I know Jesus now!"

I reached out and hugged this man who'd been my deadly enemy, who'd arrested me from time to time over the years. And now we shed tears of joy over each other's shoulders.

He said, "Barry, it's so strange—I used to fear you whenever I had to go onto the avenue and bring you in. I always had my gun ready. It's so great that now we can meet like this, empty-handed!"

"Yep," I said, "that wall of fear is broke down between us." We held each other by the shoulders, and I said, "You know why all this is possible? 'Cause Jesus done arrested the both of us—one from one side o' the law, an' one from the other! An' He ain't never lettin' us go!"

I tell you, we walked out of that room with our arms around each other's shoulders, sort of reunited—but this time both on the same side—on Jesus' side!

And I'll bet you never thought anything like *that* would be *the end* of *my* story!

To God be the Glory!

Epilogue

Since January 1981, Barry Mayson has acted as State Director of A Voice in the Wilderness prison ministry, a national outreach based in Milledgeville, Georgia. His work of "building churches behind the walls" is reaching all prisons and youth correction centers in South Carolina, as well as into U.S. federal and state prisons throughout the United States. Among his "congregations" are inmate fellowships along Death Rows.

He has ministered on a number of Christian radio and television programs, including the PTL Club. He travels and speaks extensively in high schools, colleges, Christian businessmen's meetings, and churches.

Barry lives with his wife, Fran, and children Rusty, Bari-Ann, and Barry, Jr., in Columbia, South Carolina.

Write:

> Barry Mayson
> 4128 Forest Drive
> Columbia, S.C. 29204

ABOUT THE AUTHORS

BARRY MAYSON, who now lives in West Columbia, South Carolina, is an ordained minister, affiliated with A Voice in the Wilderness Prison Ministries. He travels extensively to help those who are in trouble with the law and the Lord.

TONY MARCO was born in New York City and spent his childhood in many parts of the United States, as well as in Central America and Great Britain. A former warehouseman, lumber handler, personnel investigator, journalist, and college professor, he has an M.A. from Johns Hopkins University. He has written for the PTL Club and published poetry, reviews, and news features. Like Barry and Fran Mayson, Tony and his wife, who now live in Pineville, North Carolina, are born-again Christians.